Walking Trees

Teaching Teachers
in the New York City Schools

Ralph Fletcher

HEINEMANN
PORTSMOUTH, NH

Heinemann Educational Books, Inc.
361 Hanover Street   Portsmouth, NH 03801-3959
Offices and agents throughout the world

We would like to thank the teachers, children, and parents who have given their
permission to include material in this book. Every effort has been made to contact
copyright holders for permission to reprint borrowed material where necessary, but
if any oversights have occurred, we would be happy to rectify them in future
printings of this work.

The author and publisher wish to thank the following for permission to include
reprinted material in this work:

Page vii: Poem from the *Duino Elegies* by Rainer Maria Rilke. Reprinted by permission
of W. W. Norton and Company.

Page 116: Excerpt from *Lost in the Storm* by Carol Carrick, illustrated by Donald
Carrick. Copyright © 1974 by Carol and Donald Carrick. Reprinted by permission
of Clarion Books, a Houghton Mifflin company.

Page 176: "Nantucket" by William Carlos Williams: *The Collected Poems of William
Carlos Williams, 1909–1939, vol. I.* Copyright 1938 by New Directions Publishing
Corporation. U.S. and Canadian rights. Reprinted by permission.

Page 177: "His Dog" by Richard Margolis. Reprinted with permission of Macmillan
Publishing Company from *Secrets of a Small Brother* by Richard J. Margolis.

Page 197: "Fish?" from *Where the Sidewalk Ends* by Shel Silverstein. Copyright ©
1974 by Evil Eye Music, Inc. Reprinted by permission of Harper & Row, Publishers,
Inc.

Library of Congress Cataloging-in-Publication Data

Fletcher, Ralph J.
    Walking trees : teaching teachers in New York City schools / Ralph
J. Fletcher, Jr.
        p.   cm.
    ISBN 0-435-08536-0
    1. English language—Composition and exercises—Study and
teaching. 2. Teachers—In-service training—New York (N.Y.)
3. Teachers College Writing Project (Columbia University)
I. Title.
LB1576.F48   1991
808'.042'0707471—dc20   90-36357
                                                                 CIP

Cover Illustration by Jenny Greenleaf
Design by Jenny Greenleaf
Printed in the United States of America
91 92 93 94 95   10 9 8 7 6 5 4 3 2 1

for JoAnn

Who shows a child
      as he really is?
            Who sets him among the stars
and puts the measure of distance
      in his hand?
           Who makes the child's death
out of gray bread
      that gets hard
         who leaves it there
in his round mouth
      like the core
         of a lovely apple?
Murders aren't hard
     to comprehend
        But this:
to contain death
      the whole of death
         even *before* life has begun
to contain it so gently
     and not to be angry—
         this is indescribable.

              from the *Duino Elegies*
              by Rainer Maria Rilke

Walking Trees is a personal memoir of my experiences teaching teachers how to teach writing in the New York City schools during the 1985–1986 school year. Except where noted, the names and features of individuals and schools described in this work have been changed. In certain cases, I have created composite characters drawn from several actual individuals.

I have used actual names of some administrators, teachers, students, and members of the Teachers College Writing Project.

Principals: Deena Gold, Meryl Natelli, and Norm Sherman.

Teachers: Miriam Alflalo, Llewelyn Berk, Janice Bentz, Carol Cossins, Veray Darby, Sylvia Dunsky, Barbara Finkel, Marcia Marcus, Steve Meyers, Gwen Mahoney, Cera Northern, Margaret O'Farrell, Laura Poulos, Cheryl Steinberg, Rosemary Ullman, Helen Winstral, and Ruth Zander.

Students: Juliet Arkin, Raymond Brooke, Tina Castro, Demitri Demetrakapoulos, Charles Emanuele, Christopher Fasolino, Melissa Gonzalez, Lori Ann Haas, John Hernandez, Stephanie Hubbard, Daniel Laguna, Anna Maria Natale, Tasos Pardalis, Ralph Rella, Linda Rosenblatt, Craig Wisniewski, Rashida Yizar.

Teachers College Writing Project: Lucy Calkins, Shelley Harwayne, Hindy List, JoAnn Curtis, Dan Fiegelson, Jenifer Hall, Georgia Heard, Martha Horn, Karen Howell, Jim Sullivan, Aida Montero, Eilleen Jones.

To all these individuals, I am grateful.

I have also used the actual numbers for the following schools: PS 79, PS 105, PS 121, PS 154, PS 201. The names for all other schools mentioned have been changed.

Acknowledgments

This book was shaped, directly and indirectly, by a number of people without whose help it would not exist today. I would particularly like to thank:

My late grandfather, Ralph Fletcher, who taught English at Durfee High School in Fall River, Massachusetts, for forty-two years and who is the original reason I am in education today;

My parents, Ralph and Jean Fletcher, two fine teachers who gave me the only gift no writer can do without—a real childhood;

My brothers and sisters—Jim, Elaine, Tom, Bob, John, Joe, Kathy, and Carolyn—for all the great stories, books, and poetry readings we shared through the years;

Steven Shapiro, who taught me by example that students are changed forever by a wonderful teacher;

Lucy Calkins, for her energy, wisdom, and vision in founding the Teachers College Writing Project, and for her remarkable confidence in me;

Shelley Harwayne, for giving me the space to find my own voice as a writing teacher;

The other members of the Teachers College Writing Project—Dan Fiegelson, Jenifer Hall, Georgia Heard, Martha Horn, Karen Howell, Eileen Jones, Hindy List, Aida Montero, and Jim Sullivan—whose community helped me survive a tough year;

Deena Gold, Meryl Natelli, Norm Sherman, and many other New York City principals I worked with who, like their teachers, do heroic work in difficult surroundings;

All the teachers who brought me into their classrooms and shared the highs and heartaches of teaching in New York City;

The city kids, who wrote with such honesty and courage about their often troubled lives;

Nancie Atwell, Robert Cohen, Suzanne Gardinier, and Jim Vojcsik, for their generous and multiple readings of this manuscript in draft;

Philippa Stratton and Dawne Boyer, for their patience and humor throughout the editing of this book;

and JoAnn Curtis, whose professional clarity flavors this book from beginning to end. No matter how many times she read *Walking Trees* in draft form, JoAnn always seemed to laugh and cry in the right places. For that, and for too many other things to mention, I am grateful.

Prologue

This book chronicles a single school year (September, 1985 to June, 1986) I spent as a staff developer for the Teachers College Writing Project. It was my job to teach New York City teachers how to teach writing. In this book I want to take a slow, thorough look at that year.

The Writing Project at Teachers College, Columbia University, is headed by Lucy Calkins (or simply "Lucy," as everyone calls her), assistant professor and a national authority on the teaching of writing. I first met her in 1981 when she had just been hired at Teachers College. When I walked into her office and said I wanted to take her course on the teaching of writing, Lucy let a long silence fill the room. I had already missed the first two classes. She was a serious woman with widespread appraising eyes, her brown hair styled in a short, boyish haircut. When she spoke, Lucy's diction was so clean it was intimidating; not a wasted word anywhere in her speech. And she was remarkably young, barely a year older than myself. She thought about it. Then, reluctantly, she handed me the syllabus and admitted me to the course.

That night, in the very first class, I got infected with the writing process bug. And with Lucy. Standing primly in front of her class, she radiated poise, intelligence, fueled by an almost religious conviction. The distinct, no-nonsense smell of change and reform was all over this woman. Listening to her was electrifying: in *this* field of education, at least, anything was possible.

I devoured those early classes and filled my notebook. Lucy defined writing as an act of "dialoguing with an emerging text." All children have stories to tell, Lucy said, quoting someone named Donald Graves. The question is, will they tell them to us? Children have always been expected to produce perfect first-draft writing. We need to allow them to do what real writers do, to write rough drafts, and revise—to discover what they have to say in the act of the writing.

One day Lucy looked directly at me and said, "You know, you could make a big impact on this field." Heady stuff. I wanted to be worthy of such a judgment.

At Lucy's invitation, I began teaching at the Teachers College summer institutes on writing. I juggled this job with my work as a freelance writer and my part-time job as a tour leader for Maritz Travel Company, for whom I worked taking corporate groups of tourists around the world. Soon I found myself alternating tours to Europe with small consulting jobs at public and private schools around New York. By the summer of 1985, when Lucy invited me to join the staff of the Writing Project, I was ready for a change. I cut up the green Air Travel Card I used as a tour leader and accepted her offer.

I joined the Writing Project just as it was beginning its third year of work in the New York City schools. The Writing Project embraced a philosophy of staff development that was as innovative as its ideas on teaching writing. In many school systems, staff development (or teacher training, as it is often called) is a shoddy exercise that takes place outside the classroom. Teachers get released from their classrooms for halfday workshops to listen to experts or consultants on a particular curriculum area. The Writing Project utilized a staff-development model whereby trainers would work with practicing teachers in their own classrooms. The training involved coaching rather than direct teaching and was based on a close relationship between trainer and teacher. It was a slow-growth model, one that recognized that real change happens gradually—a trainer and a teacher might work together for several years. The humanism underlying this approach appealed to me.

I started the school year with my share of doubts. Most of these stemmed from my own status as a writer and the monumental insecurities native to this profession. I was thirty-two years old. I had very little classroom experience; could I make the transition from writer to writing teacher? Could I take myself seriously as teacher? Would the city kids listen to me? Would the teachers? Could writing be taught at all? Would I be any good at it? And finally, what effect would teaching writing and talking writing all day long have on my own writing?

As a small child I was a fiend with the garden hose. My earliest memories conjure up that cool green hissing snake, bare feet on wet grass during the summer's twilight, a garden of flowers or new grass to be watered, the almost perfect feeling of water, endless water, coursing through the hose and out onto the moist, sweet-smelling yard. Almost perfect. The problem was that I couldn't relax enough to enjoy myself for fear that one of my parents would shut off the water. This image is branded into my parents' shared memory: Ralph Junior, their firstborn, dutifully dousing the yard with water and turning around every few seconds to warn, "Don't shut it off! Don't shut it off!"

Here, then, was my deepest and most superstitious fear about teaching writing; namely, that by talking and breathing writing all day long, I would risk "shutting it off"—cutting myself off from whatever creative stuff fueled my own writing. Knowing how superstitious this fear was didn't help. If anything, my new job would reveal to me more than once how superstitious I really was.

This book is the story of that first turbulent year I spent in the New York City schools. I do not aim to provide a blueprint for teachers who might want to incorporate writing process into their classrooms. However, I have included a brief discussion of writing process and its roots. Those familiar with the process approach to teaching writing may want to skip directly to the first chapter.

From Jean Piaget to Ivan Illich, the field of education has historically been subject to pendulum shifts in philosophy and methodology. This has held true both for the field as a whole as for the separate components of education: reading, math, science, and writing. Such shifts have often fostered frustration and cynicism among educators. Concepts that were discarded twenty years ago may become fashionable today but be scorned in another fifteen years. Grasping the significance of writing process involves an understanding of the shifting educational context from which it emerged.

In the 1950s and early 1960s, students in American schools were not writing a great deal of anything. Writing composition in both elementary and secondary schools was dominated by grammar, the disappearance of essay exams (too hard to grade), and language broken down to small components. Researchers such as Arthur Appleby reported that in a typical school day, students held their pencils for 37 percent of the time. Yet these same students almost never wrote more than a word or two at a time.

No one individual "invented" the writing process approach to teaching writing. Some cite James Britton of England for laying the foundation for process by describing three categories for functional writing—transactional, expressive, and poetic—in his book *Language And Learning* (1972). Others credit James Moffett as another important early influence.

No one, however, would disagree that research played a crucial role in the genesis of writing process. In the late 1960s and early 1970s, researchers began to report a serious contradiction between what composition textbooks taught about writing and how students actually wrote. In Janet Emig's book *The Composing Process of 12th Graders* (NCTE, 1968), the author found that, conventional advice to the contrary, many skillful writers did not outline a paper before writing it. Emig was an English professor at Rutgers University, which became one of the centers for thinking about writing process. Emig's doctoral students would make major contributions to the field.

Around this time the skill-and-drill approach to teaching grammar came under increasing attack. Another researcher, Richard Braddock, analyzed published pieces of expository writing and found that the dogma about using topic sentences simply did not hold true in such published writing.

Around this time, some educators became interested in the "Writers At Work" series being published in the *Paris Review*. These interviews demystified the strategies of professional writers and highlighted the contrast between the techniques professional writers use and the strategies teachers were asking their students to use.

It was Donald Murray, an English professor at the University of New Hampshire, who would take the "Writers At Work" information and make it accessible to educators. He did this through numerous articles on writing and through his book, *A Writer Teaches Writing* (Boynton/Cook, 1970). Murray was the first educator to talk about the writing process as having four distinct stages: rehearsing (prewriting), drafting, revising, and editing. Crucial to the writing process according to Murray is revision: a process in which the writer reformulates earlier drafts to discover and shape meaning. Previously, revision had been looked on as the editing of grammatical mistakes.

Although Murray's book had an enormous impact on the educational field, its initial impact was confined primarily to high school and college teachers.

In 1972, Jim Gray founded the Bay Area Writing Project in San Francisco. This would eventually become the National Writing Project—an organization to help train teachers to teach writing process. Today, *writing project* is usually a euphemism for a staff development network that encourages and supports the process approach to teaching writing.

In 1976, Donald Graves, a colleague of Murray's at the University of New Hampshire, secured a National Institute of Education grant to begin a two-year study entitled How Children Change As Writers. Graves worked with Lucy Calkins and Susan Sowers at Atkinson Academy, a public elementary school in Atkinson, New Hampshire. The Graves study was as revolutionary in its approach as it was in its findings. Until that study, composition research had focused on a close examination of students' written samples. In Graves's study, researchers pulled next to children's desks and watched students in the act of writing. This study concluded that Donald Murray's work and many strategies that "professional" writers were revealing about their own process had direct relevance to elementary school students as well. Out of this study would come Graves's important book *Writing: Teachers & Children At Work* as well as Lucy Calkins's influential first book, *Lessons From A Child*, the story of one child's growth in writing.

By 1977 there were writing process rumblings aplenty in the field of education. Still, the tangible effects of process in classrooms would only come gradually. In that year Graves wrote an essay entitled "Writing: An Endangered Species," in which he lamented the disappearance of writing from the public schools. A major reason for this: teachers weren't prepared to teach writing. After surveying teaching colleges and educational departments around the country, Graves found 169 courses offered on the teaching of reading and only two on the teaching of writing. He found a similar disparity in how research dollars were being spent: for every one dollar of research spent on the study of writing, three thousand were spent on the study of reading. Most of the writing research money was still being spent to look at how children achieve in writing (product) instead of how children develop as writers (process).

Not everyone embraced the writing process philosophy of teaching. Still, writing process showed it was more than a passing educational fad by making its way into the curricula of school districts across the United States. Many other strong voices in the field were beginning to be heard: Nancie Atwell, Glenda Bissex, Peter Elbow, Mary Ellen Giacobbe. Lucy Calkins would found the Teachers College Writing Project in 1981. The Writing Project's Saturday workshops drew a few hundred teachers during the first year, but by 1987 as many as twenty-five hundred teachers from the New York metropolitan area were giving up a day off to attend.

But few educators would disagree that Donald Murray and Donald Graves remain the spiritual fathers of the writing process approach in this country. They continue to have a major influence on the field. At conferences around the country, their names are still spoken with reverence.

Part One

Subterranean Teaching

--- ✳ ---

Selective Mute

--- ✳ ---

In a crowded Bronx classroom I choose a child to watch. Miranda Carp. She sits in one corner of the crowded room, a thin, brown-eyed child with delicate bones and curly hair the color of aspen leaves in the fall. Twin blue ribbons, pink dress with white tights, black shoes. The child radiates the overwhelming sense of the sheer physical care her parents have provided bringing her thus far through life. I sneak up behind and peek over her shoulder. Clean bold letters grace her paper.

I am in training. On this particular morning Jenifer Hall, Jim Sullivan, and I are getting our feet wet working in a first-grade classroom in the Bronx, of all places. At first this struck me as funny: I had half-marveled that tough Bronx kids don't skip directly from infancy to the street. Shelley Harwayne, codirector of the Teachers College Writing Project, has suggested we each pick a child to study. The two other teacher trainers-to-be have obediently fanned out around the room, stalking their own subjects. Jim has marched right over to a voluble, Cabbage Patch-faced boy; I can see the two of them engaged in intense dialogue, like old friends.

Jenifer has staked out a lovely, tall Hispanic girl being simultaneously courted by four boys in the class. They rush up to her with stories—drawings, really—that detail their hopes of marrying, honeymooning, living in a big house with her. Humbly, acutely aware of their audience, the boys present their stories to the dark-eyed girl. She reads them without comment before returning to her own serene work.

Not my Miranda. Nothing serene about her. I have chosen her

carefully, having thumbed through the entire class of children before settling here. The child works furiously, head down, arms splayed out over the desk, her whole being forced down onto the page through her clenched pencil.

"Miranda, can I talk to you about your story?" I speak soothingly, sorely aware of the tone of my voice, body language, facial energy. But I'm trying not to be too self-conscious, either. Loosen up, Fletch, I remind myself, you're a natural with kids.

Or am I? Miranda does not answer, nor does she make any attempt to cover her writing. Most five- and six-year-olds begin "writing" with elaborate drawings rich in complex symbolism and idiosyncratic meaning. Miranda writes only words, ferociously executing one letter before beginning the next. Already she has filled three small pages.

My SiSSdr	My sister
kass me. Then	kicks me. Then
I kak har	I kick her
balk.	back.
My Sissad	My sister
Hass me baczze	hates me because
sa katt me	she kicked me
Yisday	yesterday.
Then I tell My	Then I tell my
Mather. My Mather	mother. My mother
Sazz naiting.	says nothing.

I read and reread the large letters, straining to decipher the girl's invented spelling.

"You have a little sister?" I finally ask. This query does not even merit a glance; Miranda continues to write. The intensity of her work excites the three other children at her table. They shove their half-finished pages in my face, all the while keeping careful track of Miranda's progress.

"Mrs. Cohen, Miranda's makin' her story even longer!" one boy yells to his teacher. "She's makin' another page! She's gonna make a whole book—like a lie-berry book!"

No doubt about it, Miranda Carp is a find: real ethnographic paydirt. I am proud of her, proud of myself for finding her. I will pit her against Jim's Cabbage Patch boy and Jenifer's Latin beauty any day of the week. Miranda is an artist, a creative cauldron, aflame with such drive and obsessiveness that you can't help but wonder about its source. She makes *me* want to sit down and write. So why won't she talk to me?

"Miranda," I say, louder than before, forcing myself into her view. "Can't you tell me something about your story?"

Nothing.

"Just a little?"

A touch on my shoulder. Turning, I see Mrs. Cohen standing behind me. She is a tall, bony woman in her early forties who wears a funereal black dress and cylindrical earrings made from what looks like black coral. Twenty years in the classroom have left a residue of weary tenderness on her face.

"You won't get much luck that way, I'm afraid. Miranda is a selective mute."

"A what?"

"Selective mute. She's already been tested five times down at the district office. She *can* talk—she just chooses not to, at least not to adults." She points to a Chinese girl seated beside Miranda. "She *allegedly* talked to Elsa. She's never talked to me."

"Why?"

"Who knows? The school psychologist says it's not that rare. Selective mutes are usually dealing with some kind of trauma—probably from home. As you can see, Miranda isn't exactly wild about her little sister." Mrs. Cohen sighs. "She's got a ton bottled up inside her. Writing seems like her only outlet."

Jenifer, Jim, and I had just taken jobs as the newest teacher trainers for the Teachers College Writing Project. This position entailed nothing less than teaching New York City teachers how to teach writing. The afternoon spent in Mrs. Cohen's class marked the beginning of our apprenticeship.

I would first have to master the nuts and bolts of "launching," or beginning a writing process classroom. This meant helping teachers set up a classroom where children could use some of the strategies professional writers use—choosing their own topics, working at their own paces, drafting and revising, editing and publishing—and assuming far more responsibility for their writing than they had ever assumed before. To this end Jenifer, Jim, and I began visiting city schools to conduct numerous mock classroom launches in preparation for the real thing.

September 21, 1985. Jenifer Hall and I are at a junior high in the Flatbush section of Brooklyn. Even at 8 AM you can feel that the day will be a scorcher. The school has a white brick front and gleaming gold letters: The Nat Turner Learning Center. Inside, the air is cooler. Hallways jammed with students sporting sun dresses, light blouses, t-shirts, a crop of bare shoulders. I would have expected rampant restlessness from students on such a summery day. And a Friday to boot. But the students seem subdued, a bit sleepy, and somehow relieved to be filing off to class.

Our first class is not until 9:00. Jenifer and I head down to the teachers' cafeteria. We walk down a flight of stairs and follow a taped yellow line for seventy-five paces. I once spent a day touring the Rikers Island prison facility for an article I was working on. With its colorless walls, ubiquitous locks and wire-reinforced windows, the prison bore a distinct similarity to the basement of this junior high. I'm not sure if this should be construed as a critique of this particular school, a compliment to Rikers, or a simple observation that at some basic level all mass institutions resemble one another.

The teachers' cafeteria itself is a stuffy room with three rows of formica tables, plastic school chairs, and three narrow windows at one end fitted with frosted glass that prevents the influx of unadulterated sunlight. Small, ash-stained, reusable pie plates are stationed on each table. There are two doors with exit signs and, just above, additional EXIT signs in case you aren't sure. A box for recyclable cans. One large gray industrial trash container. A soda machine: I watch a teacher open it and yank out a Tab.

There are perhaps ten other teachers in the room who sip coffee, smoke, leaf sleepily through newspapers. A feeling of gritty, conspiratorial fatigue. As we approach the food line, a balding, overweight teacher frowns down at us.

"Sampling our culinary delights?" he asks. "You'll be sorry. . . ."

This teacher proceeds to introduce himself: Peter Matthews, an eighth-grade English teacher with "exactly three years, seven months, thirteen days, five hours, and thirty-three minutes till retirement." Not knowing what else to do, I congratulate him. It turns out that we are scheduled to visit his room during first period.

"What do you have there?" Peter asks the cook, pointing at a large try covered with wax paper. The woman behind the counter lifts the wax paper, unveiling thick gorgeous slices of watermelon. In that joyless room the sight of those juicy slices seems almost miraculous.

"Well, will you look at that?" Peter mutters. "All right, sure. Give me a couple pieces. And a couple for my friends here."

The watermelon is sweet, firm, succulent. Twenty-five cents a slice. Peter, Jenifer, and I find a table together and eat slowly without saying a word. In the table behind us, two men are talking softly. I think I hear one of them say, "Latin girls are the best-kept secret in New York," but perhaps I only imagine it. When I glance over at them, the men lower their voices even further. Another white male teacher about my age joins us. He lights a cigarette and glances at me.

"Sub?"

I wipe watermelon juice off my chin and explain my purpose in the school.

"Ah, the writing process," he says with a faint smile.

"You've heard of it?"

"Sure," he says. "Last year writing process was hot in this district. This year thinking skills are the big thing. Writing process isn't new anymore. Next year it'll be something else."

He sips his coffee. It occurs to me that I don't know his name; it now seems too late to ask.

"In education, just keeping track of what's in, what's out, I'll tell you, it's enough to make you tired."

"What do you do?" Jenifer asks.

"Special Ed," he grunts. "Statue of Liberty curriculum."

"Huh?"

"You know: give me your tired, your poor . . ."

"Oh."

"Say, you folks need any vitamins? I can sell them to you at wholesale."

We politely decline. More teachers arrive, grim, smoking, sipping black coffee. I imagine their collective mood reflected in the color of their coffee, a coffee that all the milk in the world wouldn't lighten. One teacher offers to sell us jewelry. Cheap. Another teacher has "rock-bottom deals" on Caribbean cruises. This exotic underground economy fascinates me. Later, I ask one of the veteran teacher trainers about it.

"Lots of city teachers have second jobs," she says. "They need it to supplement their incomes."

After breakfast we follow Peter Matthews upstairs. The hallways are filled with Hispanics, blacks, a smattering of whites. Shouts, jostlings, and the salt-sourish smell of young bodies. Even with the heat lots of kids are wearing hooded sweatshirts or shirts with light jackets over them. One boy saunters past with a toothbrush in his mouth and languidly appraises us. His black high-top sneakers are untied. We pass two boys soul-shaking with each other, invoking a slow and rhythmic rap beat to greet each other:

"Willie, my man, my sin, my soul,
His hair look like one great big bowl. . . ."

In a cul-de-sac between banks of lockers, we surprise two teens engaged in some vigorous French kissing. They have black hair with identical short haircuts; at first I cannot tell boy from girl.

"All right, enough of that!" Peter bellows. The teens jump apart—I imagine each of them frantically reeling in their tongues. "What do you think this is—a motel? Get to your class!"

"Hormones," Jenifer says, smiling.

"Vertical intercourse," Peter mutters.

When we reach Peter's room, he asks us to wait outside for a moment. He closes the door behind him. Inside, we can hear him softening up his eighth-grade students for our visit.

"I want you to LISTEN. There is a gentleman and a lady outside from COLUMBIA UNIVERSITY, do you understand, Troy? They're here to work with you on your WRITING. Now, this is IMPORTANT and I fully expect you to be on your best behavior, and I'm not going to tolerate any NONSENSE from anyone, is that CLEAR?"

The door opens.

"Come in," Peter says with a flourish.

I can feel thirty-odd sets of eyes looking us over as we file in. Jenifer has bravely volunteered to start the workshop, and as she walks to the front of the class I think to myself, it won't work here. No way. Not with these big ones. They won't write. Not the smirking ones in the back, the guys with the python biceps and skintight t-shirts, the busty girls with their eyeshadow, lipstick, bad skin, and eerie bedroom eyes. Amidst the musky perfume, I smell an impending disaster.

Jenifer compounds my distress by addressing the students as "boys and girls." I cringe. Boys and girls! Most of the "boys" are bigger than I am. I wait for them to start hooting, but they do not hoot. Nor do they laugh when Jenifer suggests that they choose an important event from their own lives to write about.

The kids start to write. Some start shyly, some sullenly, some skittishly. One fat boy in back keeps fooling around with the boy next to him, not getting down to work, so I go back to talk to him.

"Go ahead," I say, pointing to his paper. "I know you've got lots to say."

"I do," he said, his dark laughing eyes suddenly serious. "I'm very smart. I'm a gifted child."

"You've got a gifted belly, we all know that," interjects the boy next to him. The class cracks up.

"Enough!" Peter Matthews bellows. "Sean, come outside with me— NOW!"

While Peter straightens out Sean, I move around the room and try to confer with students on their writing. The one-on-one writing conference is central to the writing workshop. In Australia they call this the "conference method of teaching writing." Yet it doesn't take long to discover that writing conferences are anything but easy, particularly with adolescent students like these writing about crack, sex, putting a baby up for adoption.

I find one very small boy feverishly working on a piece entitled "Chester The Molester." It's about a fifteen-year-old boy going out with a nine-year-old girl. A fair-skinned girl is writing how her "bug-eyed" math teacher is always "scoping me out." Though she doesn't look at me, her eyes narrow and she leans forward when I pause behind her. Another boy is writing about how he didn't want to go to Florida: "My girlfriend was getting on good with me and I was getting 'paid' almost every day." I'd never heard of the expression before.

"Does that mean what I think it means?" I ask him.

"Yeah," he says with a shy smile.

Carmen, a Latin girl with flawless features, is writing a piece entitled "All About My Mother." I kneel down beside her.

"You mother, huh?" I say. The girl nods politely. Great. Now what? I recall a tip about writing conferences that Shelley Harwayne had given me earlier: make eye contact with the student. Get the student's eyes off the paper. I look Carmen straight in the eyes and try again.

"Looks to me like you've picked an awful big topic, Carmen. You know, instead of telling us all about your mother, you might consider describing something special about her. That's one way of handling a big topic—finding a part of it you can handle in a piece of writing like this. Can you think of something like that? Is there something special you and your mother do together?"

"Well, we dress alike sometimes." Her voice is hushed, gravelly, the finest sandpaper.

"You do?"

"Yeah. Like sometimes we both wear these funny hats, and people on the subway be looking at us. Sometimes we wear these polka dot blouses. People be taking us for sisters."

"How old is your mother?"

"Thirty."

"And how old are you?"

"Fourteen."

I leave Carmen writing about how she and her mother dress up, and I'm feeling pretty good. Not a bad conference. Shelley Harwyne would have been proud—maybe even Lucy. Peter wanders past, and I speak to him about what appears to be the underlying issue in Carmen's story—the mother, robbed of youth by an early pregnancy, dressing up as a teenager and competing with her own daughter.

"Isn't that pretty weird?" I ask Peter.

"You'd better not ask me what's weird and what's not," Peter says slowly. I can't tell if he's smiling or wincing. "I've been teaching here fifteen years. I'm not the best person to ask something like that."

Share time. At the front of the room, I ask for volunteers to read their writing to the class. Several hands shoot up. Surprised, I call on Carlos, a wiry Hispanic boy with glasses. Instead of coming to the front of the class, Carlos stands at his desk and reads:

"Jealousy"

Last year when my mother broke up with her boyfriend I was so excited. I hated the man. He was always around, he always called. I hated him. But one thing I couldn't figure out was why I hated him. I guess I was jealous. When he was around my mother acted so happy. I often wondered why she didn't feel that way about my father.

My mother and her boyfriend were always in the bedroom. I only saw her when she came to the kitchen or to the bathroom. He never went to the bathroom or to the kitchen because he knew I would say something about their relationship.

At times I feel like striking him or saying something mean and I will. I need to express my feelings. Later I called my mother an adultress, but later she told me that she was never married to my father. That hurt me so much. I often tell my mother that she will have plenty of time to see men when I am grown. But she is a 51 year old woman and she is up the hill. But no matter I still don't like her boyfriend or any man who shows interest in her.

Stunned silence.

"What you doin' tellin' your family business in front of everybody for?" one husky girl demands.

"Yeah," a boy at the other side of the class says. "You should be axin' your mama before you write somethin' like that."

"I don't care if she likes it or not," Carlos replies, shrugging.

"Yeah, but—"

"Raise your hand," I say. "If you have something to say, raise your hand. Carlos will call on you."

"Carmen," Carlos says, pointing.

"Well, I think it's good you read that to us. It takes courage. I wish I was that brave." Carmen wheels on the husky girl. "You can't decide what's right for him to read. If he wants to read it, he can read it. It's up to him."

"You don't go tellin' your business in public," the husky girl says, folding her arms as if the matter is settled. "You just don't do it."

I let the debate rage a few minutes more before Carlos sits down with the class split about the merits of reading such a personal piece of writing. With only five minutes left in the class, several other students still want to read their writing. I call on Lindy, a slender girl, perhaps Indian or Pakistani, who moves quickly to the front of the room.

"I have a brother who's different from other kids," she reads in a clear, low voice. "He doesn't live with us. He lives in Florida because he needs special care. He has something called alateral schlerosis. This is also known as Lou Gherig's disease. We only get to see him twice a year."

Just then, just as Lindy reads the word "twice," I hear a catch in her voice, as soft and unmistakable as the safety being taken off a rifle, and somehow just as ominous. Am I the only one who hears it? She reads two more sentences.

"The last time I saw him he had a card for me. He—" The girl bursts into tears. The class freezes. Peter Matthews freezes. Sitting on a desk at one side of the room, I find my hands welded to the sides of the desk. I cannot move, and yet I must. Someone must.

Something remarkable happens. Wordlessly, the girl sitting at the desk next to Lindy's gets out of her seat and hurries to the front of the class. She takes the story out of Lindy's hand and puts her arm around her friend's shoulder. While Lindy sobs quietly, the girl continues reading the story to the class. Peter, Jenifer, and I remain frozen.

During our on-the-job-training with Shelley Harwayne, Jenifer Hall and I worked closely together. I was grateful for Jenifer—it made a huge difference being able to go through such an intense experience with another person. Jenifer and I phoned each other nightly to exchange stories and notes, encourage each other, and commiserate about the innumerable snafus in the schools we visited: scheduling foul-ups, poor directions, bad neighborhoods, absent teachers, impossible principals, and the grinding sadness of public schools.

"Some of these little kids are so damn weird," I tell her over the phone. "This first grader today asks me if I have a pair of sharp scissors.

"'Why?' I ask him.

"''Cause I don't want you to cut me up,' he says."

Jenifer tells me about a difficult day she spent in a Bronx kindergarten.

"Kindergarten! Their first week of school and I'm trying to do writing process with them! I'm trying to get them to sit still, and they keep doing this weird thing with their hands on the floor. Like they're passing little buttons or something. 'Stop that!' I tell them. 'Sit still!' But I couldn't get them to stay seated. Then I see them: ants! The floor is covered with ants! No wonder they wouldn't sit still."

Certain training days did prove to be disastrous. It might sound savvy to submit that in hindsight such days were pregnant with early warnings, telltale signals of doom I chose to ignore. Not so. Many of my early disasters took place on glorious days, promise-crammed, perfumed by clear autumn air, the kind of days that made up the best part of my own childhood, days that seemed created solely for children. On such days I felt privileged simply to be with children, breathing in the aroma. On such days I had no inkling of what lay in store for me.

Exhibit A. I am parking my car in Queens. A typical Queens neighborhood, not quite suburban, not quite city, the small homes representing in many cases an immigrant family's first toehold in America. Small brick houses, wrought iron gates, statuettes in the tiny yards. Knots of children appear on the sidewalk beside me. Sitting in my car, I am aware of the magnetic force a school exerts, pulling children out of these little homes, away from their parents, creating a swift and irresistible current through the neighborhood. It pulls me out of my own car, sweeping me along with the current, into the schoolyard and through the old front doors.

Seeing me sign the guest book (which dates back to 1953, the year of my birth), the school secretary favors me with a conspiritorial smile and whispers, "Personally, I wouldn't sign *anything* around here." Maybe that should have alerted me: the playful warning, the rare secretarial smile. But I am not warned. Instead, I dutifully head to my first classroom: Mrs. Haritakis's.

Mrs. Haritakis is out sick—the substitute teacher does not seem particularly thrilled to see me. She is a jowly woman, perhaps fifty, with a set expression as she stands, hands on hips, in front of thirty second graders.

"Shut up!" she screams. "Listen. You're going to write today. Understand? You're going to be *creative!*"

Standing before the class, I can feel the eyes of the second graders all over my face. The children represent a veritable United Nations: Asians, Hispanics, blacks, and whites. I am beginning this writing workshop with the same uneasy knowledge I have had throughout the training: this is nothing more than a mock launch, like one of those simulated test flights astronauts endure before embarking on the real thing. I will spend an hour with these children and, most likely, never see them again. I am haunted by the image of launching children into some kind of curriculum limbo. After I leave, what kind of writing instruction will they have this year? Assigned topics? Copying stories off the blackboard?

I try to tell myself it doesn't matter. Lucy Calkins has been clear on this point.

"You'll be helping kids all year," she said. "These classes are for the benefit of *you*, to practice, to make mistakes."

I gather the second graders on the floor in one corner of the class and invite the children to write. Nearby, at her desk, the sub shuffles papers. "You can write about whatever you want," I hear myself saying to the children. "Only try to write about something that's important to you. Don't waste time writing about something that doesn't matter."

Many of the kids have devilish, we've-got-a-sub-today expressions on their faces, but as I talk I can sense them beginning to listen. Encouraged, I swing into a few examples of what *I* might write about. I lead off with a story from my own childhood: the night I got lost at a country fair in Marshfield, Massachusetts.

"Once, when I was just seven years old, I — "

The door opens. The class turns unanimously to regard the intruder: a diminutive Japanese girl shyly bearing a box of Dunkin Donut "munchkin" donut centers. It turns out that the school has a custom whereby, on their birthdays, children bring around "munchkins" to the school teachers. The class and I wait while the sub chooses a chocolate-covered munchkin. Politely, I decline.

Back to my story. I get to the point where I am lost, on the brink of tears, searching out my folks in a mass of humanity. The door opens again.

"Office needs lunch money!" a boy breathlessly announces. This prompts a confused showing of hands as to which students have paid for hot lunch and which have not. In taking out his money, one boy spills a pocketful of change onto the floor sparking a near donnybrook as kids scramble around to pick up pennies, nickels, dimes, quarters.

Things deteriorate from there. In the second class, smack in the middle of my introductory talk, an errant bell sounds. And sounds. I wait. Fifteen seconds. Twenty. Glancing at the teacher in the room, I mouth, "How long?"

"A minute and a half," she replies wearily. "They've been trying to fix it since last year."

And still it goes on, my own personal horror movie, an invisible boll weevil boring into my brain. The kids ignore it.

The third classroom I visit is empty. A teacher across the hall informs me that the children are in the auditorium practicing for a play. I return to the Main Office and sit down to collect my thoughts.

The Main Office is the perfect place to take the pulse of a school — the only arguably better place is the teachers' lunchroom. I sit back to peruse my surroundings. At my right, a bulletin board displays the names and photos of the Students Of The Month. The names feel exotic in my mouth as I attempt to pronounce them: Euen Mee Shin,

Seung Tek Kim, Veneet Garg, Stella Cherepashensky, Kosquite Ellis, Philip Yoor, Wajhia Karmizada, Vibas Sharma.

To my left, the UFT (Union of Federated Teachers) Bulletin Board: a newly inaugurated Burn-out Hotline, information on retroactive pay increases, weekly meetings, etc. Next to that there is a large poster detailing

CERTAIN COMMUNICABLE DISEASES
REASONS FOR EXCLUSION FROM/READMISSION TO SCHOOL

I am studying the subtle difference between scabies and mites when two students race into the office.

"Our hamster is loose!" one of the boys, perhaps eight years old, shouts. "And we can't catch it!"

"What class?" a secretary asks wearily.

"4–332. Mrs. Shine."

At this moment a large balding teacher comes whistling into the office. I do a double take; the man is a dead ringer for the actor Peter Boyle.

"Mr. Harrison," the secretary tells him. "A hamster has gotten loose in 4–332."

"Catching loose hamsters is not part of my job," Harrison replies without missing a beat. He grabs the New York Times from his mailbox and exits, still whistling.

The principal, Howard Sleznick, a short, stumpy man with a twitch at his right eyebrow, enters, baring some impressive dental work. He is wearing a pea green dinosaur tie; there is a stain of some sort, mustard, perhaps, on one of the tiny Stegasauruses. Sleznick deals decisively with the hamster crisis, dispatching a custodian to "clear up the situation." I introduce myself.

"Oh, you're the one here to do the Lucy Calkins Writing Program, right?" he asks.

"Right, the writing process."

"Splendid, splendid," he replies. "Welcome. Hope you're enjoying the school. You don't find schools like this in the city. This school really doesn't exist in New York City. It's a figment of somebody's imagination. The best-kept secret in the Big Apple. Would you like to sign our guest book?"

Sleznick magnanimously offers to provide me with a school lunch: hot dogs, sauerkraut, baked beans, applesauce, milk. Politely, I decline.

In the afternoon, I enter a fourth-grade class. The kids are big and cynical. They snicker at the story I tell from my childhood—the first time I have been snickered at by school children—and pass the period gossiping, griping, trading insults. The class is torn by wicked subcurrents between students. Two tall boys at opposite sides of the room, Manuel and Ricky, seem particularly hostile to each other and spend their time making loud observations about each other's intelligence. During the share time, I reluctantly let Manuel read his story about how he got his leg ripped open by his brother's saw.

"What kind of blood was it?" a girl asks Manuel.

"Puerto Rican blood," Ricky mutters, just loud enough for everyone to hear.

"Ooooooh!" the class croons delightedly as Manuel levels an icy stare at Ricky. I manage to leave the room before the inevitable fight erupts.

In my final class, with third graders, I try one more time. I have heard third grade described as the perfect grade: the children old enough to be able to read and write fluently but not yet tainted by the cynicism and cliquishness of the upper grades. To model the kind of topics the kids might choose to write about, I decide to read the students some first-rate literature, in this case a personal favorite, *The Relatives Came* by Cynthia Rylant. I gather the children on the floor and open the book. But my reading gets summarily punctuated by a loud hot-dog-sauerkraut-and-beans-fueled fart coming from one of the children. The blast makes a distinct, two-note melody, starting high, diving low, sending the kids into uncontrollable paroxisms of hilarity. I cannot compete with it.

After school, utterly defeated, I limp back to my office at Teachers College. A bit of graffiti adorning one of the college men's rooms does little to cheer me up:

Those who can, do.
Those who can't, teach.
Those who can't teach, teach teachers.

That evening I have dinner with Steve "Machine Gun" Mosely and Bill O'Reilly, friends I had worked with for several years during my years as a tour leader. O'Reilly and Mosely have just returned from a month-long tour to St. Moritz, the Swiss Alps. They spill out tales of decadent expense account dinners, ancient and almost unbearably good red wine, romance with Swiss chambermaids, Mercedes rental cars. . . . Had I really once been part of such a world? The question is almost too painful to articulate, even to myself. What on earth had prompted me to take the job as a teacher trainer in the first place?

And yet my fall training included fabulous days as well. I was having a great deal more fun than I had expected. For one thing it was wonderful being able to work so closely with kids. This unexpected pleasure sustained itself all year long. I cannot quite explain why. Maybe it had something to do with the remarkable attention—I want to say *obsession*—children are capable of bringing to a moment. Perhaps it had to do with the ethnic variety of the children and my own fascination with the American "melting pot." Some of my ideas were admittedly romantic. Talking to children born in Pakistan, Afghanistan, Colombia, and Egypt, it would occur to me that they carried forth from their ancestors the actual genes and blood and energy of the great civilizations before them: the Egyptians, the Romans, the Aztecs, and the Celts.

Or maybe it had more to do with the children's surprising shows of affection—as well as my unsatisfied desire to have children of my own and the fact that I'd been working in childless worlds (writing, tour guiding) for so long. This much is true: as I worked with kids, some part of me that had long been frostbitten now began to thaw.

And there was a constant mystery at the heart of every classroom I entered. What would these children write about today? What snatches of their past or emerging selves would they scribble onto the paper?

As a child I used to cast my fishing rod out into a night forest, into the heart of the woods, imagining that I might catch a creature of strange and astounding beauty who did not need water, who subsisted on the darkness alone. One summer, while the other neighborhood kids played kick-the-can or capture-the-flag, I fished patiently for this creature, night after night, while the spaces between the huge pines filled with darkness, until my mother called me inside. Now, in a similar way, whenever I invited kids to write their important stories, I imagined myself fishing deep and virgin waters. Most children had never before been challenged to write about the important issues in their lives. I never tired of wondering what I might catch.

Sometimes it was only a phrase in a kid's writing that caught my eye—a boy describing himself running into the house after getting stung by a bee "like a video that's stuck on fast forward." Often a child's writing contained streaks of odd beauty, such as this piece by a third grade Chinese girl:

My Second Sister

My second sister died because she was born too early. Her name is Tamika. She died on January 1, 1981. She is now eight years old. She died in California. She was the size of a Math Book when she died. I miss her a lot.

Certain stories had a pleasing folksiness, as with the homespun philosophy woven into third grader Craig's piece:

The Shovel Man

One day when I was five I woke at 6:00. I went out to shovel the snow. Sometimes my neighbors paid me $5.00. But money doesn't count. Love and friendship counts. You are just doing it for fun. Then when my mother woke up she saw me. She said, "Come back to bed." But I still shoveled the snow.

I spent two memorable days in a very poor Brooklyn elementary school. New York City schools go thirty-three years before they come up for serious repainting; this particular school must have been right at the thirty-three year mark. The dim hallways featured huge ragged stalactites of paint hanging from the ceiling. In a fourth-grade class I visited, a Vietnamese girl named Minh sat down and wrote this story in less than twenty minutes.

When I Was Coming To America

When I came out from Vietnam I was only 3 or 4 years old. I took a big ship. I was on the ocean. The big waves was coming and the ship had a leak on the bottom of the ship. The ship had a lot of floors. The toilet had no doors and every time when somebody goes to the toilet the stuff on the toilet splash right on your butt and if your not lucky people who walk to get something will see you. In the ocean, they have whales, shark and dangerous animals in the ocean. My family (there were 5 of us in the ship) were hungry and thirsty. The place where we slept was very little land. Then one day we saw land but not America. It was Hong Kong. I was very sick on ship. I had a fever and I always had to throw up. So one day the police patrols came to check us. See why we were here. After they went on the ship and saw I was very sick. So they told me to get on the little police boat. They said one of my parents may come. So my mother go. Then I was in a hospital for babies.

What a find! What a piece of writing! A whole era of American history embodied in this skinny little girl. Though Minh did not have time to finish the story, she did allow me to take it back to Teachers College. I promised to bring it back the next day.

The following morning, when I return to Brooklyn, I am witness to a stunning effect of nature: the skyscrapers all bathed in clean morning light and juxtaposed against a background of dark clouds. A squall moving in. Sailing down the FDR, just as I pass the United Nations building, I realize with a sick heart that I have left Minh's piece of writing back in my office. First thing, I take her outside the classroom to apologize.

"That's okay," she says softly. "I'll just keep going from where I left off. I remember the story."

When I Was Coming To America.
(Continuing from p. 1)

I was up to the part when I didn't know what happened when I was in the hospital because I got a kind of needle shot that made me sleepy. After a few days I went back to the ship. The ship started again. We went for many days and nights. Then one day we stop (I am not sure where we were). We went to a beach. We had to walk on the beach. Some people got separated from their parents because the soldiers only let the people who were young enough to walk to the cabins. It was very spooky because the wolfs were howling and I was holding onto my mother's leg, but she had to hold the luggages, too. It turn night and it was dark. I finally reach to the cabins. It was very crowdy.

Then one day one of the soldiers said 5 people may go on the airplane to go to America so they pick us. I miss all my friends at the cabins. I was scared to go on the airplane, but I had to. That how I came to America.

One Hundred and Fifty Years of Experience

One curious byproduct of all the time spent in these schools: I unearthed the Elementary School Student buried inside me. I had never anticipated this job dredging up so many old fears, desires, so much pungent déjà vu, most of which I would have preferred to keep buried. I suddenly found myself prey to all sorts of quirky school demons: workbook spirits, the steamy smell from the cafeteria, the sovereign power of the Principal, the vicissitudes of teachers' whims and moods and idiosyncracies, the nonreferential sadness of childhood itself, the mystery of Knowledge, the eternal lathing of dreary classrooms on inquisitive minds. My God, I thought I had left this all behind.

I found myself visited by old school memories as well as recurrent archetypal school dreams like the one where I'm standing in front of my classmates who are howling with derision because I have somehow neglected to put on my pants. Or a sudden attack of lockjaw that prevents me from delivering an oral report to my class.

A memory, and a dream.

I am ten years old, soon to be eleven. Miss Barille, my fourth-grade teacher with whom I'm fervently in love, sits casually on the edge of her desk. She is a young woman, in her early twenties, with long blond hair and points of light sewn into her eyes. Walking through the classroom, Miss Barille leaves a deep musky smell in her wake: I think of her physical being and this aroma as two distinct presences. She has a way of looking at me that makes me want to be far better than I know I am. Today she is leading the class through a verbal exercise in math problems. We have reached the last, most difficult problem.

"All right, here goes," Miss Barille says. "Eight plus nine . . . minus five . . . times two . . . plus six . . . plus eleven."

She pauses. Piece of cake, I think to myself: forty-one. My hand shoots up. Miss Barille calls on me.

"Ralph?"

My heart starts to hammer. I have a fathomless desire to please her; at the same time my chest is choked with great swallows of doubt. Forty-one is such an odd number. How can I be so sure of it? Wasn't it likely that I'd made some slight error? In an instant I'm convinced of it. Quickly, desperately, I try to compensate. Mrs. Barille waits patiently, her scent blossoming all over the place, eyes blue and soft in her face.

"Forty-two?" I guess. She looks at me tenderly.

"Oh, Ralph," she says. "You're always just one number off."

In the dream, I am standing before a large class filled with very young children—four- and five-year-olds, mostly. The room brims with expectancy. In addition to the children, other important members of the Writing Project are crammed into the room: Lucy Calkins, Shelley Harwayne, JoAnn Curtis, Georgia Heard, Martha Horn. Plus the school principal. I am being closely watched to see how well I can teach writing to very young children.

"Are you ready?" Lucy asks me.

"All set."

"What are you going to sing?" Lucy asks.

"Sing?"

"I'm sure Shelley talked to you about that," Lucy says. "You know. You can't just talk to kids this little. They don't pay attention if you just talk. You have to *sing* to them."

Sing? It is the first I have heard of such a thing. How could I be so unprepared? What have I been doing these past weeks? Maybe I had been sick during the training when Shelley had gone over it. Maybe I have missed the training altogether.

"Oh right, sure," I say casually, fighting off a wave of panic. Lucy has stepped back. The kids gaze up, huge-eyed and expectant. Of course, I am not prepared to sing anything to anyone. It won't work. I realize that while I might possibly be able to fool the adults in the room on this singing issue, the kids will not be deceived for an instant. I am lost.

My training continues through a resplendent autumn. An earthquake churns through Mexico and leaves hundreds dead. A few days later the death toll has climbed well into the thousands. Hurricane Gloria hits New York. While the city children write about the hurricane as a "dud," my parents mourn the loss of four gigantic sycamore trees at their Long Island home. Leon Klinghoffer is brutally killed by Palestinian terrorists. The Kansas City Royals beat the St. Louis Cardinals in the World Series. Patrick Ewing plays his first game for the New York Knicks. The Knicks lose.

The on-the-job-training drew on an energy source I had never tapped before—not merely physical stamina but a kind of sustained mental concentration as well. This involved great feats of simultaneity: learning how to listen (both to students and teachers), keep an eye on the clock, keep myself wired to the nuances of the classroom environment, and all the while keep an eye on myself. With great faith in my resiliency, I watched the fluctuations of my energy level and tried to be patient with myself during days I found myself dragging.

In an effort to fine-tune my teaching skills, I begin carrying a tape recorder with me through the classrooms to record my various interactions with children. One day, driving from Brooklyn to the Bronx, I hit a traffic snag on the FDR. To kill some time, I start playing back the tape of myself teaching. Horrors! I would plunge into such blind syntactical alleyways, turn, bolt out, and begin my sentences again. Did I really speak so quickly? What ever happened to clean diction? What ever happened to the mot juste?

On the Thursday after election day, without a great deal of fanfare, Shelley Harwayne takes Jenifer Hall, Jim Sullivan, and me aside.

"Lucy and I have talked it over," she says, smiling. "We think you're ready to start. Probably next week."

"You mean training—for real?"

Shelley nods. The three of us exchange startled glances.

"Do you have any last-minute advice for us?" I ask.

"I've given you all the tips and advice I could think of," Shelley says, shrugging. "You'll be wonderful. Just relax. Be yourself. Wear comfortable clothes on Monday. And get lots of sleep this weekend. You'll need it."

I would be responsible for the staff development in two of New York City's thirty districts—one in Queens, the other in the Bronx. Jenifer has been slated to work in the South Bronx and the Flatbush section of Brooklyn—both with rock-bottom NYC reading scores, far tougher districts than my own. This bothers me. I chafe at missing the chance for an inside perspective in the schools I had read about. Schools with broken windows, urine in the halls, teachers stoned on reefer, kids for whom the school lunch is the only nutritionally complete meal they get all day. After all, that was the true inner city, wasn't it? Compared to Jenifer's, my districts seem drearily normal.

Taking a new job as a teacher trainer was concurrent with another change in my life: a new apartment in a new borough of the city. This had not been easy. My wife, Marian, and I were still recovering from a traumatic move from Manhattan's Upper West Side to the Lydig Avenue area of the Bronx. The population of this neighborhood was comprised of Russian Jews and other whites, Hispanics, and a recent influx of Albanians. We saw legions of elderly men and women, puffing along the sidewalks, heading for the kosher butchers or the bakeries. But after the initial shock (no Zabar's, no Central Park, no yuppies), we had cautiously begun to discover the pleasant surprises in our new environs: the large variety of Jewish bakeries, a five-minute walk to the Bronx Zoo and Botanical Gardens, and a scant three-minute drive to the Italian delicacies of Arthur Avenue. Maybe we would like it there after all.

But as October yielded to November, the spectacular autumn foliage in our neighborhood faded to November gray. Shorn of its leaves—which, I suspected, constituted one of the Bronx's few indigenous charms—my new borough revealed itself for what it was: gritty and grafittied, an uneasy quilt of ethnic groups wearily trying to hang onto some shred of their uniqueness.

I take Shelley's advice and get lots of sleep that weekend. Leaving my apartment building that Monday, my newly shaved skin gets smacked by a gust of damp wind. I walk down to the bank; the cash machine spits out two damp, woefully wrinkled ten-dollar bills. Never before had I received bills from a cash machine in such pathetic condition. Such a thing simply would not happen in Manhattan where, if you could not get an affordable apartment, at least you could count on cash machines that produce crisp, newly cut, neatly stacked bills.

Pocketing the tens, I retrace my steps to my car. It doesn't start. Won't even turn over. The battery appears to be dead. Two months earlier, when we bought the car from its original owner, I'd been told that it might need a new battery soon, and I never got around to replacing it. I sit fuming in the battery-dead Toyota while a grimy mist collects on the windshield. I'm not the least bit superstitious, but under the circumstances I can't help taking this deceased battery as a very bad omen.

No time for the battery—I am scheduled to be at my first school in Queens at 8:35, a scant forty minutes from now. I look around for a taxi. In Manhattan, the place would be crawling with yellow cabs. Here—nothing. Fortunately, there is a local car service around the corner. I hoist my briefcase over and find an empty car. The driver is a thin, unshaven old man, all gristle and bile. He looks like he has not slept in a month; his car reeks of sweat and stale smoke.

I get into the back seat and glance around. Just as we begin moving, a large roach shimmies up the back of the front seat. I scoot over to the other side of the car. Roaches—in a taxi, no less!

"You know you've got roaches in this cab," I tell the driver, calmly as I can manage.

"Whahhh?"

I repeat myself.

"What do you want me to do, mister?" the driver retorts. "People around here are animals, know what I mean? They get in the cab, they eat their lunch in the back seat, leave crumbs all over the place. No wonder I got roaches in here. Just be thankful it ain't rats."

I hunch down in the back seat, trying hard to feel thankful.

The ride takes us over the Whitestone Bridge and down the slick Queens Expressway. It is pouring rain, and cold, by the time we reach PS 478, a big, weathered, no-nonsense brick box of a school. No umbrella. I pay the driver, stick a yellow legal pad over my head, and bolt from the cab to the nearest school door. Locked. Another door. Same thing. I try seven separate entrances until one door gives and I can lurch, soaked, into the school.

A few minutes later I am sipping tepid coffee in the office of Elaine Rolnick, the principal. She is about my mother's age, fifty-five, with curly silver hair, watery eyes, and a severe Margaret Thatcher expression on her lips. I am startled to see these lips contort into a grin.

"You're just in time, Mr. Fletcher," she tells me. "Weather or no weather, we are about to have a 'Blocked Exit Fire Drill.' Not to be missed."

She pauses and walks behind her desk, her finger poised over the red fire alarm. "This is *real* power."

Moments later liquefactious streams of children are pouring out of the building into a soft rain. They stream out endlessly, child after child, solemn-faced, dutifully pumping feet, staying in line, the youngest boys and girls holding hands. The children are smartly dressed: the girls in stretch black pants and bright baggy sweatshirts, the boys in brand new dress shirts or Mets sweatshirts. Watching these children, I sense an invisible something missing from many of the inner city schools I had previously visited: conscientious parents. Or maybe it is simply money.

The children wait for the drill to end. A few elderly neighbors stand gawking. Two women with red unfurled "FIRE ALARM" pennants stop an annoyed motorist from turning left. And all the while a jackhammer at the blocked exit doesn't miss a beat.

At 9:00 I am back in Mrs. Rolnick's office, reading the sign above her large oak desk:

Tell me, I forget.
Show me, I remember.
Involve me, I understand.

Mrs. Rolnick hands me a beautifully typed schedule. For the next three mornings I am slated to do demonstration teaching in her school: a first-grade classroom followed by a class of fifth graders. Six to eight teachers would be watching each one-hour demonstration class. The schedule allows ample time for me to meet with the teachers after the class to discuss with them what they had seen.

I head first for Mrs. Oxner's class. I am nervous. No more mock launching, no more jettisoning kids into some kind of curriculum limbo.

This is the real thing. The hallways are decorated with Norman Rockwell prints. I find these prints, with their insufferably cute depictions of childhood, oddly reassuring. These are just little kids, the paintings seem to be saying, and little kids aren't out to do anybody harm. Everything will be fine.

A big splashy turkey adorns the door to Mrs. Oxner's room. Inside, even before I fidget under the inquiring eyes of the children, before I exchange pleasantries with Mrs. Oxner and the four other teachers waiting for me, I am skewered by the dazzling visual complexity of this first-grade classroom, a sensation reminiscent of the first time I took off the back of my IBM PC and the machine's terrible innards were bared to my eyes. Everything here is done in miniature; all the pieces fall under the same diminutive logic and all, somehow, fit together. On the blackboard are an attendance chart, large thermometer, calendar, and weather watcher—all arranged under the archetypal illustrated alphabet. Lists galore: Favorite Foods. Class Jobs. Child of the Month. Our Favorite Holidays. Days of the Week. Do's and Don'ts (no biting). Art Center (fingerpaints, Playdough, crayons), Science Center (plants, dinosaurs, body parts, and a huge poster: "Who's Hibernating?"), Play Center (blocks, sandbox, play kitchen, and cupboard), Reading Center. More lists along the closets: Class Birthday lists, Short Vowels, Long Vowels. And strung on a clothesline across the room, twenty-five cotton-crested paper-bag puppets. The classroom is every bit as bewildering as the control panel to a rocket, a high-tech spaceship that I have been designated to "launch."

Just as I enter, one little voice pipes out, "The writer!" The children stare up at me from their seats. Mrs. Oxner smiles at me. She is a slender woman, perhaps forty-five, with graying hair cut in the straight schoolgirlish style of the 1960s.

"Boys and girls, this is Ralph Fletcher, the writer I told you about," Mrs. Oxner says. "What do you say to Mr. Fletcher?"

In ragged chorus, "Good mor-ning Mis-ter Flet-cher."

"I'm so glad to be here," I tell them, and suddenly I mean it, I *am* glad. I can think of nothing better than spending an hour with these feverishly curious five-year-olds. "We're going to have lots of fun with writing."

"He sounds more like a *speaker* than a writer," a red-haired boy muses loudly to nobody in particular.

"Are you a p-p-p-professor?" another boy inquires.

Mrs. Oxner laughs.

"They're all yours," she says, and with an old-fashioned curtsey turns over her charges to me. The children are sitting at tables named after the major bridges of New York. Bridge by bridge, I call the children to the back of the room: Throgs Neck, Triboro, Whitestone, George Washington, Tappan Zee. They sit, cross-legged. Spellbound, fully expecting catastrophe, the children watch me lower myself into one of their Lilliputian chairs; they seem incredulous when the chair does not splinter and break.

"Boys and girls," I begin. "My name is Ralph Fletcher. You may call me Ralph, or Mr. Fletcher, whichever you please."

The children stare at me. Take my word for it: you have never really been observed until twenty-eight first graders check you out.

"I have two jobs: I'm a writer and I'm also a teacher. I have a special job as a teacher—I teach teachers. You probably didn't know that your teacher has a teacher, too, but she does. That's why all these teachers are here today—to learn more about how to teach writing. I'm going to ask you to do something special for me today. Today I'm going to ask you to pretend that I'm your teacher. All right? Pretend that Mrs. Oxner and the other teachers here are invisible. If you have any questions you can just ask me."

This wrests a chuckle from the kids.

"Does anybody know what an author is?" I ask them. Silence. After a moment a blond-haired boy directly in front of me raises his hand.

"I think a author is a bear, well, kind of like a bear or a sloth," he says, speaking in a nasally voice.

"Well, no, it's not that," I tell him, suppressing a grin.

"It's like a polar bear," a girl says. "It *is* a polar bear."

"An author is someone who writes a book," I tell them. "Authors have to decide all kinds of things: how to start, how long the story should be, what kind of pictures go with the writing. And the first thing to decide is, what should I write about?" I pause to let this idea sink in. "Let me share with you some ideas I might write about."

"I write about my family a lot," I tell them. "I'm the oldest of nine children. We have a lot of family stories we like to share. On Easter, my mother used to cook a fancy meal. When we sat down to eat Easter dinner, there was always one of those yellow marshmallow chicks on each of our plates. But one year something strange happened. When we went to sit down for Easter dinner, everybody gasped. Someone had bitten the heads off of all the marshmallow chicks."

The kids look up at me, shocked, bemused.

"Who did it?" one girl whispers.

"We all looked around," I continue. "And my brother noticed that my little sister, Kathy, had some yellow sugar at the corner of her mouth. She said she didn't do it. Even today, she says she didn't bite off those chicks' heads."*

"I think she *did* do it!" one boys says, outraged.

I share some other topics I might write about: being the oldest in a big family, when I moved from Chicago to New York, a special fishing tackle box I received as a present for my tenth birthday. Then I get the kids thinking of what they might write about and send them off to write. I am relieved to see them attack their large pieces of paper with crayons and pencil.

The kids are excited, you can feel it in the air, and their excitement gets inside of me. Whether from the children's eagerness, the teachers' rapt attentiveness, or some fortunate alignment of my own biorhythms, I feel a sudden combustion of confidence inside me. This is going to be *fun*, I say to myself, moving with the five observing teachers to the first first grader in the classroom, my first "real" writing conference—a tiny blond girl named Amber. Before I can approach her, Mrs. Oxner pulls me aside.

"I should explain a few things about Amber. She's young, a January birth who probably should have another year in kindergarten. She's pretty insecure, too—in the playground she starts to cry whenever she loses sight of her big sister. Bad family scene. When her father, who's maybe twenty-one, came to the parent conference, he was totally stoned." She pauses. "I won't be surprised if Amber has to repeat first grade."

I sit down next to her. There is a two-inch lateral scar that starts at the corner of the girl's mouth. She has already written a story in tiny letters, and after the background information Mrs. Oxner provided, I am surprised when Amber agrees to read out loud what she's written:

---

*A true story. Today, despite overwhelming evidence, Kathy continues to insist she did not bite off the chicks' heads.

I gt lst in aligzndrs	I got lost in Alexanders
in the toy conpatmit.	in the toy compartment.
I wz not hape at all.	I was not happy at all.
I wz not fenin gd.	I was not feeling good.
I wz frininde to.	I was frightened, too.
I wz I yrz old.	I was one years old.
I so a crajer tare.	I saw a stranger there.
tare wz no plese man tare.	There was no policeman there.

"Hey, this must've been scary!" I say to Amber.

Gravely, the child nods.

"Down here you wrote about the stranger. Is he important to your story?"

"Yes," she says, surprised that I would have to ask.

"Why?"

"'Cause I was afraid he would try to steal me."

"Oh! Is that important to add to your story?"

She nods solemnly. I help her tape a piece of paper to the bottom of her story so she can add in more information about the stranger.

I also confer with a perfectly beautiful, and beautifully outfitted, girl named Jessica. She is wearing an intricately woven sweater that pictures a lovely coastal scene; the two barrettes in her straight black hair pick up the blue in the sweater's ocean. Jessica is having trouble thinking of what to write about.

"I could write about my father's farm in Colombia," she says, flashing rows of straight white teeth. "He even has a pony that's mine, and I can ride it when I'm there."

"When was the last time you went to see him?" I ask.

"Just last month. My father has a lot of money. He has a house in Florida with a big swimming pool. And he has another house in New York.

"What does your father do?"

Jessica shrugs. Grins. Mrs. Oxner catches my eye as I turn away.

"I know what you're thinking," she says. "The same thing has crossed my mind."

Share time. I gather the children again and put an empty chair next to me.

"Can anyone guess who's going to sit in this chair? A very special person is going to sit here."

"The principal?"

"You?"

"The President?"

"No," I tell them. "An author is going to sit here. A real live one. One of the authors in this class. From now on, we're going to call this special chair the Author's Chair."

The children hush as Amber moves to the Author's Chair. She reads her piece about getting lost in the Alexanders "toy compartment"; her clear, tiny voice adds to the piece's fearful tone.

Next Missy reads her story:

My story is about my dog. I have a dog. And I have a mother. And I have a father. And I love my teacher, too. And I love my mother. And I love my father. And I love my mother. And I love Maribel, too. And I love Selena. And I love Erica. And I like Job. And I play with my dog. And I like the class, too. And I like November, too.

The kids are excited. A field of raised hands.

"I like your story," Rachel says. "I haven't heard such a good story in a long, long time."

"It was so funny," Christian says.

"It's adorable," Jess puts in.

"Wait a minute," says Luis. "You say your story is about your dog, but you tell how you love your mother and your father and everybody, and there's just a little about your dog at the beginning and the end."

Silence. The observing teachers look at each other, amazed. Missy gently smacks her forehead.

"I thought I was finished," she says, "and now I have lots more work to do."

Attaboy, Luis!

"Sure you didn't plant that question?" one teacher asks.

I send the kids back to their seats, table by table. Soon, only three kids remain sitting in the meeting area with me. A Japanese girl points shyly at the vacant Author's Chair.

"Could I sit in the Author's Chair?" she asks me. "Just for a minute?"

"Sure, go ahead."

She jumps up and sits down, taking a moment to get comfortable.

"Well? How does it feel?" I ask her.

"Feels great!" the girl says, beaming.

Elated, I move to Renée Shalvey's fifth-grade class. One down, two to go. After working with the first graders, these kids look enormous, their eyes shrewder, colored by dawning adolescence. I revel in the variety of issues the kids choose to write about. Boris's story is titled "Something Nasty I Did In Russia": he let go of his friend's balloons at a Russian circus. His friend now lives just five blocks away from him in Queens, but the two boys still don't speak to each other. Mike writes about the day his cat got stuck in the dryer while it was turned on; Rachel writes about having to choose between her father and mother when they divorced.

The class runs flawlessly until I confer with an unusually tall girl named Faroshta, one of several children of Afghanistan heritage in the class. Faroshta has thick dark eyebrows and long braided hair. She is writing about her summer vacation, a fairly tedious list of all the things she did over the summer: spraining her ankle, spending three weeks in Florida, going camping, worrying when her brother got lost for five hours on the beach. The teachers move closer, curious to see how I'll respond to such a piece.

"Instead of putting everything in this one piece of writing," I suggest, "you might consider writing this as a book with chapters. Do you know what I mean?" She just looks at me.

"See, one chapter might be about going to Florida. Another chapter could be about how you sprained your ankle. Like that."

Faroshta shrugs.

"Go get about five sheets of paper, and I'll show you how to do it," I say. Terrific! The perfect chance to show teachers one way of responding to a student with such a broad topic. When she returns, I take a couple sheets of paper and, with everyone watching, prepare to staple them to the back of her story.

"You don't mind, do you?" I ask.

"Do I have a choice?" she asks quietly.

Time out. I kneel beside her.

"Of course you have a choice. It's your piece of writing."

"No, go ahead. You're the teacher, right?"

A disaster? Certainly, but I decide to t'ai chi the failure of this bungled conference to explain nonchalantly to the watching teachers how important it is that students feel they own their writing and have the final say-so about revisions. And it works! The teachers nod, writing down my words. It's almost as if I *planned* it this way.

Mohammed, a serious boy with oversized black glasses, starts the share session with a piece about his old town in Pakistan.

Pakistan is a nice place. It is hot all year. We have a large house which a big family lives in. We also dress different from Americans. Children could drive cars and trucks. Over there men's are not supposed to see the ladies. When a man is getting engaged with a lady the mother and father have to choose the lady for him. If a lady is pregnant and she is not married she will have to die.

We have dirt on the road so it is very dusty. We also have chickens in our house. Some people have cows in their houses. We do not speak English we speak another language that only our people know. When the children go to school there are two or three girls and the rest are boys. We go to school every day except Friday.

Mohammed shrugs.

"That's as far as I got," he says, and seems surprised to see a dozen kids with their hands in the air, oohing and grunting, begging to ask a question.

"How come there's only a couple girls in school?" one of the girls wants to know. Mohammed shrugs.

"The girls don't want to go to school," he replies without expression.

"How come if a lady is pregnant and she's not married she has to die?" Terrence asks.

"That is our law," Mohammed replies calmly.

"How do they kill her?"

"We put her in a big tub of oil and build a fire under it," Mohammed explains. This detail satisfies some dark appetite in the children. They howl with glee.

Jason ends the share by reading "The Amazing Dobermans," a curious piece about a boy threatened by another boy, and the dogs the boy uses to protect himself. Jason reads the piece with utter sincerity; it is the lack of artifice that gives the story its charm.

"He tried to beat you up," one Oriental boy says. "Why didn't you try to beat him up?"

"Do unto others as you would have done unto you," Jason says, Confucious-like.

"That boy called you a coward," Terrence says. "How come you didn't hit him for calling you that?"

"Ah," Jason replies, smiling faintly as if he had been expecting this question. "Sticks and stones will break my bones, but names will never hurt me."

This cracks everybody up.

In the taxi from PS 478 to PS 414 I am elated, crossing my fingers, praying that my luck with today's launches will hold. A little growl sounds from my lunchless belly. But hunger gives way to surprise at how quickly the neighborhood deteriorates as we drive. The compact and neatly trimmed lawns around PS 478 grow shabbier and yield to tiny homes, burnt-out buildings, store fronts with heavy metal bars advertising DISCOUNT LIQUOR, PAWN SHOP, CHECKS CASHED HERE.

At PS 414, the secretary in the Main Office gives me the guest book to sign and directs me down to the cafeteria to find Marlon Hauser, the principal. Entering the immense room, I am assaulted by a tremendous din made by hundreds of kids eating, laughing, goofing, yelling. Decible City. At the near end of the room, three stout, heavily made-up women in dark jackets (we dubbed them "Renta-Mommies" when I was in school), all toting bullhorns, keep unsmiling watch over the kids. From time to time, one of these women raises her bullhorn to bark something ineffectual at them:

"Brian Young, get off that table! Miladred, do you want to stay after school today? 4–322, I cannot believe the way you're behaving today. . . . You ought to be ashamed of yourselves."

These admonitions don't help; the noise level continues unabated. The expressions on these aides or paraprofessionals or whoever they are profoundly depress me. An exercise in pure crowd control. When I go into a classroom I ask myself, Could I write here? In that cafeteria I find myself asking, Could I *eat* here? Could I sit for forty minutes and finish my lunch without getting indigestion?

I find Marlon Hauser in one corner of the lunchroom, talking sternly to two boys. He is a tall man, fifty-five-ish, with a great rusty Tip O'Neill nose and a slightly drooped face. With his thick white hair and direct gaze he wields a commanding presence, bringing the full weight of his authority down on the boys. One of the boys apparently does not speak English, and Hauser has to do his scolding in translation.

"This is not the park," Hauser tells the slender Hispanic boy, then pauses for the other boy to translate. "This is not the street." Pause. "Understand? *Comprende*? I don't care how you act on your block, but you're not going to do that in this school. Is that clear?"

It is as clear as it is going to get. The boys shuffle away. I introduce myself.

"Had lunch yet? Here, I'll get you a school lunch and have it sent up to my office. We can talk there before you do your first demonstration class."

Hauser's office is a jungle of greenery. I count a dozen spider plants and ivies descending from the ceiling. There are huge, wide-leafed plants on the floor; half his desk is taken up in an elaborate experiment on seed sproutings. The air has a muggy, rainforesty feel; I half-expect to be attacked by a macaw or boa constrictor. As we sit down to eat, Marlon apologizes for the scene in the cafeteria.

"Due to some atmospheric disturbance, or all the precipitation in the air, the kids have been berserk today," he says. I nod and try to figure out how to eat my lunch. The cafeteria aide has provided me with a giant submarine sandwich of indefinable coagulated white cheese and sauce. I keep searching for the meat. Unable to find it, I try cutting through the rubbery cheese which, like the proverbial poor of the world, bends but will not break.

"How are you doing there?" Hauser asks, motioning at my sub.

"Great, great," I say. "Tell me about your student body."

"As you've probably already guessed, this school draws from a completely different area than PS 478," Hauser replies. "Much poorer. This neighborhood is in what the sociologists call an 'era of transition.' We've had an exodus of whites, a drop in reading scores, and an increase in crime. I serve nearly a thousand breakfasts here every morning. Breakfasts!"

"What's the ethnic mix?"

"'Other' is our biggest majority," Hauser says. "Arabs, Latins, Haitians. You name it, we got it. And that's not all bad. Immigrants have traditionally seen the American schools as a vehicle for their children's success. They tend to see the schools as an important part of the community."

"How about your faculty?"

"Old guard with a new crop just beginning to come in." He gets up and picks a dead leaf off one of his ferns. "You want the truth? They're tired. The changes in this neighborhood have demoralized them. They just don't get the same results with second-language kids, and that bothers them."

"How receptive do you think they'll be to writing process?"

"You want the good news or the bad news?" he asks, smiling.

"Better start with the bad."

"All right." He leans forward and speaks softly, glancing several times at the closed door. "The central truth to all staff development is that *teachers are resistant to change*. Put that in bold letters above your desk. It's probably true in all human nature but particularly so in education, and for good reason. These teachers have seen every dog-and-pony show around come down from the district, only to be replaced by a new one the next year. Open court, new math, process writing, process science. So you'll find some teachers digging in their heels. Mostly the upper-grade teachers. But that's to be expected. You win good teachers over slowly to a program like this."

I grunt.

"Elementary teachers have the toughest job in all of education," Hauser continues. "They're at the bottom of the barrel. High school teachers blame their kids' inadequacies on the junior high teachers who, in turn, blame the elementary school teachers. They're every-body's scapegoat."

"I think I'm ready for the good news."

"You're working with an intelligent and experienced faculty. They're pros. They know bullshit when they see it, but if you can get them to trust you they'll follow you anywhere." He slaps the table and laughs. "Besides, they *will* teach writing this way because *I want them to*! Now, can I get you a cup of coffee?"

I head first to Donna Gereck's second-grade class. She is in the midst of a reading lesson when I arrive and doesn't seem particularly thrilled to see me. The kids are distracted during my talk with them and noisy when they start to write. A gaggle of teachers follows glumly behind as I confer with the children.

Erica, a plump girl in a heart-covered sweater, looks up at me with lovely, sad blue eyes. Her paper is covered with multi-hued rainbows of varying sizes.

"I can see you like rainbows, Erica," I say to her.

"I *love* rainbows," she replies, smiling.

"Bet you could write a whole book about rainbows."

"That's what I'm gonna do."

"You could even teach other children about rainbows," I say. "Do you know how rainbows are made?"

"Sure," she says without pausing in her drawing. "Oil and water."

"Huh?"

"When the oil mixes with the water," she explains patiently, "it makes a rainbow."

"But what about a real rainbow? In the sky."

"Well, I've never seen a rainbow in the sky," Erica says doubtfully.

"Well, you're doing a great job."

This touches me. I glance around to talk to the observing teachers about this writing conference, but they have all scattered to various parts of the classroom, and I must gather them together and request again that they please stay with me. Donna Gereck and her colleagues respond with blank looks.

I confer next with frizzy-haired Knia, who is writing with gusto on one of five sheets of paper spread out before her.

"My mother's havin' twins!" she tells me.

"Hey, that's great! You sure have something to write about, don't you?"

"Yep, sure do."

"When are the twins due?"

"I dunno, March, I think. Then there will be six people in our family."

"Six?"

"Yeah, there's only four now." She pauses and looks at me thoughtfully. "Well, there's really only three now. But this weekend there will be four people in our family because guess what? This weekend my mother's gettin' married?"

"Getting married, really?" I laugh, despite myself. "Boy, you sure do have lot to write about!"

"I know," Knia says, grinning.

Despite the noise and minor chaos, the kids seem to be enjoying the writing workshop. It's the observing teachers who are the major problem. They stroll through the classroom with noses in the air—vegetarians at a Texas steer roast. They refuse to stay with me as I confer with the students, don't take any notes, continually chat with each other even when I ask them not to. Their unspoken disapproval compounds itself as the class continues.

Afterward, I meet with all six teachers in Marlon Hauser's office greenhouse. One of the teachers whispers to Eleanor Bosch something about a poem one child was writing. This affords me the opportunity to lead off with a joke.

"I saw that poem," I say, grinning. "Move over, Emily Dickinson."

More blank looks. I am trapped in the jungle, surrounded by a pack of humorless natives. But seriously, folks . . .

"So, what did you think?" I ask them. "Did you have any questions about anything you saw today?"

Silence. Finally, one teacher speaks. She is a short, red-haired woman in her late fifties, with a taut, fingernails-on-blackboard kind of voice that instantly has me clenching my teeth.

"I'm Eleanor Bosch, fifth-grade teacher, and I don't see why you're so against giving the kids a topic," she says. "Sooner or later, they're going to have to write on an assigned topic. What's the big deal about them choosing their own topics?"

"I was told *not* to let my kids write about their lives because most of them have a poor self-image," another teacher chimes in. "Two years ago, we were told to get them writing about something else. Now, they write about their own experience. What kind of sense does that make? Next year, who knows?" She throws up her hands.

I patiently explain the rationale for asking children to start the year by writing personal narratives: how it fosters independence, allows children to make decisions and breathe authenticity into their writing, juggle the elements of a story, and take advantage of the tension between what is in the student's mind and what has been written down.

"I still don't see why there's anything wrong with giving them a topic," Mrs. Bosch interrupts. "Sometimes I just write a word onto the blackboard to give them a hint."

"If you decide to try to run a writing workshop," I say slowly, "I'm going to ask you to try letting kids write what they know. Later, I can show you how to move the kids from personal narrative to other kinds of writing."

"Let's get one thing straight," Eleanor Bosch says. "The teachers here have about 150 years' teaching experience between us. We're not exactly new at this, you know. Assigning kids topics has worked well enough so far."

I count slowly to ten, all the while wondering, How on earth did Marlon Hauser select these teachers to observe the lesson?

"Okay, you all seem to be having trouble with this topic-choice issue," I say. "But it's interesting that in today's class all of the kids came up with something to write about. Topics from their own lives."

"That was different." Mrs. Bosch objects. "You *motivated* them."

I look at her in astonishment. The nasally way she said "motivated" made it sound like a dirty word, as if I had abused the kids in some indefinable way. I try to calm down.

"If you think about it, all I did was move around the classroom showing the kids I was interested in what they were writing."

Silence.

"Before I buy anything, I research it, that's all," Eleanor Bosch says. "I just want to make sure it's the right product for me, and frankly, right now I'm not convinced that writing process *is* the right product for me."

"I appreciate your candor," I hear myself saying slowly. "But please do *me* the favor of waiting until you see the entire three-day launch before you decide for sure. Until then—" I look at the other four teachers "—try to keep an open mind."

I taxi home, utterly depressed. Later, reliving my small triumphs at PS 478 does nothing to alleviate the bad taste in my mouth from the afternoon at PS 414. Worse, I have to return there for two more afternoons.

Launch Day Two. It costs me fifty dollars to get a new battery for my Toyota. The next day's classes are virtually identical to the first: stellar results at PS 478, a foul pot of discontent brewing among the teachers at PS 414. I cannot quite shake the image of the two schools as baseball teams. Whereas PS 478 had the potential to win the pennant, PS 414 felt like a second-division team, a certified cellar dweller. Even the names of the teachers there—Bosch, Crizelli, Gereck, Gobstein, Rupp, Fink—sounded more and more like the lineup to a team of losers.

At PS 414, Marlon schedules me for a demonstration class in Eleanor Bosch's fifth-grade class. I walk into her classroom and try to muster up a shred of optimism.

"What are your kids like as a class?" I ask her. "Do you have a sense of them yet?"

"They're average," Mrs. Bosch says, making no effort to lower her voice so the students don't hear her. "Strictly average. Not a superstar among them."

Wincing, I pass out sheets of white paper; I am amazed to see one student recoil.

"I don't want this paper," she says, pushing it back to me.

"Why not?"

"That's punishment paper."

"Huh?"

"That's the paper we have to write on when we have to do a composition for punishment, or like if we have to write fifty times "I will not make noises in the lunchroom."" She shakes her head. "I don't want to write no story on that kind of paper."

Later, when I ask Eleanor Bosch about this, she doesn't try to avoid the issue.

"We can't *call* it punishment. We have them doing compositions so when the parents ask about it we can say that they're learning specific skills. But in fact it is punishment. There's no way around it with kids like this. God knows their parents don't punish them."

I am appalled.

"Don't you see how counterproductive it is if you're trying to get kids to love writing and at the same time using writing to punish them?"

"Look, they may think they have a better idea up in the ivy towers at Teachers College, but in the real world you *have* to punish kids," Eleanor Bosch retorts. "We make them write compositions because we don't have enough extra math problems or science problems to assign. You can always make them write a three-hundred-word composition on a topic."

Halfway through the class, Marlon Hauser enters. Out of the corner of my eye I can see him trying to play lightning rod and take the bulk of the teachers' static. In this capacity he is able to articulate certain things that might have been awkward for me to point out.

"Look at the class," he says to the teachers. "They're all busy writing away."

After class we all—Marlon, five teachers, and I—jam in with Marlon's ferns and spider plants. Long silence. The teachers' resistance is the most palpable presence in the room. I have lots of information to give the teachers, but under the circumstances it seems pointless.

"What are you thinking?" Marlon asks Eleanor Bosch.

"Don't ask," she retorts, laughing. "You don't want to know."

"Yes, I do."

"Well, I'm just wondering how on earth we're supposed to fit a new writing program in. We've got the reading test to get these kids ready for in February, the math test, the class play, your new science curriculum. Who are we trying to kid?"

"An hour of writing, three times a week, does seem like an awful lot," Mrs. Fink adds.

"Wait a minute," Marlon says. "Kids *should* be writing an hour a day. That seems minimal to me. It's one of the three R's. It's important."

"Sure, with some kids, maybe," Eleanor Bosch says. "IGC ["Intellectually Gifted Children"] kids will sit and write for an hour. But what about my kids? I've got kids who act out constantly, who never—"

"You mean they insist on breathing," Marlon puts in. At that, Eleanor Bosch stands up and walks out of the room.

After school, I stay to talk with Marlon Hauser. While we chat, he moves slowly around the office, and bends down to stroke his plants, pick off dead leaves, check the moisture of the soil.

"I got into this after twenty years of teaching," he says, motioning at the plants. "Before that I never knew the difference between *Cannibas minor* and poison ivy. Now I have a greenhouse at home, I'm taking courses on botany, I've got lots of the upper-grade classrooms doing experiments on seed sproutings. This summer I'm going out to Arizona, to the desert, to study desert flora. A Sierra Club seminar. Do you see what I mean?"

I confess that I do not.

"I tell teachers who are burnt out they need to learn something new," Hauser says. "That's why I'm excited about writing process. But lots of teachers don't see it what way. You've got to understand that, Ralph. Eleanor Bosch has been teaching for twenty-five years. She's the kind of teacher who already has all her dittoes ready for next year. They're numbered, too, so she can hand out ditto number one on the first day of school, ditto number two on the second. ... Understand? That's her revenge against the system. You are suggesting a radical approach to teaching—valuing what children have to say, encouraging kids to write what matters to *them*, getting the teacher to leave the front of the room and really listen to her students. She needs that like a hole in the head. She's got her dittoes."

"She has all her free time to herself," I say wonderingly. "She doesn't have to think while she's preparing."

Marlon impatiently shakes his head.

"She doesn't have to think while she's *teaching*."

Thursdays

The next day is a Thursday, not a working day in the ordinary sense. This means a reprieve from Eleanor Bosch and her cronies at PS 414.

Thursdays have always been sacred at the Writing Project, reserved for intensive meetings between Lucy Calkins, Shelley Harwayne, the teacher trainers, and researchers. It was frowned upon to miss a Thursday. Sometimes a holiday or conference would prevent our meeting on a Thursday, and Lucy would reschedule the Thursday for a Tuesday or Wednesday.

Wednesdays I'd come home whistling, knowing that the next day I would have at least a one-day's respite from resuming my upstream swim in the city schools. Thursdays represented my flirtation with routine. During the other four days of the workweek I might be working in any of a dozen schools linked by the bad roads of three city boroughs. On Thursdays I could count on gathering with the entire Writing Project at Teachers College. Teachers College and Columbia University were powerful talismans to ward off the relentless city school demons.

Thursday morning. I get up, don a faded pair of blue jeans and a flannel shirt, and whistle out to my car. Already, without breakfast, without coffee, my adrenalin is flowing; I am looking forward to airing out the Eleanor Bosch situation at our weekly meeting.

Down the Cross Bronx, to the West Side Highway, and off on the 125th Street exit. The November light is bright, harsh; the angles of every building stand out boldly, almost painfully, against the blue sky.

On such clear mornings the world seems to be imbued with a vast solidity of purpose. The asphalt exit off the Henry Hudson slopes down and goes to the ancient cobblestones by the river. Turning onto 125th Street, I can see the Cotton Club ahead on the right. Two black men wearing white aprons rush up to the car, grinning, holding packages. Up close I see that their aprons are streaked with blood. They come at me, brandishing prime sirloin, t-bones, New York strip steaks.

"How'd you like the juciest steak of your life, Jack, huh? These t-bones'd cost you fifteen bucks in the store, easy, I'll give 'em to you right now for five bucks. . . ."

I see these men at this same spot every Thursday morning. Their appearance stirs up a host of unanswered questions. Who are they? Where do they get this meat? How safe is it? How come they seem so damn happy? Seeing the steaks, I have to squelch a wave of nausea. I wave them off and continue east, away from the Hudson River, past the Cotton Club, past the McDonald's at the corner of 125th and Broadway. Even at 8:15 A.M., parking is impossible. I drive around, looking for a spot. 8:22. 8:27. Thursday meetings start at 8:30 sharp, and Lucy has, as she admits, "a thing" about lateness. Finally, I head over to Riverside, park further uptown than I'd wanted (near Grant's Tomb) and hurry toward the Writing Project office in 331 Horace Mann Hall, Teacher College, Columbia University.

Several factors—both philosophical and practical—feed into Thursdays and make it the centerpiece not only of the Writing Project but also of my workweek. These begin with the goals of the Writing Project as embodied by Lucy Calkins herself. Lucy is an unabashed educational reformer. As such, she realized early in her career that for writing process to have a lasting impact on the educational system it wouldn't be enough merely to work with students. To make a signficant mark on the system, teachers themselves would have to learn to teach writing in a new way. "Staff development" is another way of referring to this process of educating and retooling practicing teachers. Many other educational reformers had failed to factor staff development into their innovative ideas and, for this reason, saw their ideas fail to take root in the schools.

Like other teaching colleges, Teachers College has always been primarily involved in "pre-service" education—teaching teachers-to-be before they reach the classroom. While Lucy has taught popular courses on the teaching of writing, she has always had an abiding interest in "in-service" training—working with practicing teachers. This kind of staff development was complicated by the fact that most teachers had never before received quality in-service training. Many school systems did periodically engage in "turnkey" training—mass training sessions whereby a teacher was expected to internalize a new approach or curriculum area, often in a single afternoon, and emerge as an "expert." For the most part, turnkey training was a shoddy affair, and teachers knew it. Having been burned, they often reacted with suspicion at the mere mention of staff development.

Lucy envisioned a long-term staff-development project in which a trainer would develop a "mentor relationship" with a teacher and, through repeated classroom visitations, help that teacher become a more skilled writing teacher. Such a relationship might continue over several years. The fact that New York City comprised around one thousand public schools, sixty thousand teachers, and a million students made this job all the more challenging. There was always the temptation to do something splashy, to make some dramatic impact in such a gigantic system. No, Lucy said. We're going to start small, and we're going to keep the quality high. I respected that.

For the Writing Project to be successful, teacher trainers like myself would need continuous professional nourishment. This, coupled with the interaction between members and the resulting cross-pollinization of ideas was the primary rationale for regular Thursday meetings at the Writing Project.

Thursdays are about contrasts: from ragged school buildings to Teachers College's antique elegance. From working in isolation during the rest of the week to coming together, suddenly, as the Writing Project on Thursday. Thursdays are about hot croissants, muffins, fresh fruit, intense dialogue, soul searching, success stories and disasters, the opportunity to trade in the stale city school air we'd been breathing all week for some university air. People take copious notes and bolt out of the room periodically to feed parking meters or move their cars before the street sweeper comes by. Thursdays are ostensibly about professional nourishment, and for the most part that holds true, though there is a great deal of blowing off steam. Meetings are punctuated by long silences, sighs of frustration, wild laughter, and tears.

Thursday meetings take place in a narrow conference room down the hall from the Writing Project office, on the third floor of Horace Mann, the building on the northeast corner of 120th Street and Broadway. Three tables pushed together with a dozen chairs around it. Hot coffee and breakfast nourishment laid out on a table to the left as you enter.

Thirteen people comprise the heart of the Writing Project. Lucy always takes the same seat, at the far end, facing the door, making it impossible for anyone to sneak in late without her noticing. Lucy has the intangible: charisma, tons of it. When other people speak, people consider, respond; when Lucy speaks people take notes. Thursdays are dominated by Lucy's presence: her voice, intensity, and high standards pervade the meetings.

Shelley Harwayne, co-director of the Writing Project, sits at Lucy's right. Across from Shelley sits Hindy List, Language Arts Coordinator from District 15, the Writing Project's "model district" in New York City. When Lucy first came to New York City, in 1980, she did a great deal of work with District 15 teachers, in Brooklyn. Hindy and Shelley were central to Lucy's work there. District 15 features prominently in Lucy's speeches and writings.

Next to Hindy sits JoAnn Curtis, a young woman who first encountered Lucy at the University of New Hampshire. She became the Project's very first teacher trainer in 1982. Other senior trainers are Martha Horn and Georgia Heard, a poet I knew at Columbia. (Interesting to note that Lucy has generally selected people with small-town backgrounds to work as teacher trainers in tough New York City schools.) Aida Montero and Eileen Jones are teacher trainers in District 15. Jenifer Hall, Jim Sullivan, and I are the new teacher trainers. Dan Fiegelson works as a researcher for the Project.

I walk in. Naturally, all the seats are taken except for the one immediately to Lucy's left. Aida, Jenifer, and Dan smile at me when I enter. Thursdays almost always begin with "learnings"—personal and work-related insights people bring to the meeting to share. Though this exercise is optional, I always feel some pressure to bring a timely learning to each Thursday meeting. I take the last remaining seat, mumble about "no parking," pull out my notebook, and try to keep abreast of the conversation.

JOANN CURTIS: I've been reading Sarason's *Creation of Settings*, and he says that new math failed because the training teachers got was too similar to the old way they had been teaching. The kids in one class kept being told by the teacher, 'No, don't get up, don't get paper now. ...' I think it's easy for the same thing to be happening with us. Teachers need to see the deep difference between the writing workshop and the way they used to teach writing.

LUCY [*Writing furiously*]: Say more about that.

JOANN: Well, for one thing, it strikes me that the quality of the process teachers go through is not the same as the process kids go through. In some ways the kids go through a richer experience in the writing workshop.

LUCY: Right. The kids are writing. The teachers are on the outside, watching.

[*Pause*]

LUCY: That's an important point. We should come back to it. How to get the teachers more actively involved—or at least as actively involved as their kids are.

DAN FIEGELSON: Well, on a slightly different topic, I've been watching teachers who've been working together, using each other as mirrors to improve their conferring. And it's been great. All these teachers tend to talk way too much when they confer with kids, loading the kids up with information. But the teachers are really tough with each other. They don't let each other get away with anything. If a teacher has something to say to another teacher, they just say it. They don't pull any punches.

MARTHA HORN: It's funny you should mention that, because I've always worried about being too direct with teachers, like I'd hurt their feelings or something. And lately I'm learning that I can be real direct, and honest. Teachers do want help. I'm learning I don't have to hold back with them.

JIM SULLIVAN: I'm learning the power of just being honest with teachers. I was doing a launch at PS 142, and there was this one teacher who just stood in one corner of the room, arms folded, totally uninterested, during the demonstration class. When we met afterwards, the same thing happened. So I just asked her 'What gives?'

LUCY: What did she say?

JIM: 'I'm having a bad year.'

JENIFER: Some of my teachers are having a bad life.

[*Laughter*]

RALPH: Some of my principals are having a bad year. I've been thinking a lot about them this last week. We can't avoid them—they're the most powerful person in the building, usually. They're crucial to our work.

JIM: In so many ways a school building is just like a classroom. Teachers are the students; the principal runs the class.

RALPH: Right. The teachers don't trust the kids, and the principals don't trust their teachers.

JENIFER: In some cases, it's a good thing they don't.

LUCY: I'd like to put that issue on our agenda for today—better ways of working with our principals. Maybe we'll do some role plays. It's occurred to me lately that we could be getting a lot more from our principals. They're willing. All we have to do is ask. And we don't ask.

JOANN: I know we have to move on, but I just have to say I've been noticing how unappetizing some of the my schools are. Especially the teachers' rooms. In this one teachers' room, you walk in, the walls are all cracked. No professional books, no journals, no nice prints on the walls. Just drab and awful. There's this huge banner along one whole wall: 'HANG ON—JUST ONE HUNDRED NINETEEN DAYS UNTIL SUMMER VACATION.' And the only rule in the teachers' room is that you can't talk about teaching. Anything else but teaching. It's depressing.

The talk continues for another hour before there is a pause. I clear my throat.

"This may not be the right time, but I do need to talk about this one school I'm working in," I say. "Things haven't been going that well. I need some advice."

"I'm going to have to draw a line under this discussion," Lucy says. "We've got a ton of planning to do for Saturday's conference. Ralph, talk with me about that when we break for lunch."

The best, most intense discussions that take place on Thursdays happen at lunch or over drinks in late afternoon. This Thursday, Lucy has to run out to a faculty meeting and can't meet me for lunch. Instead, I head down to the Teachers College cafeteria and share the gory details of my PS 414 woes with Aida Montero.

"A hundred and fifty years of experience between them, and they're just not buying it," I tell Aida. "Any of it." She smiles.

"Listen, if I were you I wouldn't lose any sleep over it," she says.

"What do you mean?"

"Let me tell you something. We're not missionaries, okay? I'm going to tell you something surprising, but it's true. People on this planet can actually survive without writing process. That's a fact." Aida leans forward and puts her hand on my arm. "Believe it or not, millions of people are born and live their entire lives—rich, full lives—and never even hear about writing process. And you know what? They survive."

We laugh. It is exactly what I need to hear. That night I sleep the deepest sleep I've had in a month.

But the next morning, Aida's remarks notwithstanding, I wake up with anxiety chewing on my heart. The image of Eleanor Bosch, and the grating sound of her voice, makes me crawl deeper under my covers. It occurs to me that with all the miracles wrought by modern medicine, by now some clever doctors should have come up with a way to perform a *voice transplant* on a human being. How difficult could it possibly be? Teachers like Eleanor Bosch might even be required to have the quick, painless procedure (school districts would subsidize the cost) in which a discordant voice could be replaced by a wide selection of smooth, sexy, mellifluous tones. At 6:15 A.M. this idea strikes me as sheer brilliance.

Launch Day Three. Crunch Time. Put-Up-Or-Shut-Up-Time. At PS 478 Mrs. Oxner's first graders have climbed into the idea of being authors with an intensity that amazes us all. During the writing workshop, an eerie silence pervades the room while the children wrestle with crayon and pen, so much so that one little boy is prompted to remark in a whisper, "It sounds like a libarry in here!"

Raymond, a very thin black boy, sits in the author's chair at the end of the class. Everyone leans forward when Raymond reads; even so, most of the words float soundlessly away. An awkward pause follows his reading. Finally one boy raises his hand.

"I *think* it was good," he says delicately, "only I couldn't really hear it."

I ask Raymond to read his story again. He rolls his eyes at me and begins anew.

"My Baby Sister," Raymond reads slowly and a tiny bit louder. "I had a baby sister. She was beautiful. She was the beautifullest baby sister."

He looks up. Finished.

"Why did you say she was beautiful?" Felicity asks.

"She just is," Raymond says shyly.

"What makes her beautiful?" a boy wants to know.

"I don't know."

"Why did you say she was beautiful?" Abdul asks.

"I think Raymond has already answered that question," I tell the children. "You need to listen to other children's questions so you don't just repeat what someone already said. Any different questions?"

Several hands go up. Raymond points at Sean.

"Why was she beautiful?" Sean asked. Just as I am about to object, Raymond starts to speak.

"See, when the baby is inside the mother it's connected to the mother by this pipe," he explains. "And my mother ate all these good vegetables like spinach and carrots and other good food so the baby got all that good food, too. And that's what made her beautiful."

This reply satisfies the children. Case dismissed.

PS 478 is in the bag. My problem there will be how to limit the number of teachers who are interested in working with me. But the thought of returning to PS 414 fills me with dread.

I realize that something drastic—and dramatic—has to happen at PS 414 for me to have any chance at all with those teachers. On the way to my car, I pass a small bakery. Inside, behind the counter, a portly man is lifting four fresh challah loaves onto the shelf. The small room is redolent with a sweet, yeasty fragrance.

"What can I get you, son?"

"I don't know. Something for a meeting with some teachers," I tell him. "I'm doing staff development."

"Staff development," he says, pursing his lips knowingly. "For staff development you need something sticky and sweet." He points to a section of cherry and cheese danish.

"I was thinking of something lighter. Lots of teachers are on diets."

"I'm telling you: sticky and sweet," the man says patiently. "It's Friday afternoon—let 'em live a little."

He talks me into buying $11.34 worth of cherry and cheese danish. This better work, I'm thinking, as I fork over a twenty-dollar bill. When I arrive at PS 414, I immediately ask for Marlon; the secretary tells me he is out of the building. I ask her for a pot of hot coffee for my meeting with the teachers. She looks surprised and confused by such a request.

"Well, I'm not sure—"

"Mr. Hauser said it would be all right," I lie.

"Well, all right, then."

Eleanor Bosch is absent today. What a break! Her class feels so different—the kids move and talk far more freely with the weight of their teacher, the weight of her voice, lifted from their shoulders. The demonstration class goes well. When I return to Marlon's office, I find the five teachers happily munching the cheese and cherry danish. Stray bits of conversation fill my ears as I walk in: "Sure, teachers are frustrated actors. . . . Brain-damaged, the whole family is brain-damaged. . . . You've got to be an actor these days. . . . Seen his *mother?* . . . How else can you compete with TV and videos and computer games? . . ."

Marlon Hauser enters, beaming, bearing two pots of hot coffee. Behind him the office secretary comes in with sugar and—can it possibly be?— a container of fresh cream.

"Okay, Marlon," Mrs. Crizelli cackles. "What's this all about? Huh? Hot coffee? Danish? What do you want from us?"

The teachers laugh. A cynical moment, but it gives me a pang of hope. Something has happened, some subtle shifting of forces has occurred, some rare confluence of events. Maybe it is the blessed absence of Eleanor Bosch, the unexpected food, or the proximity of the weekend, but for the first time I sense the teachers actually listening when I begin talking to them.

"Let me just add a few things to what Ralph has said," Marlon says. "I've had to switch lunches, arrange for subs, and have all kinds of people babysitting your kids so you could watch these demonstration classes. You've given up three preps, and for that I thank you. We're all saying—this is important. What I want you to do is simple: let me know sometime early next week whether or not you'd like Ralph to work in your classroom."

After everything that has happened, I am astonished by Marlon's remarks, and even more amazed by the teachers' reaction.

"I might," Mrs. Crizelli murmurs, "though God knows how I'll fit it in."

"Right, the time," Mrs. Gereck says. "I like some of what I've seen, but how on earth *do* you fit this stuff in?"

"I'll help you with that," Marlon says. "That's a workable problem."

Ten minutes later I am sitting outside Marlon's office, waiting for him to return from dispatching buses. I feel exhausted and weirdly elated, like I'd just won some small but crucial victory. And slightly apprehensive, like I'm not sure I *wanted* to win.

I'm Broken Up

A strange feeling of uneasiness clung to me after I finished the launches and began follow-up visits to individual teachers' classes. I couldn't put my finger on it. On the surface, at least, things were great, especially at PS 478 where I'd made my debut as a teacher trainer. I was a star at that school, fawned over by the cute sixth-grade girls who worked in the office, featured regularly in the faculty bulletin; I even had my own sovereign mailbox where teachers left me lengthy notes. Each morning Elaine Rolnick would usher me into her office where I'd find spread out on a little table a mug of hot coffee, freshly squeezed orange juice, and a warm croissant with a pot of raspberry jam.

"An army runs on its stomach, and you're my army," she'd say with mock solemnity. "Eat!"

The teachers at PS 478 treated me equally well, though at first we all had to survive a case of the jitters. Shelley Harwayne had warned me about the tensions that went along with such follow-up visits.

"It's like the teachers are having you into their homes for the first time," she said. "They'll be nervous. But at the same time they'll be watching you. You'll have to do some proving yourself."

Beverly Darnell, a short and fearfully thin third-grade teacher, is one of the teachers who earlier watched my demonstration classes. There is a panicky glint in her wide-spaced eyes the first time I enter her classroom.

"Plot, plot, nothing but plot," she says of her students' writing. "I'm trying to slow them down enough to think about the setting, the characters. So far, they're just not getting it."

I gather the children in one corner of the room.

"Imagine we are going to create a real human being, right on this spot," I tell the third graders, motioning to the empty space next to Beverly's desk. "Let's say we put some bones together, all the bones in a person's skeleton, and then stopped. Would that be enough?"

The class shakes its collective head. "Why not?" I ask. "What else would I have to add?"

"Skin," a girl says.

A fat boy says, "A heart."

"Blood," Kim (she wears the three gold letters around her neck) says shyly. "And muscle, too."

I nod, feeling the urge I get to list their answers on the blackboard. At moments like this the impulse to wield a long, cool piece of chalk in front of children is nearly irresistible. Surely this has its source in my own schooling, that archetypal image of "real" teaching we all carry within us.

"You're right," I tell the kids. "A skeleton isn't enough by itself. And when you write a story, it's not enough just to give readers a skeleton of what happened to you. In the next few weeks, Mrs. Darnell and I are going to be talking to you about some ways you can fill out the skeletons of your own stories—to give them skin and blood and a heart—to make them whole."

There's something vaguely nauseating about this lesson: the artifical setup, strained metaphor, the coy questions whose answers I already know. I take minor solace in the fact that the lesson wasn't originally mine—I'd seen another veteran teacher trainer use it earlier in the year. Anyway, it works. I have the kids' attention. They are with me—I can feel their separate consciousnesses crowding my own. Beverly Darnell says admiringly, "That was wonderful!"

Even at PS 414 things were beginning to look up. I was working in several classrooms, enjoying my botanical talks with Marlon Hauser, had even begun to feel a sneaky affection for Eleanor Bosch. No, that's a lie. I would probably never feel any affection for Eleanor Bosch, sneaky or otherwise. But at her request, I had begun working in her classroom, which, considering everything, seemed miraculous enough.

None of it helped. The anxiety persisted and compounded itself as the weeks went by. I frequently woke during the night and had trouble falling back asleep. Awake, I was prey to old school memories; asleep, dreams of school days assaulted me. For some reason it was the bullies, the animals, the thugs of my childhood who returned en masse to torment me again. I remembered how Kevin Hilly bet a dollar with fifteen hundred different high school kids that he would shave half of his head, and then doing it, and being tough enough to collect every last dollar, and taking a vacation to the Virgin Islands with the loot. I dreamed of the time Dennis Ryan cornered me at a party, threatening to "punch my lights out" for no particular reason that I could discern, while Richie Finn, the strongest kid in school, stood behind him chanting, "C'mon, Dennis, I hear a lot of talkin', I don't see much hittin'. . . . Awful lotta talkin' Dennis, though I can't say I see much hittin'. . . ."

Weeks passed. I successfully launched other writing workshops in other schools. John Goodlad, author of *A Place Called School*, has written poignantly about the "emotional neutrality" in American classrooms, the pervasive passivity that keeps students under control. In the classrooms where I worked, kids were anything but passive. They burst into applause when I walked into the room. They wrote diligently, copiously; many of them wrote well. I should have been feeling great. I was striking a blow against the kind of sterility Goodlad talks about.

Still my anxiety persisted. I tried to follow the feeling upstream to its source. I wasn't writing; maybe that had something to do with it. In the past, not writing had spawned a great deal of tension in my life. And yet I had been prepared for this. I'd known that I would get very little writing done during this first intense year as a teacher trainer.

There was something else to consider—something more personal and sinister. My Manhattan marriage had not thrived transplanted in the Bronx. A stubborn distance had taken root between Marian and me. We fought, ignored each other, fought some more. I began seeing a therapist. He made specific suggestions about how Marian and I might work things out, but I had a bad feeling about it. Therapy was like exploring a dank underground cave with a dim flashlight; it was far larger, and far more dangerous, than I'd ever dreamed.

I found it easier to focus on educational problems than marital ones. I told myself that one reason for my nagging anxiety lay in the larger context of my work: the city schools. So many facets of the schools made so little sense; each day confronted me with a new brand of lunacy that was impossible to ignore. And I took little solace in the idea, cherished by many, that institutions like the public schools are best reformed bit by bit, program by program, instead of all at once.

During my early twenties, I traveled across the country twice with my best friend, Mark Mittelman. Each morning I watched Mark perform the same curious ritual of personal hygiene: generously dusting inside of his shoes and inside his socks with baby powder before he put them on.

"Remember," Mark would say in his most ironic voice, "the big things in life can't be right unless the little things are right. Before you tend to spiritual well-being or leading a fulfilling life, you have to take strict precautions against sweaty feet."

True enough. Big truths usually get built on top of smaller truths. Such is the premise of the scientific method. And yet as the weeks passed I found it harder and harder to build those little truths. It was more and more difficult to restrict my vision, to teach teachers about teaching writing without first facing the larger issues that the city schools presented. One such issue was the mammoth discrepancy between the conditions in the affluent schools and the schools in the poorer neighborhoods.

Take PS 478 and PS 414 in Queens. It is hard to put them in the same sentence, let alone conceive of them as part of the same district, the same school system. They represented two different worlds, fueled by vastly different expectations of the kids and adults who inhabited it, the parents who sent their children. And yet the schools were funded by the same tax pool, administered by the same chancellor who had been appointed by the same popularly elected mayor. It didn't make sense.

One of my schools, PS 468, was located in a huge apartment complex in the Bronx. As a child I remember driving with my father past Long Island City in Queens, gawking out the station wagon windows at the immense stacked honeycomb of apartments, astonished that people would choose such a condensed, swarming kind of existence. My father would explain how people had their shirts dry-cleaned there, went to the schools and restaurants and cinemas and clothing stores of the monstrous complex.

"They've got everything they need," my father said. "They don't have to go anywhere else." The reverence in my father's voice only fueled my dismay. I'd get an eerie feeling in the pit of my stomach as we drove past—as if I were getting a glimpse of the not-too-distant-future—and hunkered down lower in my seat.

In an effort to make better sense out of all the schools I was working in, I had begun dividing them into three categories: "A schools" (strong, upstanding), "B schools" (fair to middling), and "C schools" (weak and/or hopeless). These distinctions were not etched in stone; sometimes I would realize that I'd misfiled a school. Sometimes a weak school like PS 414 would sneak into the "B" category simply because of a principal like Marlon Hauser who had not given up on his teachers and students.

PS 468, however, had all the elements of a bonafide "C" school: low reading scores and staff morale, little parental support. But the biggest problem was Andrew Reilly, the veteran principal. He was a short, burly man with a thick mustache and a great, gleaming bald head. After nine years at PS 468, he had honed down his school routine to the absolute minimum. Arriving at 8:00 A.M., he would immediately change into his gym uniform. Mornings you might see him roaming the hallways in shorts, sneakers, and a Navy crew t-shirt in preparation for his daily workout, a faint jockish scent in his wake. Andrew Reilly never once stayed to talk with me after school. By 3:00 P.M. he was history. He had the reputation of beating the buses out of the school parking lot. And he was proud of it.

One morning he phoned me to remind me that I was scheduled to visit his school the following day. Such a reminder from Reilly was unusual, and I commented on it.

"There'll be a reporter visiting the school, so I want all new programs operating," he explained without a trace of irony.

I arrive at PS 468 one morning in late November, park next to a car with a bumper sticker ("SPECIAL ED DOES IT IN THE LEAST RESTRICTIVE ENVIRONMENT") and head toward the school. Bitter cold, barbed wire atop the wire fence, slate gray skies, some aides or teachers angrily herding the bundled-up kids inside. It is windy, and the cries of reproach from the supervising adults swirl up along with a scatter of dead leaves. I try to convince myself that there is some hopeful edge to this grim scene.

Usually I walk all the way around the southern entrance; this time, however, the biting wind emboldens me to try the doors at the western entrance. I walk in to a foyer where a group of men and women stand, eyeing me suspiciously.

"Help you?" one woman barks, clipboard in hand.

"Yes, I'm Ralph Fletcher from the Teachers College Writing Project." No winner here—all I get are blank looks. "I do writing with some of the teachers here."

"This is the Auditory Child Unit," the woman replies. "You'd better go around to the main entrance. There's no way for you to sign in here."

I am not superstitious, but I cannot help but take this minor rejection hard. My own personal bad omen for the day. I make my way through the front door. The new feel of PS 468 initially suggests a progressive, well-run, innovative school. This is misleading. Within moments of entering the school, I feel its peculiar spirit envelop my body. Enter me. And change me. The auras of the saddest and strangest schools I worked in remained inside me for a long time. Even after returning home, I'd feel the school still part of me, meshed with the dirt in my hands, like the salt in the deepest air of your lungs after a day at the beach. It always took a rousing hot shower to help me begin feeling like myself again.

The clock says 8:20. Thirty minutes before I visit my first class. No hot coffee, croissant, and raspberry jam for me in this school. In fact, there is no locker to hang my coat—I must carry it with me all day. The school has but one distinguishing characteristic: a magnificent private bathroom—a penthouse of a bathroom, really—sequestered behind a door in Reilly's office. In a moment of largesse Reilly once invited me to use it, and I do use it, religiously. For it is marvelously large and remote—a world utterly apart from the city school system. I make a beeline for it now and lock the heavy door behind me. The door (solid teak?) has an ornate, old-fashioned brass doorknob with the raised words "PUBLIC SCHOOL"; it closes with a heavy, satisfying "thwump." Inside I am in an airy room with three hanging plants, two long windows, a small bookcase full of well-thumbed volumes of poetry (James Dickey, Walt Whitman, William Carlos Williams) beside the toilet, which features a richly grained wooden seat. A shower with an aristocratic mauve and cream print shower curtain. Last, as a lovely afterthought, there is a tiny radio that breathes classical music into the room when I switch it on.

Most of the principals I worked with allowed me to use their own personal bathrooms; access to this seat of power constituted one of the tiny schoolboy thrills I got from the job. But no principal's bathroom came close to Andrew Reilly's. How he had managed to build such a retreat, I had no idea. I didn't want to know. PS 468 was a "C" school with an "A" bathroom, a bathroom that represented (along with his shorts, sneakers, and Navy t-shirt) Andrew Reilly's stunning revenge against the system.

Now, I sit in that bathroom and do what I do every morning at PS 468—lie low, read poetry, listen to classical music, stare out the window at the sky, try to give myself the illusion of infinite space and time, far from the world of test and curriculum, until the very last possible moment when I must quit this refuge and head to a class.

I stop at the main office. The secretary hands me a hastily scrawled schedule of the teachers I would visit. I glance down the list and try to decipher the names: Resager, Rabincoff, Federico, Anniboli, Smith, Tullman. The sight of their scribbled names recalls my first visit to PS 468, when Andrew Reilly took me into his office, shut the door, and offered this brutal assessment of his teachers:

Fern Resager. "Fern has been teaching fifth grade for thousands and thousands of years. I think she was born here. If she was ever a good teacher, it was a long time ago."

Myrna Rabincoff. "A very sincere scatterbrain. Creative but none too bright."

John Federico. "A part-time teacher, which means I don't get much teaching out of him. Often late. I give him a negative final review every year, and he never argues with it. John loves me. He'll do anything for me—anything but improve."

Val Anniboli. "My most creative teacher. Val has more energy than you or I put together, and she's starting to lose it. A sensational body ... you've never seen a better figure on a woman forty years old."

Florence Smith. "Bitter woman, forty, married once for two months, dates millions of men and tells you all about them. Not a wonderful teacher, or a human being, for that matter."

Jim Tullmann. "Owns two laundrymats and a bar. Will probably end up in jail one day. Very marginal teacher. I need him because he's the only teacher I have who can handle the really tough kids."

I look over the list. Once again the names strike me as the batting lineup for a second-division baseball team. And what is my role? Manager? Designated hitter? Ump? Mascot?

While I try to screw up my courage to face these classrooms, a dark-haired woman and a ten-year-old boy walk into the office. The boy is a miniature Rocky Balboa, handsome with black and stormy eyes. I lean forward to catch the conversation.

MOTHER [*To office secretary*]: He's just not getting along with his teacher. Is there any way we can move him to another class?

SECRETARY [*Looking doubtfully at boy*]: Well, it's pretty late in the year. I don't know what teacher—

MOTHER: No, I know that. But if we could just, you know, move him . . .

SECRETARY [*To boy*]: All right, I'll see what I can do. I'll talk to Mr. Reilly. But if we do, you've got to behave better, young man. We can't have you acting up in a new class—the new teacher won't stand for it.

MOTHER [*Loudly to son*]: You think your teacher will stand for it? She won't. What's wrong with you? What do you expect me to do with you? [*Pause. The boy looks down, says nothing.*] You don't start behaving yourself, I'm going to send you to stay with your father. Wherever he is. Even if he doesn't want you.

The boy's face is expressionless.

They exit. Moments later a thin black boy in a faded green New York Jets sweatshirt enters and stands behind the big gray counter. He speaks softly to the secretary.

"What's that, Raymond? Speak up, son."

"I said my mother died over the weekend."

The secretary stops shuffling her papers.

"I'm sorry to hear that, Raymond. I know she was awfully sick."

Raymond nods, turns around, and walks away. His face, too, is expressionless. The secretary just looks at me, shaking her head.

"Six kids, and no father, either," she says. "The kids have been staying with an aunt. What on earth is going to happen to those children now?"

I head first to Fern Resager's fifth-grade class—almost always a bad way to start the day. The students are chatting with each other; when I enter they burst into applause, momentarily glad to see me, and quickly resume talking. Fern is a corpulent woman whose years of goading, yelling, berating kids have deposited her in the chair at the front of the class, a snarling lump of inertia. It does not look like she'll be moving from there for a long time.

What should I say to Fern? Earlier in the year I spoke to her about improving her writing conferences, but now the idea that she could rise from that position, with her blue balloon dress and enormous haunches, and confer with students at their desks strikes me as preposterous.

This is not a writing process classroom—not even close to it. So why am I working with this woman? Paralyzed by the sadness of it, I stand next to Fern, trying to kill time until I can leave. I realize I should take a stand with her, draw this moment to a crisis, force her hand one way or the other. But somehow, in this thin morning light, I lack the strength to do so. We talk about the weather, the Libyan situation, some delectable Boston cream pie she sampled recently at a wedding. The decibel level in the class rises steadily. Just when it begins to be intolerable, without even looking at the kids or missing a beat in her conversation with me, Fern reaches over and bangs a little bell on the corner of her desk. The class quiets. A vase of silence has suddenly materialized; out of it Fern looks up expectantly. We continue small-talking and move to the subject of discipline. The classroom noise builds: louder, louder, louder.

"You never have to worry about coming into my class," Fern is telling me. "My kids behave. I'll break their heads if they start acting up. Really. I may sound like a tough person. I'm not. But I am a big one for respect." She bangs on her bell: ding-ding-ding! Instant quiet. "Know what I mean? If I get trouble from a kid, I send a note home to his parents. I tell them the kid doesn't shape up he's going to repeat the grade. Period. Notes like that perform miracles in a class. You send home one note like that and all twenty-nine kids get the cure. .Know what I mean?"

Ding-ding-ding!

I escape Fern Resager's class ASAP. More applause when I enter Myrna Rabincoff's second-grade class, but it does little to warm my heart. Already, the day seems lost. The kids in Myrna's room are trying to figure out how to address me. I've given them a choice, and they are still wrestling with it.

"Hi, Mr. Fletcher . . . Hi, Ralph . . . Hi, Mr. Ralph . . ."

Myrna Rabincoff wears her brown hair the way teachers in old black-and-white movies used to wear it: a prim, tight bun with not a single errant hair sticking out. I like Myrna, Reilly's "sincere scatterbrain" comment notwithstanding. She looks her students right in the eye and touches them when she talks to them. She listens hard when kids talk about their writing. She tries. She cares about children.

I talk first to one little boy with an oversized head and two bottom teeth missing. The piece of paper in front of him is blank.

"What are you going to write about?" I ask. The boy looks surprised.

"Oh, I'm not in here," he says seriously.

"What do you mean?" I ask, laughing.

"I'm not in here," he says again, shrugging. "I'm broken up."

"Broken up?" Images of a broken family, broken dreams, a broken heart clamor in my head. "What do you mean?"

"I'm broken up," he says again, as if there is nothing more to say. Myrna steps in to explain.

"His teacher is out today, so Mr. Reilly had to break up his class and put a handful of students in each of the second-grade classes," she says. "Happens all the time around here. Quite a challenge dealing with that on top of everything else."

"Why didn't they hire a sub?"

She laughs sadly.

"Mr. Reilly has trouble getting subs here. People just don't want to come out here to work. We never get enough subs."

On cue, Andrew Reilly himself strides into the class, stroking his thick mustache. PS 468 is, like all schools, a reflection of Andrew Reilly himself. This was the first truism I encountered in the city schools. Just as classrooms reflect the persona of the teacher, schools embody the principal's persona. Reilly's brashness and indifference ultimately trickle down to the students. In his white Reeboks and bright white socks, Reilly makes a dashing figure. In a different life he would have made a fine Canadian Royal Mounty. Everyone turns to admire the thick hair on his muscular legs. One of the boys whistles.

"Cut that out," he booms. "You've all seen me this way before."

"Hello, Andy," I say and immediately wince. "I mean *Andrew*." He has corrected me on this before, and I do not want to offend this man. Above everything I fear that he will take away my privilege of using his remote and ethereal bathroom. At that moment, I have an almost physical hunger to hear the solid "thwump" of that heavy door closing behind me.

"Mr. Fletcher." His words are crisp, clipped. "I would have caught up with you earlier, but we had a crisis on the second floor. Seems we may have a flasher in the third grade."

"One of mine from last year?" Mrs. Rabincoff asks.

"Yes. Billy."

"Billy." She nods grimly.

"I can't confirm it yet. All I have to go on is the word of two third-grade girls who say he flashed at them — frontally, the girls claim — when they walked by the boys' room. I've called in his parents."

He turns to leave and stops abruptly next to Konstantin. The boy has been writing about Colonel Khaddaffi attacking the United States. The Libyan leader has been in the news frequently, trading threats with President Reagan.

"Why is he writing this?" Reilly asks me.

"What do you mean?" I ask, surprised. "It's an important topic for him. He's worried about it."

"He shouldn't be writing about this in here," Reilly says, taking Konstantin's paper and folding it. "This subject matter is far more appropriate in Current Events."

Exit Reilly.

"I wish he wouldn't dress like that," Myrna Rabincoff says. "It's hard enough to get kids to respect you without him prancing around like a marathon runner. I think it's wrong."

My efforts to work with Myrna Robincoff are thwarted by the pandemonium caused by a mother bringing in some kind of toy prizes, a boy who needs to talk to his brother, two boys who want to demonstrate a wax volcano they have constructed, a monitor with a note for Myrna. In every classroom I visit, interruptions persist. At the suggestion of Martha Horn, I have begun hoisting around a large DO NOT DISTURB sign and taping it to the door of each classroom I enter. This does little to help. Errant room telephones ring, but no one answers when I pick up the phone. The French teacher, the music teacher, the science cluster invariably arrive early. Standing in those classrooms, I imagine myself as one of those figures in a biology textbook upon which one transparency after another — Special Ed, Glee Club, Storytelling, Talents Unlimited, Thinking Skills, Remedial Reading, Boy Scouts, Class Play, Resource Room, Enrichment — are piled.

John Federico's fifth-grade class represents my last stop before lunch. Strong smell of rabbits and ferrets wafting from the back of the room. John is a muscular, handsome man with a peculiarly lethargic demeanor. I haven't been able to get a fix on this man. He always seems happy to see me, talks amiably about his students as well as his rabbits, but takes little interest in the one-on-one writing conferences I have with his students. Instead, he trails behind me and busies himself putting small, healthy snacks—little packets of raisins, a few pistachio nuts, a slice of apple—onto the desks of each kid I confer with. I find this gesture so oddly tender that I have not yet been able to muster the nerve to object to it.

I hazard a school lunch with the teachers: applesauce, carrots, and what Val Anniboli calls "UFO's": Unidentified Fried Objects. The teachers and I get into a discussion about interruptions.

"This morning a big woman in a bright white outfit knocks on my door," John Federico says. "Says she's the dental hygienist and can she talk to the kids. What the hell—I let her in."

"You can't fight it," Fern agrees. "You've just got to roll with it. Today it's candy sales. Tomorrow it's something else."

The talk turns to a major problem all my teachers face: how to find time in the school day to do sustained writing with students.

"I like what Lucy Calkins says," Myrna Rabincoff says. "Cut out all the crap in the day. And we've got tons of it. We're supposed to teach so much junk. What I end up doing is writing lesson plans that satisfy Mr. Reilly. Then, when I get into my classroom, I teach what I want. What's important. I call it *subterranean teaching*."

Florence Smith, a trim, black-haired woman in slacks and white blouse, is yelling at her kids when I come in.

"Carlos, get to work. There's no room for you to be out of your seat. Melissa! Spit out your gum, sit in the back of the room. I won't have that nonsense in here. . . . Give me that (ripping a book out of one boy's hands). . . . See that? Write, Adolph, do you know what that word means? The union doesn't look favorably on teachers who strangle their students. Know what I mean? Election Day is a national holiday, you CAPitalize it, haven't you learned that yet? What planet are you on, anyway?"

Florence Smith is bad news all the way. I've got to talk to Reilly about some of these teachers. If this is the best he has, I'm in trouble. I'm in the wrong school. Meanwhile, I try to ignore Florence and move around the classroom. One girl, Tina, shyly shows me the draft of an incident that recently occurred in the class:

When My Teacher Got Scared

One Day at 2:00 pm a strange big bug climbed on the blackboard and jumped all around the class room. My teacher jumped off her chair and scremed. All the boys in the class room ran after the bug. One of the boys hit it with an erasor, and it turned white. It hid near the teacher's desk. So the boys ran after it. Then it just stood there so they boys could kill it. It was trying to comit suaside. So the boys killed it. Poor bug.

I love this story, the precise reporting, the author's empathy with the bug's perspective. The girl brightens at my response, and I am reminded of something Ralph Peterson once said: "To affect someone you have to first allow yourself to be affected by them." I'd like to mention this to Florence; unfortunately, she seems to have left the room.

Tina and I get into a conversation about the difference between scenes and narration. There is a Judy Blume book on her desk. I open it and show her a passage filled with dialogue.

"Sometimes authors try writing part of a story as a scene, with dialogue and action," I suggest. "It gives the reader a real picture of what happened. Like watching a movie."

"Yeah," Tina says. "I could try that."

Tina goes back to her seat and starts work on the second draft of her story. Twenty minutes later, she shows me this piece of writing:

When My Teacher Got Scared

Look Nick "said" what is that big thing? Oh my God "said" Mrs. Smith. Kill it! Kill it! Come on "said" Lenney let's kill that bug. Louis hit it with the erasor "said" Scott. No don't hit it with your hands "said" Mrs. Smith. Mrs. Smith, Louis hit the bug with your erasor "said" Victor. Look it jumped behind the book shelf "said" Lenney. Let's get it "said" the boys. Step on it "said" Barbara and Zakiya! It is dead "said" Mrs. Smith. Now since you boys got out of your seats you will receive a punishment. A 100 word composition.

Florence reads the piece over my shoulder, shaking her head.

"Can you believe it? Fifth grade and can't use quotations right. I oughtta be working at Bloomingdale's."

"Yes, but look at what she's done," I point out. I'm excited. In *Errors and Expectations*, Mina Shaughnessey talks about the importance of seeing the intelligence behind student errors in grammar and usage. Tina's piece is a perfect example of this.

"First, she's taken the risk to try quotation marks. Second, she knows that quotation marks have to be linked with spoken words, and she does that. Third, she knows that grammatical rules have to be used consistently, and she uses it consistently."

"Consistently wrong, you mean," Florence retorts. Quietly, in one corner of the room, a boy murmurs something to another.

"That's it, Victor," she says to him. "You can miss the class trip to the Aquarium. You're not going. You *are* going to learn that you can't disrupt this class whenever you get the urge."

Her voice punishes, needles, hammers, berates. And yet there is a streak of desperation in it, too. During my first visit to PS 468 I deemed Florence Smith a classic candidate for a voice transplant. But after a few visits I began to realize that a voice transplant would be, at best, a superficial solution. The reasons for Florence Smith's tone of voice have roots far deeper than her vocal chords. It has been said that some effort should be made to weed out teachers who don't love children. But there are many teachers who don't even *like* children. Somehow, strict safeguards must be built into the system to prevent them from working with children.

Finally, I can go home. I leave the school, take a deep breath of cold outside air, and remember with relief the greater world. Across the street, some older boys are playing baseball on an asphalt lot. I stop to watch. One boy misses a catch—the baseball rolls all the way to me. I pick it up. Grip it. Feel its honest weight. In one gaze I take in the neat stitching, the scuffs and grass stains, MADE IN HAITI. One of the boys waves at me. When I throw it back, he catches it cleanly.

"Thanks!"

It hits me: that act, throwing back an errant baseball, is the most useful thing I've done all day.

On the way home, I stop at a little barber shop near my apartment on Lydig Avenue, an unpretentious place run by three old European Jews. I have become very fond of it. I lay myself back on the chair and close my eyes while an old man goes to work cutting my hair and beard, the works, nine bucks.

"Don' worry," he says sagely. "I know how to cut beard."

After seating me and wrapping a clean sheet around me, my barber goes back to talking with the other elderly men seated in the back of the shop. The shop is a popular drop-in spot for many old men in the neighborhood, most of whom have plenty of extra time to kill. They were there when I arrived, but they were not waiting for haircuts; they all deferred to me when I walked in. After listening to principals and teachers and children all day long, it is blissful to let the indecipherable Russian, Yiddish, and German words roll over me, to ignore the meaning and concentrate instead on the music of the sounds.

The barber shop is masculine in an Old World kind of way; the barbers are fastidious in a way I have never encountered in American barbers. Beyond my hair and beard, they busy themselves with trimming hair of mine I had never before considered cutting: cheek fuzz, nostril hair, ear hair, even my eyebrows. Before they finish, a very hot moist towel is pressed down onto my face and, for an instant, I am transported to my own little steam bath.

Now, with a start, I realize that my barber is addressing me. He is balding and elvish with great laughing blue eyes that inspire enormous confidence. You would buy bread from this man, you would let him fix your favorite watch; were he a doctor you would undress to let him listen to your heart.

"There," he says, holding a mirror below my chin so I might see the job he's done cutting the beard. "How's that?"

"Beautiful," I say, struck dumb by the precision of his work. There is nothing more to say. "Beautiful."

"You don' cut beard," the old man is saying. "You sculpt beard. You know how I learn how to cut beard so well?"

I shake my head.

"During the war. The Nazis brought all my people and me to Dachau. They were going to kill me, but they need someone to cut hair and trim beards. Can you do it? they ask me. I never cut hair in my life but I say, Of course I can do it. So they let me try. And I do a good job so they keep me alive. That how I learn how to cut beard."

For a few hours this encounter works its magic and makes my own problems seem properly trivial. But toward 10 P.M., the familiar anxiety signals its return with a thin, metallic taste at the back of my mouth. I find myself thinking of a quotation by Jacob Javitz my brother

Jim etched in one of his bronze sculptures: "If we stand at all we stand on the shoulders of great teachers." I think of Fern Resager and Florence Smith. We aren't standing on the shoulders of such teachers. We aren't even sitting.

Just before falling asleep, I get a mental picture of that slender black boy in the Jets t-shirt I'd seen in the main office. His face was expressionless. My mother died over the weekend. What was that, Raymond? I said my mother died over the weekend. Father gone, mother dead, six children survivors. What on earth would happen to him?

There were reasons aplenty for my school-based anxiety. Fortunately, I hit on some tangible antidotes for this feeling: humor, for one thing. As much as possible, I laughed. No doubt about it, these bouts of laughter contained varying degrees of desperation, but I rarely stopped to dissect them. I took them as they came, diseased and strangled notes of disbelief as well as full-bodied mirth. A generous sense of humor seemed essential to surviving this job. In some indefinable way, the laughter kept me clean.

I spend one day at a school entirely devoted to preschool and kindergarten children. (Being around so many tiny ones allows me to indulge fantasies of being a seven-foot basketball star.) In one class, I try to show the kindergarten children some everyday reasons adults have for writing: jotting lists, writing notes, etc. Under the gaze of their young teacher, Miss Rogers, I help the kids make a list of their favorite people. They call out the names—Michael Jackson, Hulk Hogan, Dwight Gooden, Don Mattingly—and I list them on a large chart.

"Here's one favorite person we can't forget to put on our list," I say, and carefully print "Miss Rogers." The kids look from the list to me and back to the list again.

"Does anyone know what that says?" I ask. A girl raises her hand.

"Madonna?" she asks.

The humor of young children often had a weird, inscrutable edge. In a second-grade class, two girls approach me during the writing workshop. Their names are Drit and Andrea.

"You know," Drit says, "we don't like each other."

"No, we *hate* each other," Andrea says happily.

"Is that right?"

"Yeah, so what we do is we like to pretend we're on different planets," Drit explains. "I'm on Venus."

"I'm on Mars," Andrea says. "That way we don't have to talk to each other. Ever."

These friendly enemies walk away together, glowing in the ingenious solution to their problem.

One day Ramona, a first-grade girl wearing striped leg warmers under a white corduroy dress, decides to write about me. This necessitates an interview.

"What's your name?" Ramona asks. "Your *whole* name."

"Ralph Joseph Fletcher."

"Ralph Joseph Fletcher." She asks me to spell it, and writes it down, lips pursed. "How old are you?"

"Thirty-two."

"You're kidding. My mother's only twenty-seven. Any children?"

"No."

"Do you have a wife?"

"Yes."

"That's too bad—my mom's divorced. Do you know your wife's name?"

"Yes, I do."

"Could you spell it?"

During the rest of the class she would rush over to look into my face, searching out the color of my eyes or hair, then race back to insert the new information into her story.

Later, in this class, the children gather to share their stories with the group. One little boy gets up to read.

"Once upon a time," he begins. All the children laugh. The boy looks up, annoyed, and begins again.

"Once upon a time, there—" but the kids laugh even harder.

"Michael," Ramona says tactfully, "we don't begin our stories 'once upon a time' anymore."

I was consistently touched by the affection of children, particularly the youngest ones. Many kids were needy as hungry tomcats, leaning hard against me whenever I talked with them, starving for the attention they weren't getting at home. Yet I was just as often struck by the singular quality of young children's love: patient, untainted by any demand for reciprocity. During her first week as a teacher trainer, Jenifer Hall gathered the children at the beginning of the class. Just before the children started to write, one boy approached Jenifer, put his arm around her, and said, "Miss Hall, I like your attitude!"

One blustery morning, in a Bronx first grade, Lauren and Monique pull me aside. The girls take a deep breath, screw up their courage, and exchange several nervous glances.

"Mr. Fletcher, Lauren loves you," Monique says at last. "She wants to marry you."

"Well, I didn't say I want to marry him," Lauren corrects her friend gently. She turns to me and her eyes soften. "But I do love you."

Lauren is six years old, very light-skinned with a hint of Asian blood, remarkably blond, deep blue eyes. She sits close to me whenever I gather the children together, and I notice how her eyes drop when I glance at her, as if she is fast becoming aware that her beauty might one day be a burden. But now she looks up expectantly and does not drop her eyes. Her words, and the sincerity with which she said them, ring in the air: but I do love you. I can tell that she means it, I am not a little awed by this love, and I have not the slightest idea what to say. Awkward pause.

"Well, why don't you write about it," I suggest lamely.

When Lauren returns to her seat, the other children are eager to hear her account of this meeting.

"Did you tell him?" someone hisses.

"Yes."

"What did he say?"

"He said I should write about it," Lauren replies, rolling her eyes.

Certain classroom scenes are so bizarre there is nothing to do but laugh. One morning during a workshop with twelve elementary school teachers, I am talking about how important it is to speak naturally and humanly to children. I've learned that it is usually better to say such things to a large group where those teachers who most need to hear it can avoid feeling singled out.

Immediately after this workshop, I visit one teacher's class and find her talking to her children over a hand-held cordless microphone! This spectacle appalls me beyond words; there is nothing to do but stumble into the hallway while spasms of hard, silent laughter rack my chest. Oh, that's a good one! A portable mike! Would she also use it for her one-to-one conferences with individual kids? Oh, it was too much. It hurt, but it was funny. I finish laughing with tears in my eyes.

Later I talk to the teacher about her sound system.

"I have one dead vocal cord," she says, pointing to her throat. "Work-related malpractice. The suit's been in the courts for years."

Now for the good news: I was becoming famous, in a manner of speaking. Kids by the hundreds knew my name, gossiped about me, told and retold my stories, disparaged and admired me, everywhere: in the hallways, outside the school, in the supermarkets and pizzerias of my neighborhood. Though I rarely knew their names, they invariably called out, "Hey, Ralph!", suggesting how much bigger I loomed on their mental horizons than they loomed on mine. I began to get an odd notion of myself replicated in the psyches of all these children, people who would grow up to marry and have serious jobs, commit serious crimes, be somebody's grandmother or grandfather in sixty years hence. During the year this concept of my replicated self would return again and again to me, like a part of myself torn away and distributed in bits to all these young minds, a private company for the first time selling its stock to the public.

Having achieved this level of fame, I found that kids were not above making fanciful connections between their lives and my own. They were quite stubborn about these links, regardless of whether or not they were true.

"You know my mother, don't you?" one second-grade boy in Queens says to me.

"No, I don't think I do."

"Yes, you do," he insists, smiling up as if to say, why deny it? "I saw you talking to her the other day."

"I read one of your books," a third-grade girl informs me. "They had a copy in the library."

"Are you sure?" I ask dubiously. The odds that a Queens library would stock the slender out-of-print volume of poetry I have published (*The Magic Nest*) were remote, at best.

"I loved it," she tells me, undaunted. "It was *great!*"

Another girl tells me she knows where I live.

"Where?" I ask.

"Right here in Queens, off Kissena. I saw you going into your house."

"No, I live in the Bronx," I tell her. "Come to think of it, I don't think I've ever been in anyone's house in Queens."

"Oh, you're just foolin' me. I know you live here. I *saw* you."

At PS 478 Elaine Rolnick asks me to work with Thelma Perry, a fourth-grade teacher slated to have back surgery in a few weeks. I shouldn't do it, I tell her, it's a poor investment of my time, but Elaine asks me to visit Thelma Perry as a personal favor. Elaine's morning breakfasts for me have been one of the few, regular bright spots this fall, so savory and varied that I cannot easily resist this request, so I schedule a forty-five-minute visit at the very end of the day.

Thelma is a tall black woman, forty-five, high-energy. Her students (who have not been told about their teacher's operation and ensuing absence) are mostly "second-language learners," which means, in this case, that they speak Spanish at home.

Despite the impending operation, Thelma seems excited about writing process. She introduces me to her charges as a poet, short story writer, and magazine writer; the children are as awed as if she'd told them I was E. B. White. They write with great gusto during the workshop, right up to 2:45 P.M. Three minutes to the bell. I thank Thelma and turn to leave. My exit is blocked by four faces and four pieces of paper dancing before me.

"What?"

"Can we have your autograph?" one girl asks.

"Really?" I laugh, utterly disarmed.

"Yes, really." An Indian boy thrusts a piece of paper at me. What the hell. I take it and lean down.

"What's your name?"

"Maburak."

"How do you spell that?" I lean forward; it is becoming impossible to hear. Looking up I am amazed that the entire class of fourth graders has formed a long sinuous line behind Maburak. The kids jostle for position; when one girl tries to approach the front of the line, the other kids nearly riot.

"Hey! You can't do that! Get in the back of the line! Mrs. Perry, Shana's cutting! You're not in line!"

Taking Maburak's paper, I sign something I imagine my baseball heroes would have signed: "For Maburak, best wishes, and keep writing. Ralph Fletcher." I sign another but by now there is near-pandemonium in the class. Thelma gives me a meaningful look. I stop to look down at the pleading faces interspersed with bits of white paper.

"Hey, it's much too noisy in here," I tell them. "I'm going to be here three weeks in a row. I'll sign autographs then."

"No!" one girl says. "I want to be able to show my parents I met a real author."

"Why don't you just tell them about me?"

"No, please." She thrusts the paper at me. "They won't *believe* me unless I get your autograph."

"Sorry, I'll sign autographs next week," I say. Exit Ralph. I leave with the sounds of the children, deeply disappointed, filtering back to their seats.

Next week I return, wondering if the kids have lost their appetite for my autograph. I cannot suppress the pleasure I feel at discovering that they have not. At the end of the class, after a stern talking-to by Thelma, the children quietly line up for me to start signing.

"Why do you want *my* autograph?" I ask one boy.

"I dunno. You're a writer, aren't you?"

"How about you?" I ask an Oriental boy named Long. "Why do you want my autograph?"

"What is 'autograph'?" he asks innocently.

"These kids want me to write my autograph on a piece of paper," I tell him. "My name."

He doesn't understand. Neither do I.

I sign one girl's paper: "For Linda, keep up the good work." Linda shows it to a friend. Her friend thinks it reads: "Keep up the good ink." They argue over it.

A month later, just after Thelma leaves school for her operation, I return to her class. I explain to the sub that I will not be working with her on the writing process, but will wait and work with Thelma when she returns in March. I explain this to the children. They are severely disappointed. Cheated. No teacher, and now no me. I see the looks of betrayal on their faces.

The sound starts low and grows steadily. Booooo. The kids are booing me. My autograph hounds. I leave sheepishly and pull the door softly shut behind, but the boos spill out into the hallway after me.

Writing process marks a shift away from a narrow focus on the finished products kids write. The underlying premise is that students who gain a solid footing in writing strategies show a corresponding improvement in their finished products.

And yet I found that in the end I cared a great deal about the written products kids produced. I scoured my classrooms for fabulous pieces of writing. I knew that on these gems rode my best chances for anesthetizing whatever anxieties plagued me. When a kid wrote something terrific my job began to make sense. Powerful writing by children made me feel justified being in the schools and helped me overlook a great deal of school insanity.

Surprisingly, the best pieces of student writing did not always come from the best classrooms. Often they were sprinkled randomly throughout the best as well as the worst classrooms I visited. This randomness was reminiscent of a day I spent digging quartz "diamonds" in Herkimer, New York—I was struck by how often the dullest brown stones would, when cracked, break open to yield billiant double-terminated crystals of astonishing clarity.

At PS 105, in my own neighborhood, I worked in Miriam Alflalo's fifth-grade classroom. One boy, Danny Laguna, had a raging crush on Miss Alflalo; one day she sheepishly showed me this piece of writing he had dedicated to her.

My Prettyest Teacher

It was September 9, 1985, I came to school. It was the first day of school. When I got there, there she was the most prettyest teacher in the world. Her name was Miss. Alflalo. When I saw her I wanted to be in her class. I will do anything to be in her class. And guess what—I was in her class. The class was 5–422. I was so happy I could drop dead. I ran home and told my mother that I was in the prettyest teacher's class. I gave her every detail about her. My brother said "I wish my teacher was that pretty." I laughed and said "nobody is more prettyer than my teacher." I would like her to be my 5th grade teacher. I would always like to help her. She said she brought us Christmas presents. I call her mommy. She lets me come up to clean the room. I also call her cutie, sweetie pie, and pumpkin. She is very very bright and smart. I want to go to her house and clean it.

This writing gem made me laugh out loud. Another boy in that school, a second grader in Helen Winstral's class, wrote this piece:

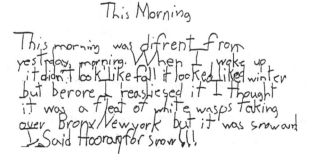

This Morning

This morning was difrent from yesterday morning. When I woke up it didn't look like fall it looked like winter but berore I reasliesed it I thought it was a fleat of white wasps taking over Bronx/Newyork but it was snow and I said Hooray for snow!!!

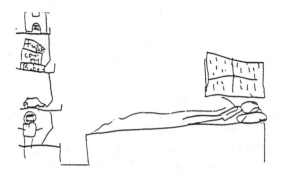

A fleet of white wasps taking over Bronx, New York! I thought I had never read a better description of fat snowflakes in late fall. I loved this piece of writing. I lusted after it. I wished I had written it. It gave me a deep sense of accomplishment to know that I shared some small part in this creation. Important work I was doing, inspiring children to write like this.

A few days later, during a workshop at PS 78, one teacher gave me this piece of writing by one of her first graders:

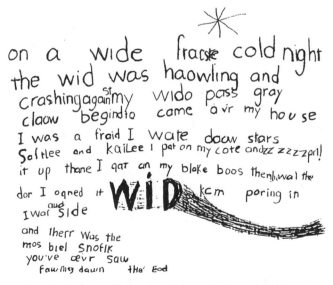

Translation: On a windy frosty cold night the wind was howling and crashing against my window panes. Gray clouds began to come over my house. I was afraid. I went downstairs softly and quietly I put on my coat and zippered! it up. Then I got on my black boots. Then I went to the door, I opened it. WIND came pouring in. I went outside. And there was the most beautiful snowflake you've ever saw falling down.

"Beautiful!" I tell her. "Could I make a copy of it?"

"Sure."

"How long have you been teaching at this school?"

"Oh, no, I don't teach here." she tells me. "I teach at a private school in New Jersey. My best friend teaches here. I'm just visiting."

"Oh." Private school. I can't hide my disappointment.

"Sorry," she says, laughing. "Do you still want me to make a copy for you?"

I nod. She heads off to the Main Office. Minutes later I have the xeroxed copy in my hands. The child's piece of writing is dazzling: I will treasure it. But now that I know it was written by a private school child, its medical effects are nil. It does very little to quell my anxiety.

Spy Incubus

———— ❊ ————

I kept finding the need to define my job—even if only to myself. The glib comeback I reserved for inquiring relatives—"I teach teachers how to teach writing"—told only a fraction of the real story.

Myrna Rabincoff's comment about *subterranean teaching* kept coming back to me. In some fundamental sense, all the teaching of teachers and teaching of children I did took place not in the full light of open inquiry and professional curiosity but underground. Underwater.

At our Thursday meetings, when the trainers came up for air, Lucy used the term *change agent* to describe key individuals in a building or district. The nature of my job, I quickly realized, was to function as a catalyst, a change agent myself. But, by design, the change would happen slowly, surreptitiously.

Sometimes I felt like a professional irritation, a bit of stubborn, indissoluble grit, deftly and deliberately planted in a school, like a tiny particle inserted into an oyster.

Other times I conceived of myself as an *incubated spy*. Incubated spies are dedicated individuals from one country or organization who are quietly introduced at a young age into another country or organization for the purpose of intelligence-gathering or espionage. Such spies are extremely difficult to detect and root out. They eat the same food, breathe the same air, read the same newspaper headlines, hear the same popular music over the radio, bask in the same sunlight as their hosts. But all the while the incubated spy watches and waits. Finally his day arrives. He strikes.

Sometimes I felt like an incubated spy myself, watching and waiting for those days when I could make some small, significant change in the huge, and hugely indifferent, city school system.

The undercover nature of my job was partly rooted in the issue of gender. Racing from class to noisy class, school to school, the thought kept nagging at me: where were the men? It was not unusual to spend several consecutive days in schools without seeing any men at all. True, they did exist at either ends of the school community—as principals or custodians—but in the trenches, in the classrooms themselves, they were glaringly absent. In the city schools the male scent was a remarkably weak one, as if it had been abandoned a long time ago.

This made me something of an anomaly, and my special status generated as many problems as privileges. Often, the office secretaries would scratch their heads and shrug at my request to be directed to the nearest men's room.

"Well, there's a little boys' room on the other side of the cafeteria, will that be all right?"

Kids had their own troubles coming to grips with my gender. Dozens of students instinctively addressed me as "Mrs. Fletcher" before they'd shake their heads, sheepishly, and try again.

The days I worked at PS 105, on Holland Avenue, the Bronx, were a pleasure. I could get up, get dressed, and walk to school through my neighborhood past the kosher butchers, past the old barbers, past the old Jews squeezing avocados in the fruit stands. The walk to PS 105 took less than five minutes. I often ran into kids I knew on the street, or teachers at Six Brothers Diner on White Plains Road.

When I enter Margaret O'Farrell's first-grade class, she grabs me excitedly. Margaret speaks to me in a public voice that is intended for her students as well.

"Mr. Fletcher, we've been talking about the color pink," she says, eyes scanning the class. "Some of the girls and boys thought that only girls wear pink. But you're wearing a pink shirt, aren't you? Do you see that, boys and girls?"

Everyone scrutinizes my shirt. It is, in fact, a salmon pink. A Chinese girl raises her hand; Mrs. O'Farrell points to her.

"Yes, Amy?"

"But he's not a man," the child objects. "He's a teacher."

Ouch.

Other times I enjoyed the luxury of the private use of what few men's restrooms existed in the buildings. In most schools both the principal and custodian had exclusive use of his or her own personal bathroom. Since there were no other men in the school, I figured the public men's room became the property of mine alone.

One day I decided to test this theory. I entered one of those scarcely used men's rooms and placed four tiny bits of tissue paper on the toilet seat. Returning to the school two weeks later, I was delighted to find the four bits of tissue paper exactly where I had planted them.

So it was a mixture of curiosity and professional loneliness that made me look closely at those men I did encounter within the city schools.

At PS 468 I spent a great deal of time in John Federico's class, trying to figure him out. I kept thinking of Andrew Reilly's appraisal of John: "John will do anything for me—anything but improve." For several weeks he was the only male teacher I worked with, and I fussed over him the way a set of parents might fret over their only child. I found John to be unflaggingly courteous, attentive, and intelligent; nonetheless, his writing workshop was disastrous.

Typical scene: John leans casually back at his desk chair while a couple of students stand around him. Shirt sleeves rolled up to bare the thick sinews on his forearms. I'd put him at about forty, with thick, curly brown hair and the pale and liquid eyes of a priest. Sweet stink of rabbits perfuming the air. Some students are writing at their desks. Most are chatting quietly or munching one of the healthy snacks John has doled out. He grins, winks, flips me a little pack of Sun Maid Golden Raisins when I approach his desk.

"How're you doing?" I ask.

"Great." He grins up at me, open-faced and expectant.

"So. What do you think we should do with the kids today? What do you think they need?"

"I'm game for just about anything," he says, shrugging.

"I thought I might introduce the idea of proofreading—editing—to the kids. Think they're ready for that?"

"Great, sure," John says affably. A playful light comes into his eyes. "This morning I told the class a story about when I was a boy. Right, class?"

"Yeah," one girl, Surena, says with a frowning roll of her eyes. "He tried to tell us he was just a head when he was born."

"I was," John deadpans. "My mother used to carry me around like a football. That's the way I was until I was eighteen."

"Were you shaving then?" Evon asks.

"Yes."

"How?"

"My father shaved me," John explains. "Anyway, one day my father took me to a bar and sat me—just a head, remember—on the stool next to him. The bartender asked what I wanted to drink, and I told him to give me a scotch. I drank it down and an amazing thing happened. I grew a body! My father and I couldn't believe it! The bartender gave me another scotch. I drank it down and—guess what?"

"He grew arms," Selena says with a can-you-believe-this-stuff smile.

"That's right—arms. The bartender brought me another scotch. I drank it down and it was amazing! I grew legs. Now I was whole."

"But you didn't have any clothes," Sherri points out. "You could've got arrested. Indecent exposure."

"They dug up some clothes for me right on the spot. There I was, a whole man, and the bartender poured out another shot of scotch. I drank that down. And you know what happened? I fell forward on the bar. Dead. I died right there in the bar. And the moral of the story, class?"

In weary unison: "He shoulda quit while he was a head."

I tried to smile. I had learned that you could tell a great deal about teachers by the kind of humor that permeated their classes. John Federico's comic interludes always left me unsettled. I had no idea what to make of this strange theater being replayed for my benefit. To demonstrate his casual style—to relieve boredom? What?

In John Federico I smelled a burned-out teacher. For the past few weeks I'd been studying this phenomenon, trying to catalogue the various ways teachers burned out. Some seemed to shrivel up and go tired and sad-eyed. A great wounded silence invaded their classrooms and the kids could sense it living and breathing alongside them. Other teachers went all brittle and tight inside until some kid fiddling with somebody else's eraser could send them off into wild spasms of rage. The kids understood that kind, too, and learned quickly to tiptoe around them.

Others, like John Federico, perhaps, went all slack-smiling and loose when they burned out, greasing each new interruption with a shrug of their shoulders, a roll of their eyes, a languid grin. I suspected that John's drive and enthusiasm for teaching had long been gradually reduced to carbon and ashes, and the affability, bad jokes, and wholesome snacks he served up to his kids were nothing more than smoke screens to mask this fact.

One day, during a quick lunch with John at the local pizzeria, I learned that John was a nationally ranked racquetball player, a photographer, and a writer.

"I like to write at night, when everyone else has gone to bed. I write at a desk I have set up down in my basement, right next to the furnace. The perfect place for writing. Perfect."

It turned out that John had gone through his own intense search for meaning—five years of wrestling with questions about God, death, the soul, etc.

"Yeah, I did the guru bit in India, everything. It was driving me crazy. On the outside I had everything under control, I was Mr. Together, but I was a pressure cooker inside. It was like being in a burning house. Finally, after about five years of sitting there, asking myself why the fire had started, and how I should put it out, it hit me that the first thing I had to do was get the hell out of the house. Later on you discover that finding the answers to those questions isn't quite as important as you thought."

I saw John only about once a week; still, he occupied a great deal of my mental space when I was not with him. I liked the guy, I cherished the image of this man hunkered down at a desk in his basement somewhere out in suburbia, writing through the evening hours beside a roaring furnace. Getting to know John, his history, the larger context of his life made me more sympathetic to the man; still, the state of his writing workshop made me wonder what on earth I was doing in his room, why I wasn't working with someone genuinely interested in running a writing workshop.

One day I go into John's class and see a quizzical look on his face I'd never seen before. With a flick of his head, he motions to the back of the classroom where a tall, striking woman with bright red lips is standing next to the rabbit cage. John introduces me to her. The woman is Patricia Leonardia, mother of Melissa Leonardia, one of the third graders in the class. Up close the woman has high cheekbones and luminous green eyes. She is wearing a trace too much makeup and perfume. Still, there is an aura of intensity, of charged sexuality around her, like a heroine in a Raymond Chandler mystery. Such energy stands out boldly against the neutered tones of the classroom.

"Mrs. Leonardia has started to write," John tells me.

"I think that what you're doing is so important," Mrs. Leonardia says quickly, speaking in a low, dusky voice, and taking a small step into my personal space. Her perfume wallops me. "My daughter's gotten so excited about writing that she writes all the time. Now I've started writing. And it's just pouring out of me: stories, poems, you name it. I'm a river. I'm a flood. I can't stop it. My husband thinks I'm nuts. I'm writing all day long now. I've even got an idea for a book."

"Great."

"Here." She hands me five poems, penned in elaborate script, and stands shyly, awaiting my reaction. Romantic poems, mostly, though a few have a darker vein—particularly one titled "Puppet" in which she describes a woman (presumably herself) totally controlled by a man (presumably her husband) and paralyzed by this control, yearning for freedom. Her writing is dreadfully grandiose and purple: "scarlet blimps of joy pulsing through my chest, cascading, transcending ..." There's no other charitable way to put it. I stand for a moment, wondering what to say.

"I can see that writing has been a powerful outlet for you."

"Powerful! That's the word." She takes a step closer. "I tell you I can't stop. I wake up in the middle of the night and I've got a great idea for a poem and I go into the bathroom and write for an hour, two hours. My husband comes in and says 'What are you doing?' I can't explain it to him."

Mrs. Leonardia stays during this writing class. She doesn't talk to her daughter. She doesn't listen in on my conferences. Instead, she plants herself in a spare desk at the back of the room and writes. Relentlessly. The kids don't seem terribly surprised; after a few puzzled glances they get used to her. If anything, they seem to take their writing more seriously with Mrs. Leonardia writing in the back of the class.

When I come back the following week, John Federico is smiling again.

"Your friend is here," he says, signaling to the back of the room where vivacious Mrs. Leonardia, tall in her high heels, is waiting for me beside the rabbit cage.

Mrs. Leonardia's visits soon became a regular feature of my visits to John's class. For the time being this ritual distracts me from the deeper emotions of how to light a fire under John Federico. For five weeks running I find Patricia (she insists I call her by her first name) waiting for me, clutching a fresh batch of poems and, once a short story, when I walk into the class. Children would line up behind her, arms folded, waiting for their turn to confer with me. The kids are not awed by her presence; if my conferences with Patricia go on too long one of the children noisily clears his or her throat to signal that her time is just about up.

I walk in one day and find John's kids munching, not writing. I look around the classroom: no Patricia Leonardia. Instead there is an assigned topic—"My Magic Invention"—written on the blackboard. I try not to feel personally betrayed. John Federico, my only male teacher, spoonfeeding a topic to his kids, and a bogus topic at that. How could he do this to me?

"Where's Patricia?" I ask John.

"Gone. Mr. Reilly asked her not to visit during class. People were starting to ask questions." He winks at me. "Know what I mean?"

"Too bad." I suddenly miss her, the high-strung, lunatic energy of the lady. Without her, the classroom landscape looks drearily flat again.

"The kids seem pretty low energy," I say.

"Yeah, they do."

Mentally, I blame John for the writing lethargy. But how honest can I afford to be with this man? "John, have you ever considered the possiblity that your kids have low energy because you do?" No, that won't fly. Instead, I ask, "Why do you think that is?"

"They're not self-motivating when it comes to writing," he says. "With art, or gym, they jump right into it, no problem. With writing, they don't. I think it has to do with their perception of writing. It isn't a glamorous thing for them, and glamor motivates them. They don't turn on TV and see writers drafting and revising. They see baseball, 'Miami Vice.' There's no Little League for writers. They don't look at it as exciting."

"Yes, but the excitement about writing should be coming from the fact that they can write about the important things inside themselves," I say, realizing that I'm sounding exactly like a writing process textbook but unable to do anything but bull ahead. "But when you give them an assignment . . ."

"You're right," he says, motioning at the blackboard. "It's *deus ex machina*. It's not a real writing experience. I know what you said—the oil a writer needs to run on has to come from deep inside. And I agree with you. But these kids don't seem to know how to get in touch with it."

Pause.

"How are you doing?" I ask.

"Not so great," he admits, opening another tiny box of raisins. "This job is so damn isolating, you know? No one ever comes into the room. You stop learning. Did you read the article in the *Times* today about teachers who left the field? They were almost all happy. They didn't miss it. No regrets. Most of them found jobs that paid more, were less stressful, more rewarding. Their only regret is that they didn't leave earlier. In the next five years over a million teachers are going to retire or leave teaching. And you're looking at one of them."

Pause.

"How's your writing going, John?"

"No, it's not going so good. I'm not doing *anything*." He grimaces. "It *kills* me. I've got so much talent and it's going to waste." He pauses and looks down. "I hate myself."

"Hey, don't be so hard on yourself, John," I say, slapping his shoulder. He looks away from me, his jaw working furiously.

"But I am hard on myself, and I *should* be."

That wouldn't be the last time I would play therapist to one of the teachers I worked with. But in light of John's past struggles, this interaction seems ominous, and I enter his classroom nervously two weeks later. He is sitting, Buddha-like per usual, at his desk. Come to think of it, I never once saw him pull his muscular frame up from the desk to confer with students at their desks.

"I'm going to a retreat this weekend given by Milton Ward," John says. "Have you heard of him? He's written a lot of books. The best is *Your Unfallible Instinct*. He has some interesting ideas about the difference between being *in* the universe and *of* it."

"Oh."

"Do you realize that your body, every atomic particle in your body, orginally came from the earth? And practically every particle on the earth—except the meteorites—originally came from the sun." He beams at me.

"I'm with you." In fact I'd aired out a similar idea a dozen years earlier with some college friends.

"Don't you see?" He sits forward. "You aren't separate from the universe. You're a *part* of it. If they removed you from the universe it would be less that much. You aren't *in* the universe, you are *of* it."

"And?"

John laughs. This is the happiest I have ever seen him.

"Well, if you are *of* the universe, there's nothing more to do, is there? There's nothing to achieve. What more could you achieve than being part of this universe?"

So that explains his passivity. Nothing more to teaching than to nurture students with nuts, raisins, love. No wonder his writing workshop is in a shambles. How could he possibly reconcile the aggressive insight and energy required in individual writing conferences with this cosmic vision?

"Do you believe that?" I ask him. "That there's nothing more to achieve?"

"I don't think it's a belief," John says. "It's a fact."

By this time there are a half-dozen third graders standing around John's desk.

"I have nothing to write about," one girl whines.

"Why don't you write about that?" John replies smoothly, winking at me.

In early December, I am in Flushing, Queens. At 8:35 A.M. I park my car and head toward the school. A sudden shriek from overhead. I glance up and what I see instinctively makes me duck: a gleaming 747 jet, barely two hundred feet in the air, descending for a landing at nearby LaGuardia.

The day begins with some demonstration teaching in a fifth-grade classroom, a place that features a million-dollar view of the old Worlds Fair grounds. This almost makes up for the fact that the school lies directly in the path of approaching aircraft. Jets continually rake the class with their high-decibel screech and drown out my voice. Brenda Stillman is the fifth-grade teacher, a stocky young woman with a blood-red blouse.

"For some reason it's always worse on Mondays," Brenda says. "Last Monday I counted 112 jets. Before lunch."

One of the teachers observing my lesson is a sleepy-eyed man, a few years shy of fifty, with dark hair and deep facial lines of fatigue. His name is Steve Meyers, another fifth-grade teacher in the school. Watching him at the back of the class, yawning and sipping a styrofoam cup of coffee, I find myself imagining the years of classroom dust and grit worn into the lines in his face. I can't get this thought out of my mind.

After the class, I meet for a conference with the three fifth-grade teachers: Brenda Stillman, Steve Meyers, and Terry Sowinski. Meyers's eyelids grow heavy as I explain the philosophical underpinnings of the writing workshop. Soon there is a pleasured and rhythmic breathing sounding from the man. Brenda nudges him hard and he sits up with a jolt.

"Sorry." He favors me with a sleepy Jack Nicholson grin. "Has anyone ever told you you've got a very soothing voice?"

"Steven, behave yourself," Brenda says.

I ask the teachers what they'd noticed about the demonstration class.

"One thing I noticed," Steve says to me, "is you didn't give them any little rules about writing. Like—think before you write. Organize your ideas. You just got them writing."

"He didn't have to," Brenda puts in.

"No, you don't understand," Steve tells her. "He sees things differently from us. He's a writer. He notices different things."

"What did you notice about the writing conferences?" I ask them.

"You really put the kids on the spot," Steve says.

"Not really," I say. "I just talked to them."

"Yes, really," Steve says, smiling, and all of a sudden he doesn't look so tired. "Come on. You talk to them with the expectation that they produce a good piece of writing. You don't accept just any old thing. You have high expectations and they know it. That's putting them on the spot. And it's a damn good thing, too."

Next Monday, when I return to the school it is freezing cold inside.

"I should've told you to wear a sweater," Steve says when I enter his classroom. "They turn off the heat over the weekend. It's always frigid here on Mondays. Damn custodians run the school!"

Standing at his desk, Steve looks even more exhausted than he did the last time I saw him. One of his students stands at the coffee machine plugged in behind Steve's desk, fixing him a cup of coffee.

"I'm a part-time lawyer, just finished a three-day trial," he says. "Divorce. Nasty stuff." He fills me in on the nasty details.

"Did you win?"

"Nah." He waves his hand. "The guy's a hotshot for John Hancock insurance company. They're represented by a big law firm that doesn't want to lose Hancock's business. So they had about fifteen lawyers working me over. I got mugged. Ridiculous."

In lieu of beginning the writing workshop, Steve shows off his kids for me. He has required each student to read one of the classics, and whips around the room asking each to tell me which one they read: *Ivanho, Swiss Family Robinson, Treasure Island, Huckleberry Finn, Lord of the Flies*. A Chinese girl tells me she read *Moby Dick*. At Steve's prompting, she explains that the Chinese have a saying (Mo-Be-Di) for an all-powerful enemy you can't beat.

"Whaddya think of that?" Steve says proudly. "Popcorn!" He barks the word at a slender boy, either Indian or Pakistani. "Tell Mr. Fletcher what you eat at home, Popcorn."

"We are vegetarians," the boy says humbly. I laugh at the nickname; his real name is Pujnabi.

"I gave him that nickname," Steve bellows proudly. "I had no intention of calling him Pujnabi all year. Now everybody calls him Popcorn. He likes it, don't you, Popcorn?"

Popcorn grins, open-faced and nodding.

"His whole *family* calls him Popcorn now," Steve says, delighted. "People are even starting to call his little brother 'Crackerjack.' Ha! It's driving his father crazy."

You can feel it in the classroom: the kids love this balding man with the courtroom voice and work-worn face.

"I always use this loud voice—hope it doesn't shock you. I taught at a junior high in Brooklyn for a long time and had to shout to be heard over the kids. I talk like this at my own house. Been here years and years and still can't get used to talking normal, so I've given up. Hey, you're gonna love these kids. Here."

He points to a stocky Japanese girl carefully straightening papers on his desk.

"That is Anna, and she is *the most important person* in this classroom. Anna knows where every record, every scrap of paper I've kept all year long is. I'm totally lost without her. When she's absent it's berserk around here. Ask them. Alice, what's the class like when Anna's not in school?"

"Confusion," the girl replies, smiling shyly.

"Listen to this," Steve says, rapid-fire. I can feel him heating up. "This morning I'm trying to get them thinking about thinking. Metacognition, isn't that what they call it? I ask one boy when he does his best thinking. 'The bathtub,' he says. 'What else is with you while you're in the bathtub?' I ask the class. 'His rubber duck,' Benny puts in, and everybody cracks up. And they know they can do that. But when it's time to work—they work."

Working in Steve Meyers's class quickly becomes my favorite part of the week, though the experience is far different from any I'd had in any other class. Let's face it, I'd become spoiled: I was used to being the writing star, applauded wildly by children the instant I walked into a class. In Steve Meyers's class, no matter how much he would deny it, he was the ringmaster. And yet he was also very serious about teaching writing. In fact, I was amazed at how naturally this fast-talking teacher/lawyer adopted the writing process. He took my suggestions and implemented them immediately.

One day I arrive and find him holding up stories from two children.

"Watch this," he tells me. To the class: "Which one is neater?"

"Sarah's," the class says.

"Which is sloppier?" he asks.

"Brian's."

"So which is probably better *as a first draft*?"

"Brian's," the kids reply.

"Why? Miranda."

"Because first drafts are supposed to be messy because you might have to add stuff and cross out—"

"That's right!" Steve thunders.

On my third visit I walk smack into gales of laughter when I enter his classroom. The kids are gathered in one corner of the room where Steve is trying to jump rope. He is failing dismally, not nearly nimble-footed enough to keep from entangling his legs in the jump rope. Each new attempt brings a loud burst of laughter from the kids.

"Hi, Ralph," he calls. "Be with you in just a minute." He tries—and gets tangled up again—to renewed laughter. As the kids file back to their seats, he grabs me on the shoulder.

"I think failure is tremendously important in education," he says breathlessly. "Think of it: Babe Ruth is one of the all-time strikeout leaders in baseball. He struck out 1,331 times! See what I mean? I want my kids to know it's okay for them to take a risk, try something new, even if it means they fail. I try to jump rope and they watch me make an ass of myself. It's important for them to see."

During the time I worked with Steve Meyers I found myself returning to an idea I'd had before, how often the best teachers seem to break the standard rules for working with kids: be predictable, don't hurt their feelings, don't poke fun at ethnic differences, don't put them down, etc. One day an Indian girl is talking to him in a heavy Indian accent.

"Mr. Meyers, I have nothing to write about."

"Yoooo have noooothing to write about?" he mimicks in the same heavy accent. The girl smiles; he smiles back and rubs the back of her neck. She purrs.

Steve's flamboyant style led to frequent clashes with Bill Scott, the principal, much to the delight of the rest of the staff. According to Steve, the reserved and perfectly attired Scott was not always amused by his antics.

"Yesterday, Scott heard all this noise coming from my class," Steve tells me. "So he motions me out into the hall."

"'This is the second time I've had to speak to you today,' he said."

"'Yes, and just think,' I told him, 'the day's not even half over yet.' The other day I went into the cafeteria and had lunch with some of the students. He spotted me eating there."

"'Why are you eating with the students?' he asks me. 'You know what the regulations are.'"

"'Look, I could eat lunch with the teachers, and listen to them talk about the kids, or I could eat with the kids, and listen to them talk about the teachers. So I figured today I'd eat with the kids.'"

"Don't you worry about getting a bad review or anything?" I asked him.

"Nah, he can't do much of anything," Steve said, grinning. "I've got a little money stashed away. As long as you've got a little money in the bank there's nothing to worry about."

My schedule takes me away from Steve Meyers's class for several weeks. The day I am scheduled to return, my car won't start and I have to take the subway. The morning finds me standing on the subway platform over White Plains Road. A gusting wind makes the platform tremble high above the ground. It is brutally cold at 7:30 A.M. The subway is late. The battered front page of a *New York Post* somersaults past, like some ragged urban tumbleweed, and I distinctly make out the surreal headlines: HEADLESS BODY FOUND IN TOPLESS BAR as the paper rolls past. I jam my hands deeper into my pockets. Still no train.

So I am in foul spirits when I arrive, late, at the school. Approaching Steve's room, I hear nothing but noise, the sounds of a wild party taking place. Inside, the scene is raucous: balloons, streamers, kids pouring drinks from gallon bottles of Coke, loud laughter, a Tears For Fears album throbbing over the portable stereo: "Shout, Shout, Let it all out . . ." A boy hands me a plate of cake. Junk food galore: chips, pretzels, popcorn. It takes me a few minutes of questioning to learn the reason for the party. The kids are celebrating Steve's return from the hospital; he had recently had balloon therapy on a blocked heart artery. Beaming, he pulls me over to his deak.

"Look at this," he says, opening up several plastic bags containing oranges, apples, bananas. "They know that this is the kind of food I have to eat. Look, someone even brought me some chicken soup. Taste that cake? Anna had it made for me in Chinatown. Kid waited two hours for them to make it. You should've seen the cards and presents they sent to the hospital. Look, I even got a bottle of wine."

I have a twinge of embarrassment; this is the first I've heard of his illness.

"Steve I didn't know—" I say, but just then Brenda Stillman comes into the room, covering her ears in mock disbelief. Steve grins and shows her the bottle of wine.

"You still got that VCR in your room?" he asks, nudging me and pulling Brenda aside where he speaks to her in a stage whisper. "Listen, tell you what you and me are gonna do. First we'll get us an X-rated video, pull down the blinds, crack this bottle, and go to town. I'm going to warn you ahead of time: making love takes me one hour. It's *always* taken me one hour. When I was twenty it took me five minutes to get my clothes off and fifty-five minutes to make love. Now it takes me fifty-five minutes to get my clothes off and five minutes to make love. Still one hour. Hey!" His bellow quiets the class. "Quiet down a little."

"You came at the right time," Brenda murmurs to me.

"Mario, c'mere," Steve says. A good-looking boy with short light hair comes up to him. With rough tenderness, Steve pulls the boy against him. "Thanks for your card, Mario, it meant a lot to me. Ralph, meet Mario. Mario came to school first day, and all he could talk about was Italy, right Mario? Italy is the greatest, Italy is the best, great soccer players, nothing can touch Italian food. So I say to Mario, 'Mario, hasn't anybody told you? The Italians are way behind the rest of the world. The Italians haven't even invented the wheel yet!' So Mario goes home. Next day his father comes in. Pissed. "'Whaddayou tellin my son for thatta they don got no wheel in Italia?' Oh, I swear to God, I cracked up, didn't I, Mario? I was rolling right on the floor. ..."

In the midst of the chaos, Steve starts telling me about the extraordinary nurses at the hospital.

"They were great to me," he says. Then, louder to the kids, "Hey, listen up! You know, those cards and things you sent to the hospital really meant a lot to me. I was awful scared in there."

The class is silent.

Anna, Steve's personal secretary, comes up to him with a glass of water and whispers something to him. He nods, reaches into his pocket, removes a vial of pills, and takes one with water. Anna doesn't leave until he has swallowed the pill.

"For my ticker," he says, patting his chest. "I don't know what I'd do without that kid. Brenda, what am I gonna do next year without Anna? It's scary even to think about it."

Three kids stand in front of the class, reading from a taped scroll made from all the individual poems the kids had written for Steve. He is touched and jokes to hide his embarrassment.

"You know, when I was about your age I was in love with this dark-skinned Mexican girl. One day she wrote me this poem: 'I love you, I love you, I love you.' Man! I was so excited I thought I'd die right there on the spot. But the rest of the poem said, 'But don't get too excited. I love horses, too.'"

The poems are short and sincere. One boy, Reznick, who was born in Ethiopia, reads with a tremulous voice:

> Roses are red
> Violets are blue
> Please come back, Mr. Meyers,
> And we'll be so happy.

"Fantastic, Reznick," Steve grins at the boy. "I guess that explains why there aren't any famous Ethiopian poets." The boy laughs. Beams.

I Think Your Mother Should Read That Book

Someone is following me. I am in a kindergarten, mostly black and Hispanic kids, and Gabrielle insists on tagging along as I move around the class conferring with kids on their writing. She is, no doubt, somebody's baby doll: plump face, clear copper skin, a pink butterfly barrette fastened to the tight braids on her head. Her hair has the delicious smell of coconut oil. While I talk to one boy, Gabrielle leans against me, chubby hand on my shoulder as I crouch down to look at his writing. She rarely speaks; still, the idea of drawing/writing interests her enough to follow my hands as I point out colors, shapes, and letters on the boy's paper.

I lead her gently back to her seat and encourage her to write. Gabrielle responds by scribbling on the giant-sized piece of paper on her desk. She sits directly in a beam of sunlight. It irradiates the back of her ear and sends an amber glow into the side of her face. All my musings about Gabrielle immediately conjure up the sweet smell of coconut oil and this warm glow on her smooth cheeks. She picks up a blue-green crayon. Gingerly, I make my exit. But a moment later she is once more glued to my side. Whenever I enter the class, the child runs up to give me a bear hug. I ask Mrs. Cohen how Gabrielle has been doing during writing time.

"Nothing," Mrs. Cohen sighs. "Or during any other time, for that matter."

After a few weeks of this I give up trying to force Gabrielle to write. Instead, I let her join my conferences with other kids. Whenever I speak I make a point of addressing Gabrielle as well, hoping that something might eventually rub off on her.

I was in a staff development project, trying to do nothing less than change the way teachers teach. Yet the most absorbing part of my job continued to be the writing conferences with individual children. From the first I was fascinated by the one-to-one writing conference, the central and most difficult part of running a writing workshop. Also the most radical. Individual writing conferences? Child-centered, individualized instruction might be fine in private schools, but in tough city classrooms with thirty or thirty-five children? Who were we trying to kid? Yet I fully believed in the concept and enjoyed the challenge of trying to implement this exotic idea in city classrooms.

Every day, as part of my demonstration teaching, I conferred with children on their writing. These encounters were supposed to take place under the watchful eye of the classroom teacher. But too often the teacher's attention would get distracted, he or she would wander off, and I'd find myself conferring with the child alone.

My days were sweet with children—hundreds of them. Or, not children, but the faces of children. Entering a classroom, those faces generated their own soft light, a radiance that was warmer and steadier than the flourescent light from the ceiling.

Hallways jammed with children in motion. Kids moving in silence, in laughter, in bunches. All of them moving through their childhoods, a block of time that would form the matrix of their lives.

During my college years, I worked summers digging cherrystones and littleneck clams on Long Island's Great South Bay. Clam digging (or "bivalve extracting" as I had printed up on a business card) developed my pectoral muscles and gave me a great tan to boot. Exhausted at night, I'd lie down, close my eyes, and see nothing but clams. Billions of clams. I couldn't get them out of my mind.

Now, after a day working the city schools, I would close my eyes and see the faces of children. Not only at night, either. Everything I saw reminded me of children. A red fire hydrant was a toddler in winter, bundled up with parka, hat, and mittens. The slots in the guardrail along the Cross Bronx Expressway were children lined up for lunch. Dead leaves blowing down the sides of the Henry Hudson were kids chasing each other at recess.

I saw Miranda Carp nearly every week. She still wrote profusely, ferociously, silently. I told myself that there were subtle cracks in her silence, that in tiny ways it had loosened and thawed. But in truth I couldn't be sure.

Lauren, that comely first grader, still told me she loved me. She blushed through the writing conferences we had together.

Minh finished the epic piece about coming to America and began writing about her tumultuous life in Vietnam.

And there were other memorable kids, plenty of them, many burdened with physical problems. A second-grade boy with a hideous burn on one-half of his face. His eyes always lit up when I came into class.

A seventh-grade girl whose brain was growing so fast it was too big for her cranium. She needed brain surgery.

A third-grade girl who had had a liver transplant six months earlier. The anti-rejection medicine made her teeth soft, her lips black, and sapped her stamina. She pulled me over to her desk to show me her stories whenever I came into the class.

A fifth-grade girl, Melanie, with a withered right arm, her "choker," she called it, who maneuvered to sit next to me during share sessions and used her withered arm to lightly touch me—arm, shoulder, back— while the other student read. Finally, I had to ask her to stop.

Aaron, a first-grade boy, with a patch over one eye and a little sign—"Under Construction"—taped to the patch. Aaron has leukemia.

Over time, through trial and error, aided by my own affinity for children, I did learn to confer pretty well. I learned how to find something—*anything*—to enjoy about each writing conference I had. Sometimes I found it on the page; sometimes in what passed between the child and myself.

"I'm gonna write about my uncle," one second-grade girl tells me. "He died when he was a hundred and five."

"Really? Was he your great uncle?"

"I should say so," she replies, surprised.

Subterranean teaching: my writing conferences often took me inside children, into their inner life. If I had been a math consultant, my conferences with children would have centered on math. If I had been a science teacher, we would have conferred about astronomy or biology. In writing conferences, children taught *me*: about their families, friends, vacation, fears, as well as what they knew about writing.

Writing conferences gave me an excuse to get to know kids well. Put another way, writing conferences were the vessels into which beginning friendships with children were poured. I never felt the rapport I developed with kids to be superfluous to these conferences, either. In a conference, I earned the right to teach writing by first spending time with a child, talking about a piece of writing, appreciating the work that had gone into it. After this initial dialogue, students were almost always willing to listen to my suggestions about how to improve their work.

At first, kids seemed far more comfortable with my regular visits than did their teachers. This made sense. Teachers may have associated my visits with evaluations and nerve-wracking formal observations. In some cases it took a long time to break down this mistrust. Kids, who rarely get the luxury of a one-to-one encounter with an adult in school, reveled in it.

In Roz Mittelman's first-grade class, I encounter Derek, a big blond boy with a large head, lavish cheeks, full pursed lips, worried eyes. Derek has an aristocratic expression, a miniature member of British Parliament, and immediately makes himself known to me.

"You know my mother," Derek tells me during my first visit to his class. "Yes, you do."

"I do?"

"Yes, she's told you all about me, don't you remember? About how I love to write stories. That's all I do all day long at home: write stories, write stories, write stories. I make them up."

Directly behind Derek I glimpse Roz Mittelman flashing me an "I'll-tell-you-about-it-later" look. Roz and I get along well. Twenty-five years earlier she and several other teachers at the school had been students at Queens College. They worked at the school under a pilot teacher-mentor program and liked it so much they ended up staying. Roz is a fine, easygoing teacher who loves her kids, gobbles up two-thirds of my ideas, and ignores the other third, which is all right with me.

Later in the class, Derek pulls me over to his desk.

"C'mere, Mr. Fletcher. Lemme show you this story I just wrote." On the paper he has written in big wobbly letters: "My Motr."

"A book about my mother," Derek says. His eyes darken. "But don't show it to her."

"Why not?"

"I don't want to surprise her," he says. "See, I've never written about her before. If she gets surprised, she might get hyper, and if she gets hyper she starts chain-smoking real bad. So don't show it to her. Okay?"

Okay.

"Derek is the child of two highly professional parents," Roz explains to me. "He's bright, and he's a little different, too. The other kids don't always know what to make of him, and I'm not sure I do, either."

Derek quickly became a mainstay in Roz's class. Much as I tried to spread myself around, he always managed to grab a prime slice of my attention.

Roz sometimes talked to the kids about her new grandson. I arrive one day and find her students gathered around her, looking at pictures of the baby.

"He smells so good," she is telling the kids. "Better than any flower you could imagine."

Derek lifts his nose and sniffs carefully.

"I think I can smell him right now!" he says.

The next week I approach Derek from behind. The first grader is decked out in a bright red BEST GRANDCHILD shirt with a dinosaur belt and He-Man wristwatch with a purple strap.

"Wait a sec," he says, straightening up. "My sensors are picking up a signal. I think there's someone behind me."

He whirls around and grins.

"Hullo, Mr. Fletcher. My rear sensors never fail. Hey, didya know what happened to me? Over the weekend I was looking at myself in the mirror and all of a sudden my eyes turned bright red like robot lights and two little windows opened up right here (on the inside of his arms) and I could see all these different colored wires in there. And I could *hear* them moving, like a machine."

I smile sympathetically.

"No, I mean it!" His eyebrows are up, his face a study in deadpan earnestness. "I'm not kidding. There's a computer-digitized robot machine inside my body. Really!"

Next week I arrive to the sight of Derek motioning me over to his desk with a swirling motion of his chubby arms, like a runway technician coaxing a jumbo jet into a hangar. I stifle a laugh and manage to put him off for a full fifteen minutes before he corrals me.

"Hey, guess what, I just gotta new computer," he tells me. "And guess what? It's got this little mouse. You just click these buttons and it moves across the screen."

"Great. What kind of computer?"

"An Apple."

"Hope your mouse doesn't take a bit out of your Apple," I joke.

"Very funny, Mr. Fletcher. Do you have a computer?"

"Yes."

"What kind?"

"An IBM."

"Well, I hope you don't get any dust caught in your 'I'." He bursts into laughter and pounds the desk with his fists.

But next week I find Derek sitting with the other kids, clenching and unclenching his hands, screwing up his adult, jowly face. He deliberately avoids looking at me. There has been an incident that morning on the bus involving his little sister. Apparently, a group of boys threw some small rocks at the girl; one of them scratched her cheek.

"Derek, will you please pay attention?" Roz asks him. "I know you're mad about what happened."

"You bet I am!" His face quivers with rage. "Those boys are gonna pay!"

"Think you might want to write about what happened to your sister?" she asks. He nods grimly.

Another boy asks Derek if he can borrow a green crayon.

"Do you care about my sister?" Derek asks him.

"Sure," the boy replies uncertainly.

"Can you come to my house today? We have to go down the street to find those guys that hurt my sister."

"Well, I don't think I can go that far. . . ."

"I thought you said you cared about my sister."

"I do, but I'm not allowed to go past my own street. Can I have this?" He picks up the crayon.

"No," Derek snaps. Sighing, the other boy leaves.

In November I meet Felicia, a pixie of a third grader with small, wide-spaced eyes and uncertain thin lips. She sits before her blank paper like a child who hasn't touched her dinner, and doesn't intend to, either. I know nothing about her; she had been absent during the demonstration classes I'd done the previous week.

"I don't feel like writing," she says, and for some reason rises to stand next to her desk. She is not very tall. Behind her, Felicia's teacher, Ruth O'Brien, mouths the word *stubborn*.

"Why not?"

"Cause I don't want to *be* a writer. I want to be a dancer, or an artist."

"Is it possible you're being difficult today?" I ask, pulling her toward me.

Felicia twists away and gives me a level stare.

"Is it possible I don't know you?" she says evenly. "Is it possible you're a stranger?"

"Mr. Fletcher was with the class all last week," Ruth says.

"I don't like people touching me who don't know me," she says.

"That makes sense," I say, feeling like I've just been nominated for the Child Molester of the Week award.

Next week I arrive and find Felicia dressed in pink lipstick, a pink and white necklace, pink dress. Nothing to write about, she says, and proceeds to march to the last abandoned row in the room whereupon she sets up three notebooks to form a kind of private cubicle with DO NOT DISTURB signs adorning each wall. From this foxhole, she blinks out at me.

"I don't feel like writing," she says. "For one thing I can't seem to get my hand to put my feelings down on paper."

"You haven't even tried today," I tell her. "Look, I'm not going to force you to write—"

"Good, cause if you did I'd punch you so hard you'd go all the way to the moon!"

"Felicia!" Ruth stares at her. "Any more talk like that and I'm sending you down to the office."

I ignore her and move on to confer with other children. During the remainder of my stay, she stands in a corner of the room, arms crossed, staring at me with a lethal gaze. When it is time for me to leave, Felicia opens the door and hands me my briefcase.

"Here's the door," she says coldly. "Goodbye."

I exit, but instead of closing the door on me, she follows me into the hall.

"Mr. Fletcher, can I talk to you?"

I look at her. "You sure weren't very pleasant today. What's going on with you?"

"I'm sorry." Sighing, she sits down on the floor next to me. "I guess I'm just not very happy these days. Writing is hard for me. I can't write about the important things in my life. They're too personal."

"What's the worst thing that could happen if you did write about them?"

"My mother would find out. She'd hit me."

"How would she find out?" I ask after a moment. "She wouldn't have to know."

"She'd find out. She knows. It's called 'mother's intuition.'"

I laugh despite myself.

"It's not funny," she says, screwing up her features. "Sometimes I start writing about something only I know I have to stop or else I'll start to cry."

"What, for example?"

"Well, my grandmother was in an old-age home, and last year she died. She was ninety-five and I'll start to cry if I write about her. I know I will." Right on cue, a fat tear breaks over the edge of her eye and skitters down her cheek. "And yesterday I saw some needles in the living room and I got worried that a needle would fall onto the floor and poke my brother in the eye while he's lying down watching TV."

"Wait a sec," I say. "You lost me. Why would you worry about something like that?"

"He just had to get a thicker pair of glasses."

"Your brother has bad eyesight?"

"Very bad." Her lower lip starts to tremble. "And I'm worried that he might go blind. I don't want him to. He's twenty-one."

Two tiny kindergarten kids scurry past, holding hands.

"I tried to write this weekend," Felicia says. "I tried to write about all the things I'm allergic to: dogs, cats, trees, grass, flowers, milk, chocolate. Well, actually the doctor just put me back on milk and chocolate."

I laugh. She flashes me that look again: wide-spaced green eyes holding back tears aplenty.

"It's not funny when you have trouble breathing and the doctor gives you a shot with a needle as big as a knife."

Later that afternoon the principal, Marlon Hauser, gives me background on Felicia: a neurotic mother who picks her up at school, refuses to let Felicia play at any other child's house.

"The mother has brought her kids up with a self-righteous sense of their own importance," Marlon says. "That can be good—up to a point. Felicia is as complex a child as we have in this school. She can be charming, even seductive at times. And manipulative. She has a way of setting up situations with other children where she gets them to react and lose control of themselves. And they get in trouble."

"You seem to have a real fix on her."

"I know my kids," Marlon replies, grinning.

My hallway conversation opens up something between Felicia and me. At home I find myself thinking about Felicia and the labyrinth of anxiety inside her. The following week I am delighted to find her writing a story about how she connived to get her father to buy her a sapphire birthstone ring.

"It says '18 carat gold' on the inside," she says, handing me the ring.

"I can't see it."

"The writing is very small," she says. "Mostly only children's eyes can see it."

Next week, Felicia is not in school. Her absence gives me a pang that surprises me. The following week she gives me a big smile when I show up in class.

"How come you were out of school last week?"

She looks up at me, a trifle embarrassed.

"Lice."

That night, when I recount this story to Marian, she nearly jumps out of bed.

"Great!" she says. "That's all I need, for you to give me a case of head lice from one of those kids you work with. Do me a big favor, Ralph, and keep a little distance between you and those kids of yours, okay?"

Conversations like this one led to some reluctant comparisons between my home life and work life. Nowadays, I realized, all my best conversations were with the children I worked with in school. The dialogue, laughter, tears I shared with kids only highlighted the deteriorating state of my marriage. Marian and I were doing a fine job of not talking about anything important. The stillness in our apartment, Marian's penchant for an ultra-clean living space, the Spartan white walls, all gave the place an unfinished feel, a sterile sheen. By contrast, my classrooms were noisy, messy, full of life. The world in which I grew up—a sprawling, large family—was much closer to my classroom world than my world at home.

Next week, Felicia has another acute case of writer's block. She sits with her head on the desk. As I leave, she follows me into the hallway again.

"I guess I haven't turned out to be what you expected, have I?" she asks.

"Do you mean with your writing?" This acute sense of disappointment seems all wrong for a nine-year-old.

"I just can't write and that's no fiction," she says, smiling sadly. She kneels beside me.

"It's all right," I tell her. "Don't be too hard on yourself. Maybe it will come later on."

"My mother says I'm a sensitive child. Sometimes I don't write because I get embarrassed. The other kids in class say things to me, but mostly the mean things they say stay in my mind. After a while it builds up."

During our talk, her face slowly changes. The hard, adult contours of her cheek and eyes soften. Looking down, I see that she has taken my hand. Is this the seductive Felicia? The manipulative Felicia? Or Felicia the kid with real problems?

"Do you have better luck writing at home?"

"Yeah, sometimes at home, sometimes in the library, but I always have trouble writing in class."

"Why don't you write something at home and mail it to me?"

She looks at me in astonishment.

"Run that by me again?"

I repeat myself.

"Okay, but I don't think you all the way understand. It's the class. It has something to do with my size. I'm small and the kids make fun of me for that. And sometimes I have a nightmare about something that happened when I was in first grade. I was still little then, but I was popular, and one day the kids all ganged up on me. I still think about that and I dream about it. It scares me. I have mainly two fears—one fear of being ganged up on, and one fear of flying in an airplane. I'm afraid it might crash. Isn't that ridiculous?"

She smiles, a thin smile, a bit desperate, but I am glad to see it. Then a shadow comes over her features.

"Can I ask you a question? Have I disappointed you this year? I know you expected a lot of writing from me."

"Felicia, you've been riding that disappointment horse for a long time, haven't you? Don't you think it might be time to get off it?"

"But it's the only horse I know how to ride." I can see her eyes starting to cloud up again. I stand up. I'm already ten minutes late for my next class.

"I've got to go."

"I always end up writing about something sad," she says. "That ends up making me cry. I don't want to cry because sometimes I'm afraid that if I start crying I might never stop...."

I return to Robin Cohen's class at PS 452. Gabrielle gives me a hug like a cross-body block: it nearly knocks me over. I lead her back to her desk and crouch down beside her chair. She takes my loose fist and playfully makes a nest for her chin. The light from outside is particularly strong today. As sunlight hits the back of Gabrielle's ear, the amber glow covering the child's face reaches beyond, nearly to me. Anything is possible in such light. I speak to her slowly, pressing a crayon into her hand, trying to tease her into some small break-through, writing the first letter of her name, drawing some coherent picture, anything. She scribbles on the page.

The ethnic balance in Fran Rogers's first-grade class is textbook perfect: Asians, blacks, Hispanics, whites, the works. Denise is an exotic-looking Latin girl, with loose joints, oversized dark eyes, and black bangs that are endearingly in need of a trim. She continually shakes thick hair out of her eyes. Denise's clothes tend to be worn, too small, and none too clean. Today she is wearing a blue striped jersey with an inch and a half of her belly, and belly button, peeking out beneath the shirt.

Denise has lagged behind the other kids in both reading and writing, and Fran is worried about it. While the Emilys and Troys and Adams and Marcys have busily produced stories with detailed pictures and rich inventive spellings, Denise has filled her pages with nothing more than pictures.

"Look," she says in a hushed voice. Her page reveals a barren landscape: small house, skinny tree.

"Hey, you're writing a story about a house and a tree."

She nods seriously.

"Can you read it to me?"

"I can't read," she says gravely.

"What's your story about?"

"My brother. Dino."

"Do you know how to write his name?"

She does not. I print it for her in large block letters. It comes as a revelation to her that Dino's name starts with the same letter as her own.

"Do you want to draw a picture of your brother?"

"No, he's in the house," she says. "I'm done. Can I go to the bathroom?"

During lunch in the teachers' room, I ask the teachers what they know about Denise.

"That kid doesn't have much to look forward to," one teacher says. "You know her situation? After the mother died, the father started going to Puerto Rico and bringing back these women—young girls, fifteen, sixteen—and shacking up with them. Pretty soon they're pregnant, Denise's got another half-sister or brother running around, and Daddy's heading back to Puerto Rico for another girl."

"The father's a real animal," another teacher agrees. "He goes after anything with a skirt on. You hear about the time he propositioned me? 'Very nice to meet you,' I told him. He bowed. 'Very nice to be seeing the woman my daughter spends so much time with. Maybe you and I could spend a little time together.' Eeeeeek!" She shudders.

"She'll get knocked up at fourteen, thirteen, however young it can be done," the first teacher puts in. The other teachers sentence the child with vigorous nods. "She'll jump into bed with the first flashy guy with money who shows any tenderness to her. Look what kind of life she's come from."

During my next visit to Fran's class, Michael spills a carton of milk all over the floor.

"All right, don't get excited," Fran says. "Get some paper towels, Michael."

But Denise pushes Michael out of the way and takes charge of the situation. First, she mops up the milk with a sponge. She uses four paper towels to soak up the residue. Then she takes another sponge, wets it, puts a few drops of detergent from under the sink on the sponge, and scrubs the spot a third time. She uses another couple of paper towels to dry the floor.

Fran and I just stare at each other. Even the other kids seem stunned.

That night I try to explain the incident to Marian.

"She didn't clean it up the way you'd expect a kid to," I tell her. "She cleaned it like an adult. Like a mother."

Carmelina is a third grader, tall and pretty with auburn hair. There is a stillness about her. One day she takes her place in the author's chair and reads the beginning of a story:

When I Wish I Wasn't The Oldest In My Family

On January 29, 1984, my baby brother was born. That year was ok, but when he learned how to walk he was terrible.

He could grab everything and ruin everything. He even picked up pencils and scribbled on the table.

In the middle of the year he started bumping everywhere. Every time he bumped, my mother would rush over and help him. He got all the attention.

I got very jealous.

Now whenever I have a problem, my mother doesn't listen to me.

Carmelina's classmates are silent after she finishes reading. Even her teacher, Mrs. Bentz, doesn't seem to know what to say. Joanne raises her hand.

"What kind of problems do you have?"

"Well, like no time for myself," she says. "Every day when I come from school I've got to take care of my three little brothers. Then I have to start supper."

The class is silent.

"Why don't you talk to your parents about it?" Roger asks.

"I've tried," Carmelina says. "See, my father has three jobs. When he's not working, he's sleeping. And my mother's refinishing the house. She comes downstairs all dirty, with paint in her hair, and she just walks past me. She doesn't listen to me."

More silence. Linda raises her hand.

"Well, I'm pretty good with little kids," she says. "Maybe I could come over sometimes and help you take care of your little brothers."

"Yeah, and I'm not a bad cook," Eterey puts in. "I'll come over and help you get supper started. Really."

An electric moment. It's obvious that the boys feel it, too, though none of them is quite brave enough to be the first to offer his own help to Carmelina.

During the following weeks, Carmelina's story expands into a chapter which, in turn, grows into a book. Whenever I confer with her, she listens attentively and incorporates any suggestions I have. She is a terrific kid, a girl who will walk the plank for anyone she believes in or who believes in her. In two weeks Carmelina returns to the author's chair to read her story to the class. She reads her "About The Author" section first:

Carmelina was born in Flushing on February 12, 1977. She moved to Whitestone two years later. Now she is eight years old.

She has three little brothers, all younger than she. One is six, one is three, and the last one is one. She has to take care of them every time her mother goes to work.

During her spare time, not that she has a lot, she likes to write stories and paint. Although Carmelina wrote many stories, this is her first published book.

The stories in this book are very true. Carmelina does have problems at home, as you could see in this book.

Carmelina's story has a five part dedication:

Dedicated

To all the children that are
the oldest in their family.

To all the children that have
pesty brothers and sisters.

To all the hard-working
mothers and fathers.

To all the babies that need
a sister or brother.

To Mrs. Bentz for talking to
me about my family.

The class is silent after Carmelina finishes reading her book. Finally, Eric's hand goes up.

"What are you going to do with your book?" he asks.

Carmelina shrugs shyly. Pause.

"I think you should give that book to your mother," Eric says deliberately. "I think your mother should read that book."

Carmelina looks at Mrs. Bentz who, in turn, smiles back at her. A wordless murmur ripples through the gathered children. You can just feel them relishing the thought of Carmelina's mother reading that book.

December 22. My last day of work before the holiday break. You have never really lived through a holiday season unless you have spent it in an elementary school and experienced firsthand the hallways and classrooms gone berserk with Christmas and Hanukkah paraphernalia: snowflakes, snowmen, Santa Claus dolls and puppets, presents, menorahs, red and green ribbon, garlands, paper chains, holiday concerts, bake sales. . . .

But at PS 452, the holiday madness is muted. No decorations in the halls. No special feeling in the air. I run into Robin Cohen at 8:25 A.M.

"Happy holidays," she says.

"Not here. What's going on?"

"Let me show you something. Wait right here." She dashes off, returns two minutes later with a sheet of paper, and hands it to me. "From our fearless leader."

ADMINISTRATIVE MEMORANDUM #34

TO: ALL STAFF
FROM: Elaine Gruenberg, Principal
DATE: December 17, 1985
SUBJECT: Pre-Holiday Discipline

At this time of year, as before the spring recess and the end of the school year, all schools encounter problems which derive from the excitement and rising spirit of the children and staff. It is of the utmost importance that we employ all our professional skills in an effort to avoid accidents and incidents which may mar the joy of the season. It is our obligation to maintain a "business as usual" environment so that we may quell the crescendo.

As indicated at our September conference and discussed on other occasions, there are to be no classroom holiday parties. There is also no need to show films in the classroom or auditorium for the sole purpose of entertainment inasmuch as the G.O. movies, which are to be shown December 21 and 22, and the holiday assemblies, are meant to serve as special treats for all our children. We have often lamented together the shortage of time in a given school day, month, or year, with respect to the many demands of the curriculum, pull-out programs, and mandates for instruction. Holiday parties and films unrelated to curriculum are a waste of the instructional time we so sorely need.

I am also requesting that teachers exercise extreme vigilance with regard to school rules and regulations and movement of classes through the halls. Our mutual efforts in behalf of an orderly student body, fully occupied and engaged in meaningful work until 3:00 P.M. on December 23, will provide the appropriate learning environment.

Teachers are advised that if they receive any requests for parties from parents or any pressure, of any kind, relating to this subject, the parent (or other individual) may be referred to the principal. If you have any questions or problems with regard to this memo, kindly direct your questions to me.

"Can you believe that shit?" Robin asks. "And you thought Scrooge was some guy who lived a long, long time ago."

I don't return to Robin's class until 2:00 P.M. Vacation is all but here: I can practically taste it. Gabrielle half-tackles me with her bearhug. Robin's face has a stricken look that chills my blood.

"What is it?"

"We just got back the test scores on Gabrielle." She takes a deep breath. "Her I.Q. is forty-six."

"Forty-six?" I can see the two digits in my head. Four plus six equals ten. Mrs. Cohen points at her own head.

"There's nothing much up there, I'm afraid. We're just holding her until Mrs. Gruenberg can find the right class for her."

Gabrielle is tugging on my sleeve. But now I don't know how to respond to her. Numbly, I allow her to tag along as I confer with other children around the room on their writing. She pulls me back to her desk, dark eyes twinkling, awaiting the intensity of my attention. As before, the light from the window shines on the back of her right ear and floods her cheek with a rich caramel light, a light that deepens the natural hue of her skin. For a moment we are both enveloped in it. But everything is different now. And the most chilling thing is not this sobering knowledge about Gabrielle but what I note in myself:

today I make no effort to seriously engage her, to push her beyond her limits, to dig for whatever writing I might coax out of her. Instead, I watch quietly while she scribbles on the page.

Part Two

Disequilibrium

Nobody Steals the Boots

January 6, 1986, and I'm back in the schools. It's dark at 7:55 A.M. Smudge nimbus clouds in the sky, bruise purple, backed by pastel streaks of pink and white against a distant sapphire blue. The earliest I've been up in nearly two weeks; my system has not yet made the transition from holiday to school schedule. Considering everything, I'm not feeling as rejuvenated by the vacation as I might have hoped.

Queens. The school is banked by great mounds of dirty frozen snow. Entering, I am stung by a double dose of déjà vu. First, the sweet school stink of yesteryear. But something else. My first visit to this particular school, and yet I have been to it several times before, or to one just like it in my work around New York City. The city schools were built in four or five architectural prototypes. This model opens on a small foyer. Entering, I could lose my eyes and still know exactly which way to go. Through a second set of doors, I come to a corridor guarded by a woman at a desk. Check-in point. To my left, cafeteria personnel are serving somebody's idea of breakfast to a horde of children. I sign in and indicate "Office" as my destination. I climb up one flight, steadying myself with the red painted railing, and go through another door, across the corridor, and enter the Main Office. With fifteen minutes before my first class, I sneak into the teachers' room for a cup of coffee where a knot of women are talking.

"... I was at the diner, waiting for Barbara, right? And these two men came over to me. They said, 'Are you with Nynex? We're waiting for a sales rep. We're supposed to meet her here.' 'No,' I told them.

But I couldn't believe it. I mean they thought I was a business woman. A professional. They didn't even recognize me as a teacher. ..."

My first classroom is similar to many of the rooms I worked in during the fall: crowded, noisy, not enough books, not enough heat. The children are fourth graders, all black. Many of the kids are wearing jackets, which makes the classroom feel even tighter than it is. With some difficulty, Mrs. McCall shushes the kids so I can begin the class. I talk to these kids about writing very much the way I talked to other kids about writing before the holidays.

"Being an author involves making lots of decisions. How are you going to begin your piece? How long will it be? Where will it take place? Those are things I can't decide for you. Probably the first major decision you'll have to make is: what am I going to write about? Let me share with you some things I might write about. ..."

The kids are silent. I tell them a few of my personal stories: being the oldest of a big family, getting lost at the circus, how my brother Tom had to sit under the kitchen table whenever he got in trouble. The kids' silence deepens, grows roots. I grope for their silence, trying to measure it. As a boy, I lived with my father's silences, which always perplexed and fascinated me. I tried to decipher his silences, I tried to read meaning into them. I marveled at the way he could wear his silences religiously, casually, officially, or sternly, as the occasion demanded. I saw the way he would smoothly slip from one silent guise into another. I wondered if, for him, silence might not be a language unto itself, a language beyond words, beyond love.

The silence of these children is an inscrutable as my father's. They beam back none of the enthusiasm I can hear in my own voice. Nor do they have much to say when I confer with them on their writing. One-syllable replies are about all I get. Later, I ask their teacher about it.

"Two-two-thirteen is a very angry class," Mrs. McCall explains. "I'm having a real tough time with them. The first half of the year they had a teacher, Miss Steele, a young woman they liked a lot. What happened was last week the teacher of the fifth grade IGC [gifted] class got a district job. So, Miss Steele took over the IGC class. And two-two-thirteen really felt betrayed. Not only that, but they had to move out of their old classroom so the IGC kids could move in with Miss Steele. It was a huge room filled with light. Two-two-thirteen got stuck in here. With me."

Schools are ostensibly about social cohesion. The Pledge of Allegiance, Star Spangled Banner, homework, report cards, citywide tests, talent shows—all promote at least the illusion of a social glue, a pool of common experiences that bond all public school children together.

Now, as I moved from borough to borough, school to school, it struck me how the bitter cold air and the snow around each building furthered the seductive notion of a unity, a set of democratic touchstones, between the experiences of children in various city schools. You only had to take two steps inside the school buildings to see how laughable this notion really was. Vast inequities existed between public schools. Everything from the appearance, rigor, reading scores, and ethnic makeup of city schools accurately reflected the surrounding neighborhoods more than any serious effort at a unity of quality education. There were worlds in the few miles that separated the schools of Laurelton, Queens (District 29), from the schools of Bayside, Queens (District 26).

Teacher trainers at the Writing Project were occasionally hired by suburban school districts to do staff development in writing. My schedule with New York City school districts was flexible enough to allow me to work a handful of days as a private consultant in this manner. Lucy had no objection to this arrangement—it was one way she could help us boost our relatively low Teachers College salaries.

My first consulting job takes place in a lovely elementary school on the north shore of Nassau County, Long Island. A public school, but as close to private as you can get. New paint, splashy colors, uncracked books, new desks. Spanking new incubators in each primary classroom; factory fresh Apple computers in the upper-grade classes. Blue blood all over the place. Kids with sixty-dollar haircuts, freckled snub noses, braces, Ralph Lauren shirts; kids who write about going to the Virgin Islands, Seychelles, or St. Kitts over Christmas break.

Gorgeous classrooms. In one class of gifted five-year-olds, many children have written signs and draped them over the backs of their chairs during the writing workshop:

Ples Do Not Dicterb: Xept Gronups!

All Jerks Keep Out

If You Hav A Ide For My Book Tell Me!

In that school I smell the intoxicating scent of money and privilege. It seems to buoy up the teachers as well as the kids.

Sandy, a young third-grade teacher, asks me to observe her mini-lesson. She first explains the purpose of this lesson: to make her students more aware of rich language. Her children sit without comment or apparent surprise when she begins the class by handing out squares of Hershey's chocolate. Even I get one.

"Go ahead, eat it," she urges. We eat. "It's chocolate. Delicious, isn't it? But now I want you to try something else."

Sandy reaches into a Bloomingdale's shopping bag beside her desk and takes out a white box. When she opens it, I can see that it is a box of truffles. Truffles! Even at ten feet, I pick up the tantalizing scent of those prim little squares. Saliva pools in my mouth as she begins doling them out.

"Go ahead. Eat it. Taste it. Mmmmmm. Isn't that good? Wow! Can you taste the difference? That's not just chocolate. That's *rich* chocolate."

Nodding, riding the same truffle dream, we taste the difference, swift, dramatic. While we suck and savor and swallow, Sandy continues talking, making the smooth transition from the gastronomic to the cognitive.

"Now, then. Let me read something to you: 'The wind blew hard at the beach that day.' Nothing wrong with that. That writing is good and delicious—just like the first piece of chocolate we ate. But now let me read something else."

Sandy opens a picture book (*Lost In The Storm* by Carol Carrick) and reads, "'The wind blew sand in their faces and rolled balls of dried seaweed along the beach.'" She looks up. "There! Do you hear the difference? 'The wind blew sand in their faces and rolled balls of dried seaweed along the beach.' That's *rich* language—like the second piece of chocolate we ate. Can you *taste* the difference?"

The kids nod; Sandy turns to me, beaming.

The feel of that school and the taste of those truffles (she insisted I take the rest of them home with me) lingers with me the following day. I spend the day with JoAnn Curtis, in one of her District 5 schools on 137th Street, Harlem. Drab walls, peeling paint, overcrowded classrooms. Kids with bad teeth. I try to imagine these Harlem teachers shelling out ten or twenty dollars for various grades of fine chocolate.

I try to picture how the city kids would react. I try to imagine them primly sitting there like those suburban school kids, tasting, nodding, listening. The picture will not come into focus.

We enter a second-grade class. The kids have just arrived. They take off their coats. They stand for the obligatory Pledge of Allegiance. Poor black kids with enormous odds against them. They face the flag. They put their right hands over their hearts. Their voices are clear and strong. While they recite, I think of those public school kids in Sandy's class, pledging allegiance to the flag of north shore Long Island. Same flag. Same words. Different Americas.

In that second-grade class, a thin boy runs up to me. He is handsome and dirty, excited by this new male presence in the classroom. His black glasses have rims that have cracked and been poorly taped back together. Brown corduroy shirt with sleeves far too long for his skinny arms. He approaches me with both arms extended.

"Can you help me roll up these sleeves, Mister?"

"Sure." I have to unroll them first. The fabric is threadbare. Both sleeves are missing buttons. The boy tells me his name is Eric.

"Do you have something to write about today?" I ask Eric.

"Oh yeah!" Eric says, opening his eyes wide and starting to breathe fast from excitement. The words spill out of him. "My brother, right? Him and me washes cars, right? And this weekend we went over these people's house. And it was a place where all the houses was big. Real big! And we went into this house and these people there was watching TV, right? And the TV was bigger than my Papa! Yeah, and the people that lives there, right? They take their boots off before they go inside the house, and, and, and they leave the boots outside the door, on like the porch, and nobody steals the boots!" He shakes his head in astonishment. "Nobody steals the boots! That's the kind of place it was!"

That afternoon JoAnn and I talk on the ride back to Teachers College. The visit has depressed me.

"What's the point of all this writing stuff anyway?" I say to her. "Who are we trying to fool? Most of these kids will never become writers. Most of them will never go to college."

"You're right," JoAnn replies. "Lots of them won't. But writing matters a lot for these kids, because it gives them a way to make sense of their lives. That's what happens when kids start to write their stories. That's the real benefit."

January 22, 1986, the day Martin Luther King's birthday is celebrated. So far January has been a month of contrasts. Today, I am consulting again, this time at a private school near Morristown, New Jersey. Lovely place: the ivied main building has been designed like a wheel with classroom pods on the outside, a lavish library at the hub, and numerous corridors to empty children from classrooms into the library. A kind of architectural embodiment of a literature-based curriculum. Very clever. Very nice. The classrooms have an average of eight children per teacher. The kids are handsome, alert, freckled. White. Boys in blazers and ties. Girls in tweed skirts and white blouses. Many of the children have colored circles pinned to their chests: white, yellow, green, blue. When I ask the headmaster about it, he gives me a sly smile.

"I'm glad you asked," he says. "In honor of Martin Luther King's birthday and the Civil Rights movement, we're giving our kids a little taste of apartheid."

"Apartheid?"

"We've randomly divided up our student body," he explains. "The kids wearing white circles represent the whites in South Africa. The privileged class. Today they have free run of the school — within reason, of course. The other students will all experience some degree of discrimination. Yellows, greens, and blues will have to carry identification at all times. We'll stop them periodically and check their I.D. If they don't have it, they'll be detained. You'll notice signs around the school: NO BLUES. NO GREENS. Students wearing blue or green circles will have to follow those signs. If they don't, they will be punished. Right before lunch, we'll have an assembly. The whites will get the choice seats. Blues will sit on the floor, on the side. Greens will stand in back. Later, we'll ask kids to write about it. To describe how it felt. We're trying to bring the concept of apartheid down to terms they can grapple with."

"What happens after lunch?" I ask, feeling myself getting angry. "Jailings? Beatings? A hunger strike?"

He smiles at me.

"The experiment will last only until lunch. We just want to give these children some feeling of what apartheid is like."

"And later, when some kid's mother is driving her to her ballet lesson, in a Jaguar or a Porsche, how much apartheid do you think she'll remember?"

"It's a start," the headmaster says. "It's just intended to give kids a taste of apartheid. That's all. It may seem superficial to you, but we thought it would be well worth the effort."

On Thursday afternoon, after our regular meeting, I meet at the Amsterdam Café with several Project trainers. We drink beer and swap horror stories about the city schools. A fat kid who got caught in his desk and couldn't get out. A boy who paid a girl to take down her pants in the bathroom for his best friend to eyeball. After awhile we are joined by Donna Fredricks, who teaches first grade in Harlem and has been working with JoAnn Curtis. The conversation shifts to all the wrenching changes teachers have to deal with during the school year: pull-out programs, specials, school plays, new supervisors, curriculum changes, testing, unexpected behavioral problems.

"Not only that, but every year I have to break it to my kids that I'm white," Donna says quietly. "They take it pretty hard."

"What?!"

"I'm serious," she says. "It usually happens right around this time, in January, around Martin Luther King's birthday, when I'm talking to the kids about slavery, the Civil Rights movement. My kids start feeling pretty negative about white people. Finally, I tell them; 'You know, boys and girls, not all white people are bad. I'm white.' It happened today. You should've seen my kids. Shock. Total silence. A couple kids started laughing. They didn't believe me."

"How could they not believe you?" I ask. Donna is as white as I am.

"They don't. They tell me, 'No, Tamika is lighter than you and she's black. You're darker than Darryl, too.' 'No, I am white,' I tell them. 'I really am.' It takes the kids a long time to accept this. Some of them never do. But after that, things in class are a little different. I don't know. The kids seem a little more careful with me."

January 27: Brooklyn. Bone-rattling cold. I'm breakfasting in a diner just over the Brooklyn Bridge at 7:45 A.M., watching the clock the whole time. I risk getting a ticket if I don't move my car by 8 A.M. Then I head toward The Nat Turner Learning Center for a return visit. Strange to be back among older adolescent kids. Near the auditorium, Bill Bricker, my best teacher at the school, introduces me to a tall black girl.

"Mr. Fletcher, I'd like you to meet Tanya, one of the best and bravest writers." I shake her hand. "Tanya, can I let Mr. Fletcher read your piece?"

The girl nods and hands me five pages.

The Half-Autobiography

My name is Tanya Clayton. I was born on November 22, 1972. I have four brothers and four sisters. When I was younger I was very quiet and shy until things started happening to me which changed my whole life.

When I was five years old I was child abused by my mother for two and a half years. I never knew what I did to deserve such beatings that I got. My father was not living with us at the time but all the same, we were close.

In 1982 when the department of Social Service took me away from my mother I was very scared where I was going to go. The only one left to take me was my father but he was really in a world of his own. But he still took me in and that's one of the reasons why I still love him.

I was always around adults. That's probably why I'm more grown that I should be. My father was very strict but he treated me very well. He made me gain weight and brought me anything I wanted.

We were very close for two and a half years, until one day a white girl was sitting on our step crying because she had no place to go. Being that my father knew her friend who she lived with before, he took her in and she has been living with him since then, and that was three and a half years ago.

We didn't get along very well after she was there for a while. She got jealous of me because I was always being spoiled by my father and I always spent time with him. It wasn't that I was with my father all the time. It was just that she wanted to spend every minute with him. I didn't really mind but my father did, so he always used to yell at her about being jealous of me because I was his blood and she wasn't.

For three years my father and I were very close.

That was when everything changed little by little. I felt like I was in bondage or jail because I didn't go out. I wasn't like any other person my age. I guess that's why I like to stand out amongst a crowd and be known.

I was always an A or B student even in 4th grade. Although I was absent a lot I still made it to 5th grade.

But as I said my life changed. No one could control me no matter what they did, not even my father could stop me from being ignorant and disobedient.

In late April my life really changed when my father sexually molested me. I was so confused and up set that I cryed all day long in school. When I got home my father and I talked and he promised it wouldn't happen again, but it did.

I never told anybody what was going on because I was scared at first. My father said he could deny it. But after a while I started to hate him like I never hated anybody in my life.

I finally got to the point where I was going to kill him!

In early August I called my sister, Milagrose. When I told her she didn't believe me but when I told her it was hard enough for me to say it and mean it she believed me—especially after I started crying. The next day she called me and told me to pack as much as I could and she would pick me up.

When she picked me up she took me to her best friend Peppi's house. I stayed with him for a month.

I had to go to the hospital for six days to get tests taken.

On September 5th I went to court. The judge decided that I wasn't going to live with any of my family for a while. They put me in a Cony Island Group Home.

So far I have had four fights with other girls but I'm coming along okay.

Tanya smiles shyly while I try to figure out how to react. What can I possibly say? And yet there she is, standing beside me, politely waiting. Bill has walked away, leaving the two of us alone.

"How are things at the shelter you're at now?" I ask.

"Okay." She speaks quietly.

"They're treating you all right?"

She nods. I take a deep breath.

"This is some kind of story," I tell her.

"Yeah." Awkward pause. Then Tanya starts to speak. "I like to write. I feel good while I'm writing, like things are going to get better because I understand them better. I'd like to be a writer when I grow up." She motions at her story. "What do you think of it?"

She looks at me. My first instinct is to reach out, touch her shoulder. Then again, maybe I shouldn't.

"It's honest," I tell her. "There's plenty of pain in this piece of writing. But strength, too. You've got powerful stuff to write about, and you know how to get out of the way of your story."

"What's your favorite part?" she asks.

"This." I point to her title, "The Half-Autobiography." "There's something hopeful about that. You've got the whole other half of your life ahead of you."

Educators and Managers

On my first visit to PS 121 I run into an angry black man who pickets with a hand-made sign outside the school: MY SON IS BEING DENIED HIS RIGHT TO AN EDUCATION. Another sign propped up against the tree charges NATELLI IS A RACIST. I try to sneak past, but the man buttonholes me.

"How would you like it if your son was discriminated in school?"

"Well, I—"

"You wouldn't like it a bit, would you? My son has been railroaded out of this school. A school that my tax dollars are going to support. On a technicality."

"Has he been expelled?"

"Suspended! For two weeks! And his mother and me were never given the chance to meet with Natelli or his teachers. It's outrageous! Let me tell you, mister, I intend to call the papers, the radio stations, and stay out here as long as it takes until my son gets justice."

With an abrupt gesture the man dismisses me and begins chanting loudly: "Na-tel-li is a ra-cist! Na-tel-li is a ra-cist! Na-tel-li is a ra-cist! Na-tel-li is a ra-cist!"

Entering the principal's office, I see a small black child, perhaps a second grader, wearing a dirty white jersey under a brown jacket, sitting at one end of a conference table. She is absorbed in her breakfast—Rice Krispies, corn muffin, chocolate milk—and I stand for a moment watching the girl carefully spoon the cereal into her mouth while the principal finishes a phone call. I wonder what the child is doing there. Maybe the principal has a special program whereby each day a different child has breakfast in her office. Nice idea.

"Meryl Natelli," she says loudly, standing and grabbing my hand. She is a big buxom woman, her arms and hands heavy with gold jewelry. "You must be Ralph. I've heard all about you."

"Nice to meet you," I say. The angry chant from the man picketing outside filters into the office. "Sounds like you've got a friend out there."

"Oh, yes," she laughs, motioning me to take the seat next to the child. "Some case, that one. He's the father of a fourth-grade boy. Kid has been terrorizing the school. Literally. Beating up kids, disrupting assemblies, insolent to teachers, disregarding rules ... Three times I asked his parents to come in for a conference. Three times I warned them that the child was close to a full-blown suspension. They ignored me. They thought I was bluffing. I wasn't. So I suspended him. The superintendent backs me 100 percent. So do the teachers in this school. Ask the other teachers about it. Ask the black teachers about this racist nonsense."

"Does it bother you?" I ask, motioning outside.

"No!" She laughs. She glances at the girl eating breakfast, and reaches over to stroke her neck. Meryl, formerly a kindergarten supervisor and assistant principal in Manhattan, is a second-year principal.

"I took it slow the first year. Coffee? You know what they say about being a new principal. The first year you sit back and watch. The second year you start making changes." She laughs again. "Well, I started last year. And the teachers had lots of complaints."

"Complaints?"

"Complaints filed through the U.F.T. Liaison Committee. They said I was trying to make them do the impossible. In fact, I was just trying to get them to do what they're supposed to do."

She pauses to look at the child eating breakfast. The room is silent: the picketer outside seems to have gone on break.

"It's true that the academic caliber of kids here has gone down the past few years. A lot more single parent families, for one thing. That's been around a long time, but in the past there was always an extended family—aunts and grandparents—to support it. No more. Nowadays more single parents are by themselves, out on a limb. Plus, there's more substance abuse in the home. So we're seeing kids that are much more needy. My teachers are feeling the heat. And I'm putting pressure on them, too. That's life. We're all getting paid to do the best we can."

We start setting up a schedule for my visits. I mention an upcoming all-day conference on writing process at Teachers College.

"It would be great if some of your teachers could come," I say. Meryl sighs.

"I'll post it, but don't hold your breath," Meryl says. "I mention conferences and workshops around here to my teachers until I'm blue in the face. I tell them I'll pay for their lunch, I'll pay for their parking. They rarely show any interest. I tell teachers that they should be learning something new every day. Some of them understand that— others give me this glazed look. I call it the Stepford Wife Syndrome."

"You're kidding, right?"

By way of response, Meryl just glares at me.

Meryl has to juggle teachers' prep times to make the schedule work. On the way out, I ask the little girl sitting with us: "How did you get to eat your breakfast in the principal's office?"

"I was cold," the girl says softly, touching my hand. "Feel. Cold."

"Feel better now?" Meryl asks. The girl nods. "All right, you can go down to your class. I want you to come see me before you go home, okay?" Somberly, the girl nods. As she leaves, Meryl shakes her head.

"Look at that: kid's wearing pajamas, for Chrissakes. She came to school dressed like that. No breakfast, either. There's no excuse for that. I got on the phone and gave the parents hell. The mother had gone to work; the father told me her big brother was supposed to make sure she got dressed and got fed before she left. He didn't."

"Does that happen often?"

"Don't ask."

I visit PS 121 next on a frigid day. Kids are dragon-breathing, yelling, racing into the school. The lone picketer, wearing earmuffs and a green army jacket, is making his rounds, carrying a large "PS 121 IS A RACIST SCHOOL" sign. The kids, nearly all black, ignore him. It hits me: on this issue Meryl Natelli *won't* budge. This guy is wasting his time. For the first time I feel a little sorry for him.

Inside, Meryl has a huge pink flower in her silver hair in honor of Puerto Rican Heritage Appreciation Day. She thrusts a cylinder at me and shakes it like a tambourine.

"We're collecting for the volcano victims in Colombia. Come on, Ralph, cough up."

Meryl picks that day to shadow me. In Cera Northern's classroom—a combination of first and second graders—I ask the children to join me in the meeting area. Meryl settles her large body onto one of the tiny chairs. Some of the girls are wearing dresses and balk at sitting on the floor.

"Down here," I urge. "It's all right. It's not dirty."

Meryl lets out a great laugh, slaps her knees.

"My ex-husband used the same line on me ten years ago. And you know what? It worked."

In the next class, I confer with Denton, a first grader with very short hair and liquid brown eyes. He has written a story:

A Date Wihe a Vampier	A Date with a Vampire
I day my Fother wint out	One day my father went out
with a vampier	with a vampire.
he wnte with a lady vampier	He went out with a lady vampire.
sehe dit him oness	She bit him once.
sehe bet him I more time	She bit him one more time.
then seh bit him agine	Then she bit him again.
vampires are very dadly	Vampires are very deadly.

This wrests an appreciative laugh from Meryl. I commend Denton on how hard he has worked to spell out the words.

"I noticed that you spelled 'bit' three different ways," I tell him. "Look, here you spelled it d-i-t. Here you spelled it b-e-t, and here you spelled it b-i-t. Which one do you think is right?"

Without hesitation, Denton points to b-i-t.

"Right! Maybe you can go back and change the other two." To the classroom teacher I say, "It seemed like he was drafting the spelling of the word. I'd guess Denton is a pretty good reader"—here the teacher nods—"so he's got enough of a sight vocabulary that when he sees the correct spelling of the word he recognizes it. This writing conference was just a matter of making him aware of what he knows and holding him accountable to it."

All of this sounds pretty smart, even to me. Meryl is beaming.

"Marvelous!" Meryl says to the teacher. "Did you see how he did that? So subtle, no big thing, and Denton ended up correcting the errors himself."

This little interaction wins Meryl's confidence in me. After that, she insists on personally introducing me to her teachers and pointing out her favorite kids to me.

"Robert!" she calls to one skinny boy. "Come over here." She kneels down and pulls Robert against her; the boy's shy face dissolves into an involuntary grin. "Robert has the distinction of being the school pornographer. Robert, show Mr. Fletcher the picture you drew of me."

He races off and returns moments later with a ground-level view of Meryl Natelli: blood-red lipstick, copious jewelry, her head peering out from between two enormous breasts.

"I guess he drew it that way because he's always looking up at me. My boobs are the only thing he can see. Talk about perspective! This kid's got it, doesn't he? I told his mother I want the picture but she says no way, she's going to put it up on the wall at home!"

One unexpected perk in my role as a teacher trainer with university credentials: I discovered that I came into the school on a rough kind of professional parity with the principal. These men and women talked to me, complained and confided in me. Some were hungry to talk educational theory; others seemed to anticipate my company like people in a hospital who look forward to a visitor, anybody, who can break up the monotony of the four walls and stale air.

On my first visit to one Bronx elementary school, I approach the back entrance of the school along with a tall, handsome man adorned in black: black hair and mustache, black Russian fur hat, black mourner's coat. As we walk toward the double doors, five boys race up behind us. Seeing the man in black, they jam on their brakes.

"Where are you going?" he asks them.

Uneasily, they motion inside.

"You know you don't use this entrance." His voice is an alloy of patience and weariness. "Go through the front. How many times do I have to tell you?"

The boys leave. Sad-eyed, he turns to me.

"Fifteen years of pretending I give a fuck which door the kids use." He extends his hand. "Stephen Rawley. I'm the principal around here."

Rawley and I hit it off. I'd poke my head into his office each morning before I started my rounds to the various classrooms, and he'd keep me there to talk. At 8 A.M. we talked about poetry. Rawley liked the big serious poets: Whitman, Keats, Wordsworth, Wallace Stevens, T. S. Eliot, Matthew Arnold. He wrinkled up his nose when I mentioned Galway Kinnell and Seamus Heaney; he has very little use for contemporary poetry.

"They all write these little verses," he says. "I don't mean short, I mean little. It's almost like somebody told them not to bite off too much that's important. I think that, at some point at least, a poet has to sing. Whitman sang. Wallace Stevens sang, too, even though his music was a bit softer and more refined than Whitman's. Which of the modern poets really sing?"

My work at Rawley's school goes well. From the beginning, I notice two things these teachers have in common. They are all young women, around twenty-five. And uniformly attractive. In the morning, the teachers' room reminds me of nothing so much as a training school for stewardesses, filled with clusters of pretty women. I wonder, is this some kind of training school for new teachers? I always mean to ask Rawley about this, but I never get around to it, because he and I talk about so many other things.

At first I spend ten minutes with Rawley each morning in his office, then fifteen, soon a half-hour. Before long he is scheduling me to have lunch with him at a good local restaurant. During these repasts, which often stretch beyond two hours, our talks range from God, Freud, Darwin, Bruno Bettelheim and the importance of exposing children to the uncut versions of fairy tales, bilingual education, the educational voucher system, crack. Rawley likes to reminisce about his years as a teacher.

"I student-taught at a huge high school," he says at lunch one day. "I was scared, let me tell you. My first class had twenty-nine twelfth graders. They looked enormous to me. I was just twenty-three myself. Anyway, the class went OK, a few laughs in the wrong places, but OK. When the bell rang one of the girls came up to me, handed me a note, and left. I ducked into the men's room to read it. It said, "'Mr. Rawley, I enjoyed your class, but there's something I think I ought to tell you. See, you have this way of tensing up your butt whenever you start writing on the board. Just thought you'd want to know. Some of the kids were starting to laugh at it. Filomena (braided hair, second row).'

"What the hell do you do about that? Next day in that class when I saw Filomena my heart started doing backflips. I got up and started teaching—about Hamlet, I think. When I turned to write something on the board I heard a girl cough, significantly. So I carefully untensed my butt, first the right half, then the left. When I turned around she winked at me. I'm still grateful to that girl."

"The Western mind is not conditioned to dealing with paradox," Rawley says at lunch one day. He has just attended my workshop on bringing literature into the writing workshop, and it has him excited. "That's one of the great things about children's literature—it helps us deal with paradox."

"You mean it helps children."

"No, I mean the child that lives inside us all. See, that's why what you do is so appealing to both children and adults. By talking about great children's books you're letting people get back in touch with the child that's still alive inside them."

He pauses and looks at me.

"There's a lot of spirit inside all of us. It's trying to get out. We've got to help it get out. Literature may be one way of doing that."

"You're sounding awfully religious all of a sudden."

"It's dangerous, like religion," Rawley replies. "You see, literature is a threat to people, just the way writing is, and it's a threat because it involves self-knowledge. All of us have a beast inside us. It's when you forget that, when you deny the existence of the beast, that you get into trouble. That's why self-knowledge is so scary for people—people don't want to get in touch with their dark sides."

I glance at my watch: nearly 2 P.M. Rawley rises. Reaches for the check.

"Speaking of dark sides, how 'bout a peek at some genuine unadulterated moon rocks? We got 'em on Friday, and these babies are absolutely not to be missed. I had to go all the way up to Albany to take a seminar about Integrating Moon Rocks into the Science Curriculum...."

Above everything, Rawley, like most of the principals with whom I worked, seemed intellectually lonely, in dire need of a sounding board, a professional friend, someone to swap theories and commiserate with. I fill that role. It helps, no doubt, that I am not part of the immediate school culture and the politics enshrouding it.

PS 79 is located in the Whitestone section of Queens. I first encounter the school on January 14, during a driving snowstorm. It's not until I enter the Main Office that I detect something out of whack here. A typical Main Office in most respects jammed with mailboxes, clock, posters, bulletin boards, secretaries. But the room is bright with fresh flowers and colorful fingerpaints. Big plate of homemade pinwheel cookies sitting on the counter. The secretaries, two attractive, well-dressed women, smile as if they have actually been looking forward to my arrival. Am I in a New York City school or what? Puzzled, disoriented, I introduce myself. A moment later a tall, slender woman with curly red hair emerges from her office and puts my hand in both of hers.

"Welcome," she says, smiling. "I'm Deena Gold."

Above Deena's desk there is a poster of Charlie Brown's friend Lucy sitting at her desk and asking the teacher, "Do you want us to write what we think, or what we think you want us to think?" This is a good omen, and the omen holds. Deena Gold knows writing process. Having coordinated the writing process staff development in another district, Deena speaks the language: launches, folders, revision, inventive spelling, Lucy Calkins, Donald Murray, Don Graves, the works.

"Look." Deena hands me a pile of papers. "Those are from one of my teachers. Those are the stories and booklets she wrote as a little girl. She dug them up and brought them in to share with her class. Isn't that wonderful? The kids were fascinated."

Over coffee, Deena briefs me on her faculty.

"It's an older faculty," she says. "Experienced. High standards but they tend to be overly structured, locked in at times. I think they need to understand the process kids go through when they learn. That's what writing process does, and that's why I'm hopeful it'll help loosen up some of my teachers here. Tell me, how has your work been going in other schools?"

"Good, mostly." It's the first time I've been asked such a question by a principal, and I pause to think about it. "Some teachers really take to it. But with certain bad, burnt-out teachers, it's tough sledding. I—"

"Wait a second," Deena says. "A burnt-out teacher is not necessarily the same as a bad teacher. I make a distinction between the two."

"What do you mean?"

"A burnt-out teacher you can revive and rejuvenate. Down deep a burnt-out teacher still cares, still works hard. She is a professional. Bad teachers are different. Bad teachers are bad right from the start, usually. The best thing that could happen is for a bad teacher to retire."

"But they don't."

"Not always, not if they have tenure."

"Doesn't it bother you to have to assign kids to a bad teacher?" I ask.

"Sure it does." She smiles sadly. "It kills you but it's a fact of life. I have to deal with it as a principal, and I've had to deal with it as a parent, too. My son practically was destroyed by a certain teacher in junior high. Mr. Turner. Four years later my younger son Billy was put into Mr. Turner's class. I marched right down to the school and talked to the principal. 'I'm sorry,' I told him, 'but we have a strict family policy of sacrificing only one child to Mr. Turner.' The principal understood. Billy was moved into another class."

I pass most of that morning visiting cheery classrooms, amazed that such schools actually exist in the city system and that I have been lucky enough to snare one for my own. By the time I leave, at lunch, I'm just beginning to get used to it.

But next week this same disorientation wallops me when I walk into PS 79. The classroom-based staff development used by the Writing Project required teacher trainers to make several jolting adjustments to new settings in a single day. An angry fifth-grade teacher lecturing students. Dimmed rooms awash with slumbering five-year-olds. LD kids and LEP (Limited English Proficiency) kids and IGC kids. Affluent schools and impoverished schools. Just when you started getting comfortable somewhere—BANG!—time to move to the next class, the next school. These quick scene changes kept me in a perpetual state of imbalance. But PS 79 presented me with a new kind of adjustment problem: the splashes of color in the Main Office, the huge central photo entitled "We Are The Children Of PS 79," fresh flowers on all the desks, laughter, somebody humming, an enormous letter along one wall written from the children of one second grade class to Deena Gold.

And in the Main Office, what a smell! A coffee-like aroma, but richer than coffee, more like cappuccino or espresso. The sixth-grade monitors, two avatars of efficiency, have a cup of hot java in my hands practically before I can remove my coat. Even at 8:20 A.M., this is a place you want to be. I find myself glancing around, seeking out clues. It's hard to avoid the idea that this office embodies Deena Gold's persona. The solicitous monitors, even the smiling school secretaries, somehow seem extensions of Deena herself.

Today Deena gives me a school tour. The place is bright, cheery, open—the classrooms far more reminiscent of certain suburban class-rooms I'd seen than city classrooms. Deena fawns, cajoles, teases her teachers. In Gail Falcoff's beautiful first-grade classroom, Deena shakes her head in disbelief. "As a child you simply could not spend a year in a room like this without learning to read. It's just not possible."

Like Meryl Natelli, Deena has an extraordinary rapport with the kids. In Marsha Marcus's first-grade class, she smiles at one boy. He is handsome, with blond, slicked-back hair and a genuine three-piece suit. I stifle a laugh and make a note to ask Deena about this kid who reminds me of nothing so much as a sweet-faced first-grade gangster. Moving next to a very serious boy, Deena stops, crouches, motions me over.

"Mr. Fletcher, I'd like you to meet Demitri Demetrakapolous. There's *nothing* that Demitri can't do, right Demitri?" She squeezes the boy—he offers the barest hint of a smile—before she moves on.

Back in Deena's office, we finalize our plans for my first four visits. Out in the hall, a group of children pass by; the office is flooded with gales of rich, full laughter.

"Hear that?" Deena asks. "You can tell worlds about a class by how much they laugh. I mean *really* laugh. Those are Rosemary Ullman's children. It's amazing how many times you can hear kids in the hallway and pick out their teacher by the quality of their laughter."

She stops to pour us both a cup of coffee.

"Funny. With all the wonderful teachers I've worked with, it's the horror stories that tend to stick in your mind. A few years ago, I had this one teacher who was assigning her students to write birthday cards to her daughter. And that's not a tenth of it."

"What happened?"

"A kid finally said something about it. Another year one of my teachers had a child who was doing so-so work, didn't always do his homework, didn't work that hard. He came from a family with a family business, and when he grew up he knew there would be a job for him to work in the business. There was no pressure for him to win a scholarship, no expectation that he'd even go to college. All right, so maybe he wasn't working as hard as he could have been. Still, he was the nicest kid, not a mean bone in his body. But his teacher really went for him, started putting pressure on him, sending notes home to his parents. I finally had to call her into my office. 'He's third from the bottom of the class,' the teacher told me. I said, 'Someone has to be at the bottom, someone has to be second from the bottom, and someone has to be third from the bottom. Not everybody is a scholar.' It was an inappropriate expectation for that child."

"It seems hard for teachers to adjust their expectations for individual students."

"That's right, but that's why writing process is so important. It teaches teachers to become responsive to each child in the class."

"How do you think it'll go here?" I ask her. She shrugs.

"Don't get your hopes up too high," she says. "Writing process is an approach that asks teachers to give students some measure of independence, some control over their own learning. That's a hard thing for teachers to give children when they've never really had it for themselves."

1:35 P.M. Stephen Rawley and I are locked in a postprandial discussion at a Chinese restaurant. I am edgy; today I have decided to ask him about the abundance of pretty young women on his staff. But first I must wait while Rawley finishes his discourse on the principals in the city system.

"There are basically two kinds of principals in the city schools," he is saying. "The educators, and the managers. The educators tend to be women. Not always—I like to think I'm an educator—but they tend to be. They can't keep their noses out of classrooms, they go to conferences and take tons of notes, they talk theory, they're always getting excited about what's going on in their school. They view the piles of paperwork as a nuisance that gets in the way of their real job: giving kids the best education they possibly can. The managers tend to be men. You know, the old-boy network. The managers don't go too wild over classroom instruction. But the paperwork doesn't bother them, either. They sit in their offices, they fill out the forms, they tend to the daily emergencies that come up in their schools. They survive. And maybe they're the smart ones."

"Why?"

"Because there's really no hope for the city school system. Not really. Sure, there are a few pockets of excellence here and there, and some good new ideas. But as a whole the system is unsalvageable. Kaput."

Pause. He sips the last of his water. After this last comment, my question seems trivial. I decide to ask it anyway.

"Stephen, I've been meaning to ask you something. So many of your teachers, I don't know, they seem so young. So pretty. Is that just coincidental? Am I crazy, or is there something going on?"

Rawley smiles a bit ruefully and motions for the check. He looks me straight in the eyes.

"You're right," he says quietly. "I do tend to hire them that way. It's deliberate. That sounds terrible, doesn't it? But listen. I want you to understand me on this. Maybe it's a rationalization. If so, so be it. I have never, and would never, take any liberties with my staff. But here's how I figure it. I have a tough job in a tough setting. And if I can hire teachers, good teachers, who can make the job just the littlest bit more pleasant for me ... Well, do you see what I mean? Would you condemn me for that?"

He is looking at me, and I have no idea what to say. One thing is clear: hiring pretty women to staff his classrooms represents Rawley's revenge against the system.

In the tour business, tour guides go by this rule of thumb: a small percentage of tourists will be marvelous, most will pass through without distinguishing themselves in any positive or negative way, and 10 percent will drive you to the very brink of your endurance. That 10 percent makes you wish you never took the job in the first place.

Sometimes I got lucky and landed a sweetheart group, or a thoroughly despicable bunch of tourists, but over the long haul I found that 10 percent figure to be pretty accurate. I'd extend that troublesome 10 percent to include other players in the travel business: flight attendants and other airline personnel, hotel clerks and maids, bus drivers, maitre d's, even tour guides. In fact, I have strong suspicions that this figure represents some yet-to-be-proven absolute in (human) nature, such as the speed of light, Planck's Constant, or pi.

So I was not surprised to find that among the majority of wonderful (or at least tolerable) children and teachers with whom I worked, roughly 10 percent of them gave me nightmares and made me wish I were building furniture and crunching numbers on a computer. This also applied to principals.

Deena Gold, Marlon Hauser, Meryl Natelli, and Elaine Rolnick were typical of the best principals I worked with: smart, tough, quirky, compassionate. Human. There were others, of course, such as Andrew Reilly. (Who, by the way, the last time I saw him, was sitting in his office attired in full workout regalia watching a giant television set: "In seven minutes my mother-in-law is going to be on Phil Donahue. If I miss it, I'll never hear the end of it. Sit down.") But these principals only made me more appreciative of the real gems I found.

January 26. I wake to a blizzard. My initial reaction—(childish delight)—gets replaced in quick succession by worries about driving conditions, a slim hope for school cancellation, a temptation to call in sick. Sighing, I rise to face the day.

PS 201 is located on 164th Street in Queens, a stone's throw from Queens College. I ease over the icy Triboro Bridge and arrive at the school unscathed. I am directed from the Main Office down to the auditorium where the principal, Norm Sherman, stands before seven or eight hundred seated children. The kids are all bundled up, some still sleepy, yawning, others jabbering away, enervated by the storm. High decibels reign. Norm raises two fingers on his right hand—the old peace sign invoked now as the pay attention/shut up signal. Slowly, a hush inhabits the big, tired room. Norm speaks calmly.

"Today is a school day. That's the way we're going to play it." He pauses here for effect. "I know you're excited about the snow, but let's all remember what we're here for. Lunch will be inside. I want everyone to think and be careful when leaving the school. The last thing we want is to start the year off with an accident."

He pauses again. The kids wait, snug in their bulky jackets and winter parkas.

"In the international news, President Reagan is concerned about the election in the Philippines," Norm says. "The fear is that Ferdinand Marcos may try to run a fraudulent [he says this word slowly, and pauses to let it sink in] election; that is, his party might destroy ballets for other candidates. President Reagan is also concerned about Mr. Quaddaffi, the president of Libya. Our government feels that Mr. Quaddaffi and his country have been the cause of a great deal of terrorism in the world. President Reagan has warned Mr. Quaddaffi about this several times. Now then, as for school news, I want to remind you that today is the Talent Show that so many of you have worked so hard for. I wish you luck. . . ."

I sit in the back, trying to squelch a smile, transfixed by the delicious juxtaposition of Quaddaffi and the school talent show.

"Please stand for the pledge," Norm says. All stand, myself included, drawn upward by an irresistible force. "Auditorium: pledge!" At exactly 8:21 A.M. I place my right hand over the heart.

After dismissing the various classes, Norm stays to deal with three boys. By the set expressions on their faces, it is apparent that they are expecting to be punished. When I reach the front of the auditorium, Norm is addressing a chubby boy.

"You're not listening to me, Clarence. The point is, your sister doesn't need you to be her policeman."

"Yes, but Mr. Sherman that's my baby sister," the boy says, crying a little. "I can't have anybody beating on my baby sister. I can't have that."

"We agree on that, Clarence. If anybody starts trouble with your sister, you come and get me or any one of the teachers on the playground. All right?"

Clarence nods reluctantly. Norm turns to the two other boys.

"Raymond, go to the office. I'll talk to you there. Marvin, you put your *right* hand over your heart while doing the pledge. Now go to your class. I don't want to hear a peep out of you today. Do we understand each other? Mr. Fletcher, how do you do?"

He thrusts his hand at me and gives me an old-fashioned hearty handshake. I have to stride rapidly to keep up with him as we leave the deserted auditorium.

"I loved your talk about world events," I say. Norm smiles.

"I know lots of that stuff goes over their heads, but I still think it's important to expose them to it. These kids come from parents who don't read newspapers, lots of them. I want to introduce them to the idea that the world is a bigger place than Queens, New York."

In his office, Norm goes over the day's schedule with me. As usual, my demonstration teaching will turn the school upside down. Hours of extra secretarial time have been required to reschedule classroom teachers, juggle their prep periods, and hire substitute teachers. Am I really worth all this? At one point Norm takes a phone call.

"It's an emergency," he says to me covering the phone. "A parent. I'll be with you in five minutes."

I duck into Norm's bathroom. There is an Apple computer perched on the toilet seat; I gingerly lower it onto the floor.

At the end of the day I meet with Norm again. Most principals merely poked their heads into my demonstration classes to make sure the observing teachers were there and paying attention. I was surprised and flattered when Norm stayed for entire demonstration classes, listening, nodding, scribbling pages of notes. Bearded, heavyset, with no-nonsense glasses, Norm looked as much like a research scientist or rabbinical scholar as an elementary school principal. What I liked immediately about Norm was his reasonableness, his *norm*alness in the frenetic city schools. He was enthusiastic about the demonstration classes he had seen.

"You were fantastic!" Norm tells me. "This is one of the most exciting ideas I've seen in education for a long time, and I don't say that lightly. I don't like educational fads. Too many ideas in education are like women's hemlines: up one year, down the next. But this is terrific! You were wonderful with the kids and the teachers."

I leave the school, glowing. Hang onto this feeling, Ralph, I'm telling myself. Someday you're going to want to remember how good this feels.

I return to my car. A parking ticket is tucked under my windshield wiper. Thirty-five dollars for parking by a fire hydrant. I look around and see the hydrant for the first time, three-fourths buried in a mound of plowed snow.

What was I supposed to remember?

Next morning, and every morning I work at PS 201, I make sure to get up early enough to catch Norm's State-of-the-World address. Though I had abandoned the practice of grading the schools I worked in (the perverse pleasure wore off quicker than I'd expected), I still occasionally indulged myself. PS 201 was a B school, but the presence of Norm Sherman made me forget its drawbacks and bump it to an A−.

After quieting the children, Norm begins speaking slowly and deliberately. The kindergarten kids and first graders sit in the front rows closest to Norm, the older children in back.

"Good morning, boys and girls. Today is January 27th, 1986. Some of you may have heard that two people in Westchester County have died after swallowing Tylenol capsules. Investigators have now proven that those capsules had been tampered with. What that means is that somebody apparently put poison in the capsules. The police are trying to figure out who did this, and why they would do such a thing. Until that time, remember: do *not* take any Tylenol pills or capsules."

Subdued buzzing from the assembled kids. Norm pauses while a teacher leads a small group of children into the auditorium. She pushes a very thin boy in his wheelchair, followed by a boy moving slowly with the aid of a walker, two Downs Syndrome children, and three girls, their grinning faces pinched with the telltale mark of retardation.

"Good morning," Norm smiles at them. He waits until they have taken their places before he continues.

"Today the spaceship *Voyager 2* will move within fifty thousand miles of the planet Uranus. Scientists are excited about this because they don't know a great deal about Uranus and they're hoping to get photographs back from it."

From here Norm launches into the pros and cons about allowing the children to have outside recess after lunch. He considers this issue with the same gravity as the Tylenol scare, or *Voyager 2*'s brush with Uranus.

"It's not so much the cold weather, it's the wind we're concerned with," Norm explains. "I'll have a more definite answer for you just before lunch. Now, for school news. Tickets will be on sale at lunch today for Friday's concert. I ask all of you to remind your parents not to bring babies or small children to the concert. Oh, I almost forgot, tomorrow, as most of you know, Christa McAuliffe, a teacher, will become the first civilian ever to go into space. We'll be seeing history in the making. I know that several classes have done projects on this exciting event, and these will be on display for the rest of the week in the cafeteria for everyone to see. . . ."

I Was Eating My Lunch
When She Died

January 28, 1986, dawns clear and cold. Heading over the Whitestone Bridge I stumble into a reverie about Beth Byers, my first school sweetheart, in sixth grade, a girl I hadn't thought about in years. She had long, looping curls and wide eyes I would glimpse at certain times appraising me from across the classroom and yet—damn! I missed my exit. Trying to backtrack, I run into a swarm of rush-hour traffic and arrive at PS 201 rattled, too late for a quick cup of coffee at the nearby Dunkin Donuts, too late even to hear Norm Sherman's soothing morning address, which I make a point of never missing. Bad way to start the day. I run into the Main Office, grab my schedule, and race off to my first class.

11:00 A.M. I am meeting with eight kindergarten teachers in the teachers' room. Norm has requested this workshop and arranged a "mass coverage"—entertaining the kindergarten children by setting up a large television screen in the cafeteria so they can all watch the launch of the *Challenger* while I work with their teachers.

The teachers' room is small and depressing: residual smoke from someone's morning cigarette, bad coffee, ugly walls. There is a bumper sticker on the wall: I'M NOT DEAF—I'M IGNORING YOU. The teachers look tired. I sense more relief at having a free period than any abiding interest in writing process. I gather my notes, hearing the teachers' chatter around me.

"Coffee?"

"Coffee I'd love; this mud I can do without."

"What I'm really thirsty for is the weekend. Boy, I can almost taste it."

"Christa McAuliffe, now there's a teacher with the right idea. Get as far away from your classroom as humanly possible. If I left this planet I might just keep going."

"Let us know so we can throw you a party."

I listen to one man named Ray, about sixty, his face agreeably seamed with patience and fatigue. He is talking about a new program called PARP: Parents As Reading Partners.

"Makes all the difference in the world," Ray says, "but lots of parents don't appreciate it. They don't read to their kids. They look at it as more pressure. I got one note from a mother saying, 'Dear Mr. Williams, please don't send Nicky home with any extra reading or homework. I just don't have time for it. I don't care if he has to stay in for recess or for gym. Have him finish it in school."

"I have one girl, you know, Michelle, who was having all kinds of problems with her verbal skills," says Renée, a large bleached blond with oversized glasses and liquid eyes. She has exaggerated three-martini gestures of hand and face that seem misplaced in school. "At Parents Night I took her mother aside and said, 'I'd like you to take fifteen minutes a night and really talk to Michelle, get her talking, listen to her, so we can pull that deficiency up.' Mrs. Lewis says, 'I don't *have* fifteen minutes a day.'"

"She probably doesn't," Ray says.

"Come on, Ray," Renée says. "I raised two kids without any husband, and my kids never went to bed without a story. Who do you think you're talking to?"

"What's with parents these days?" another woman asks. "I was in a parking lot in front of Bloomingdale's last week. This young mother and her son, maybe twelve, are getting into a Jag. Steel gray. The boy holds up a wallet. 'I found this on the counter inside. What should I do with it?' The mother says, 'You can keep the money but you'd better throw the credit cards away.' Then she slams the door and backs out."

"And we're supposed to do something with kids like that," Renée says. "No wonder they call teaching a tired profession."

"If I had to do it all over now," Ray says, "I'm not sure I'd put my kids in a public school."

"What would you do, put them in one of those snooty private schools?" Renée asks.

Ray thinks for a moment.

"I'd probably try to teach them at home myself."

"I rest my case," Renée says.

"Can we get started?" I suggest.

"Didn't someone say something about lox and bagels?" one woman asks blithely.

"C'mon," says Renée, who feels a certain protectiveness toward me. "Make nice."

The door bursts open and Norm Sherman sticks in his head.

"The *Challenger* just exploded," he says. "The shuttle."

"My God," Renée whispers.

Then: silence. We stare at each other. 11:15 A.M.

"Some of the kids are upset," Norm says. "You'd better go to your classes." To me, he says, "Sorry about this, Ralph."

Rivulets of children pour out of the cafeteria in tight formation, something-important-has-just-happened written all over their faces, legs and arms moving stiffly, with difficulty, as if they are all aware that on this particular day they are walking through history. Their expressions run the emotional gamut. Shock. Sadness. Nervous smiles. Gleeful fascination.

"Mr. Fletcher, the spaceship blew up!"

"Didya see it?"

"The teacher's dead!"

"They showed it four times!"

They deliver their news and stand back, studying my reaction. My face is stung by déjà vu: twenty-three years earlier, South River School, in Marshfield, Massachusetts, when Mr. Tobin's voice came over the loudspeaker: "Boys and girls, may I have your attention please. Boys and girls, I have some very serious and very sad news to tell you. . . ."

In the hallways, two pudgy first-grade boys walk past, stoically sucking their thumbs. A few seconds later Jessica, a girl I know, skitters past saying—"We were destined for something like this to happen sooner or later—" and gives me a a tense smile before vanishing in the crowd.

In the cafeteria, someone has turned off the TV. When most of the kids have left, Ray snaps it back on again. A group of teachers and I stand around watching the explosion again and again. It isn't easy to watch, particularly the cut to the parents' reaction.

"I guess you know what kids'll be writing about today," Ray murmurs to me.

"Don't count on it," Renée says. "Bet you ten bucks this rolls right off most of them. They see so many people getting zapped and blown up and shrunk on cartoons and movies. How is this any different? Just one more TV death."

I have a meeting with the language arts coordinator that keeps me from visiting any more classrooms that day. The next morning the guy selling newspapers by the Whitestone Bridge toll plaza holds up the biggest *New York Times* headline I have ever seen: SHUTTLE EXPLODES. The radio is clotted with bulletins, theories, questions, interviews, condolences, and perspectives from around the world. On one station a psychologist discusses possible long-range damage to the psyches of America's children.

"Many children have had simple fantasies about going to space," she says. "After the explosion of the *Challenger,* it will be much more complicated for children to entertain such fantasies."

During that day, and the numb days that follow, the kids I encounter are split on the *Challenger* explosion: many ignore it; other kids are unable to write about anything else. I start gathering pieces of writing about the shuttle disaster. In all the samples, you can see the children using writing to try to make sense of the tragedy. Gregory, a first grader in Carolyn Spengler's class, writes:

The Shuttle Blownup Story
There were 7 astronauts
They lived and Died together
When the shuttle Blew up
There was a teacher
I'm Glad it Wasn't Ms Spengler
Of course it was Ms McAuliff
I'm sad it happened
I couldn't stand it no more
I didn't want to hear about
it again.

This story, like many of the shuttle stories I would read, is accompanied by a vivid three-part drawing at the bottom of the page showing an intact capsule first flying, then vibrating, and finally blossoming into a cloud of smoke. The *Challenger* disaster prompts many kindergarten and first-grade children who had been writing words to revert back to drawing to make sense of the tragedy.

It is dark when I enter Gail Reznick's first-grade class. None of the warm, raucous greeting I usually get upon arrival. The kids turn to look at me with luminous eyes.

"Mr. Fletcher, we're sitting in the dark because of something sad we're talking about," Gail says to me in a somber stage voice. "We're sad about all the astronauts who died when the *Challenger* blew up."

I nod. Gail stands and moves next to me.

"How did they take it?" I whisper.

"We were having a shuttle party, balloons, streamers, cupcakes, TV blaring, the whole shebang," she whispers back. And then it happened. Can you imagine? Nineteen out of twenty-five kids were crying."

"Do you think they'll write about it?"

"No, they won't."

I look at her, surprised. Gail's first graders are among the best writers I work with.

"They won't?"

"They decided, as a class, that they didn't want to write about it." She shrugs. "It was too sad for them. I tried to reason with them but they wouldn't budge."

I leave Gail's class with the children still sitting in the dark. In a second-grade class, Amy, a diminutive Chinese girl, writes:

How I Felt About The Explosion

I felt so sad that I felt just like you do about the explosion. I heard that a teacher died at the explosion. I ws so surprise. I felt sorry for her and the other peoples. I was eating my lunch when she died.

Janice Bentz, a third-grade teacher at PS 79, stops me in the hallway to show me a batch of letters she was just about to send off to Christa McAuliffe's family.

Dear Parents,

I am really sorry that your daughter died. People just seem to come and go in a jiffy these days.

She will never die in your hearts because you love her very very much. Everybody in my family cares about your daughter, too.

I think that she was really a very nice lady, brave and very special. If I was her I would think I was lucky because she was a teacher who was very smart and got picked. So you were very lucky to have her as your daughter.

Sincerely,
Wendy

Wendy's first sentence—"People seem to come and go in a jiffy these days"—makes me laugh despite myself.

"I know I shouldn't but—"

"I know," Janice says. "I had the same reaction."

Another of Mrs. Bentz's third graders, apparently unclear about the certainty of the astronauts' deaths, wrote:

Dear Mr. and Mrs. McAuliffe,

I have been so worried about what happened when I saw the news. I was terrified that she died. You would need a miracle to save her now.

The seven people were very brave and will alwys be heroes and a memory to America and me.

Your friend,
Tasos

Dear Parents,

What a sad thing! I was crying after your daughter died and I know you must have been crying, too. It was like someone in my own family was dead.

Love,
Alysha

P.S. I want to be your friend.

Dear McAuliffe family,

You are not alone in your sorrow. My class and I will always remember Christa as a brave hero of our time.

Love, your friend,
Danyel

Dear McAuliffe family,

I am so sorry about what happened. I saw the whole thing. I know how you feel to lose a person from your family. Everybody loved her even if she was not in their family. I don't even know her, but I love Christa McAuliffe.

Love,
Annamarie Natale

I was curious to see the responses of older children. Lori Ann Haas, a fifth grader, writes:

> When the space shuttle went up everybody was talking about it. I didn't know what everyone was talking about until it exploded. I knew. I was sad. I heard that the teacher who was killed had two children, Scott and Caroline. Could you imagine how they felt? She said she wanted to go up because she wasn't afraid. I would be afraid to go up into space. I think this should stop. Before you know it a million people will die. I mean it. It should stop.

My interest in the kids' response to this tragedy was rooted in the larger issue that had fascinated me since I'd begun working in the city schools: the attitudes toward death that kids displayed in their writing, the way they used writing to make sense of it. It was remarkable how often kids wrote about death and how honestly they wrote about it. One of the most powerful pieces kicking around the Writing Project had been written by a kindergarten child:

Translation: When you get to be a big person . . . cemetery.

I met Gabriel Borgella in a fourth-grade class at PS 161. He was short, portly, prematurely grave, like some future commissioner or circuit judge. One day he penned a story and handed it to me without comment, without even looking at me.

My Brother Is Dead

One day my brother O'Neil fall at the window in the 9th floor window. He was dead and my mother and father and my sister were sad and even me too, I was too sad about my brother. And at night when I was at my bed sleeping, I couldn't sleep, I was so scared. And I went to the living room, to think about him. And I was so sleeping and then, I went to my room and went to sleep and dream about him, and I been thinking about him.

That was the end
from Gabriel in class 4–504

Writing like this lived inside me for many days, partly because I had seen my own seventeen-year-old brother Bob killed in a car accident in 1974. But I was also haunted by Gabriel's writing itself, the strangely articulate way he communicated his sorrow and disorientation; that image of him sitting in the living room at night thinking of his brother; even the way the unusual end—"That was the end"—reinforces the tone of the whole piece.

Kids' writing about death tapped something in me. Maybe it had to do with the schools themselves, the various shades of death that schools encompass. Or maybe it had more to do with the slow demise of my own marriage. For whatever reasons, I began collecting writings on death by children. Once I started looking, I found them everywhere.

In PS 403 the halls smell like a mountain of melted cheese. I try to guess the plate du jour: macaroni 'n cheese, perhaps, or the infamous "pizza roll" I'd sampled elsewhere. In the Main Office, principal Anna Schick is racing frantically about, barking out orders, disposing of parents, making the days' announcements, handing me my schedule, pulling levers to set off bells, and beaming a taped recording of the Star Spangled Banner and the Pledge of Allegiance into the classrooms.

"It's one of those days, Ralph," she sighs. "We've got a special tennis assembly in the morning, the first-grade dance festival, rehearsal for the Talent Show ..."

She rolls her eyes. It's *always* one of those days at PS 403.

I escape to the relative sanity of a fourth-grade classroom. The teacher, a young woman with a coarse sandpaper voice, is just finishing up a spelling lesson. While waiting for her to finish, I look over the bulletin boards and discover this story:

My Baby Brother

I had a baby brother. His name was Joey. He was born early so he was very sick. He had to go to the hospital a couple of times. He was one years old when he died in the hospital. I was going to Sea Side Heights. I was in the car when he died. My mother didn't tell me until I came back. I cryed. I was very sad. My brother had a stuffed horse. He gave it to me. I cryed. My stepmother made one big tear. I loved my little brother. I played with him. His first word was Mama. He had very bad heart problems, so he went to the hospital with a blue face. I always wanted him to get older so I could play wrestling with him.

At the bottom of the page, Vinnie had drawn a little figure named "Mr. Tear," crying, with the bubble, "I love my brother." At the top of the paper the teacher has written in bright red ink: Good!

"Some piece of writing," I say when the teacher comes over.

"Isn't it? And it's true, too. I've talked to the stepmother."

"Can I make one suggestion?" I ask.

"Sure, go ahead."

I point to the big word—GOOD!—on top of the page.

"I wonder about writing something like that on a kid's paper," I say. She winces.

"I know we're not supposed to write on the kids' papers. Sometimes it's so hard to resist."

"It's not just that," I say. "It's a tragic story, not a 'Good' story. I think our basic response should recognize that. Know what I mean?"

"You're right." She smiles ruefully. "It's just that it's the best thing he's written all year. I guess I was responding to how well he wrote instead of what he was writing about."

At a Teachers College workshop, one teacher hands me the xerox of a story by a second-grade girl in her class.

My Father Died

My father died last Friday night at 7:30 P.M. You know how I know? I was watching from my window. He got dead by a car. My father is dead now.

Now I'm with my mother. My mother is an old mother now.
You should love your mother too. Your mother wants you to live.
by Amy Arias

What could I say about that one haunting sentence—"My mother is an old mother now"? What could I say about the poem written by Katherine, an eight-year-old Japanese girl?

I Love my Mother and my father,
they are my best Mother and father;
they make me go outside.
then my father kill him selfe in the Close.
At night.

Cheryl Steinberg, a bright young woman, teaches fourth grade at PS 154 in Queens. A serious teacher with high standards, Cheryl does not hesitate to let her kids know when they don't perform as well as she knows they can. She spends a lot of time correcting the mistakes in her kids' writing. I am trying to get her to enjoy her kids more, to appreciate the strengths in their writing, to relinquish some of the power in the class. Cheryl has thus far responded warily.

Early February. I am standing in front of Cheryl's fourth graders, talking about revision, of all things. It is one of those days when I can feel Cheryl's impatience weighing heavily on the kids. Their writing has been dispirited lately; Cheryl is hoping that a pep talk by me might revitalize the class. I have brought in several pages from a rough draft of a story I've been working on. I hold it up and explain the cross-outs and inserts. I explain to the kids how important rereading is to revision. The kids' faces are glazed. Something is wrong.

"Does *anybody* understand what Mr. Fletcher is talking about?" Cheryl demands. Silence. Loudly, to me "They don't understand. Say it again—more slowly this time."

A very bad day. I slink out of the room, wishing I never had to come back. But I do have to return, in a meager two weeks. When I return, every kid in class is writing furiously. The kids are absorbed, obsessed. I survey the class. One topic is more powerful than the next. I Miss You, Grandpa. When Daddy Left. My Brother Came In Drunk. Cheryl is shaking her head.

"Can you believe this?" she whispers to me. "Look. It's 12:15. These kids would write until 3:00 if I didn't stop them. Look at Derika. Two days ago I saw her writing, slumped over her desk. I told her to sit up, but when I went over to her I could see her sobbing. The tears were falling right onto the paper. Look. You can see the stains on the paper."

"What happened?"

"I stopped pretending that all stories have happy endings," Cheryl says.

"What do you mean?"

"These kids have so much pain in their lives, and the nice neat stories we were reading and talking about didn't tap that pain. So I decided to read *A Taste of Blackberries* [Doris Buchanen Smith] with the class. Do you know it? It's about a boy's best friend who gets stung by a bee one summer, and has an allergic reaction, and dies. What a tearjerker! I used up a box of tissues. The kids loved it."

I listen slowly, still thinking about what Cheryl said a minute earlier: "I stopped pretending that all stories have happy endings." How did she come up with that?

". . . and then I started really talking to the kids about my own life, you know, telling them personal stories like you did back at the beginning of the year. I told them about how my parents are moving to Florida and it's just killing me. I feel like I'm losing my right arm. Then I told them about all the plastic surgery I've had on my face, how I've always thought I was ugly. And something happened. Konstantin started writing about his grandmother's death. It's just pouring out of them. I feel guilty when I tell them to put their writing folders away."

I am thunderstruck: never in my wildest moments would I have suggested that Cheryl talk so frankly to her kids about her life. Where had she found the courage to do so? Something important has happened in this class. You can feel it. Cheryl has had a breakthrough. My first big success as a teacher trainer. How much of it had to do with me? How much of it had to do with her own honesty? How much stemmed from that book about the death of a boy's best friend that Cheryl read to her class? I leave the class elated, if confused.

In the earliest chemistry experiment I can remember doing in school, I learned that only a certain amount of sugar will dissolve in a glass of cold water. Additional sugar does not dissolve but gathers, instead, in a little mound at the bottom of the glass. If, however, you heat the water, a good deal more of the sugar will dissolve. In fact, this additional sugar will stay dissolved even *after* the hot solution has cooled down to room temperature. Try it if you don't believe me. You now possess what is known as a "supersaturated solution." Now comes the fun part: drop into the cooled supersaturated solution just the tiniest bit of dry sugar and watch the rest of the dissolved sugar appear, almost magically, and gather again in a pile at the bottom of the water.

The children I worked with were supersaturated with powerful experiences—death, divorce, birth of a new baby, moving from another country—they'd lived through, and needed just the tiniest bit of encouragement to pour them out onto the paper. I tried to give them that nudge without falling into the pitfall of making it an assignment. Whenever I spoke of the kinds of things I write about, I was careful to share topics and stories with a variety of emotions. These are my stories, I told the kids. *You* decide what to write about. Still, it was uncanny how often kids chose to write about death.

Even for young children, death often loomed as an issue that had to be chewed over and reckoned with. Evan, a first grader, uses a huge piece of paper to write a story about his mother:

My mom had a baby   I was sad   My Brthre was jumping
My mom was happy with her baby   My Brthre was
Happy   My mom saw me when I was sad

"I don't understand," I tell Evan. "Why were you sad?"

The boy looks down and lets his silence reply. I repeat my question. His silence becomes denser, darker. I ask him to read his story to the class. Surprisingly, he agrees. He reads in a soft, clear voice. The kids murmur appreciatively. But many ask Evan the same question that I did.

"Why were you sad when your mother had a baby?" Melanie wants to know. "Having a baby is supposed to be a *happy* thing."

"Yeah, why were you sad?"

Evan does not reply, does not even look at me. But when the session finishes, he goes back to his seat and adds one sentence to the bottom of his paper:

"I was sad becuas I thot that My mom was going to diy."

John Hernandez, a fifth grader at PS 105, writes an essay titled "How I Feel About Death":

> First of all I'm scared of a few little things. One: we have to go in a coffin to get buried or cremated and I do not like the sound of any of those things.
>
> I have something to say. I bet a lot of people ask about it. How are we sure we go to Heaven or Hell?
>
> Because I saw on T.V. Thursday a lady said when you die you are reborn again in a different body.
>
> I hope there is a thing called Heaven because I believe and I'm sure a lot of other million people believe in it, too.

Often the piece of writing centered on the death of a pet. Kids wrote about the demise of rabbits, rodents, lovebirds, and snakes. Stephanie, a fifth grader, wrote about her turtle. The long run-on sentences—even in the title—suggest the headlong rush of feelings provoked by the experience.

My Turtle An Unhappy Day

> My turtles name is pinellipee   But she died I was very hurt inside because she was mostly the best friend I ever had of course I do love my dog very much but pinellipee was sord of a pal when I first got her she was frightened but I patted her on the head and she knew that I loved her pinellipee died because of an amonia because at first she was a school project to see how she lives but she was more to me than just a project. The kids in my class were touching her and I think one of the kids had a cold and pinellipee caught it my mother called the Museum of Natural History because they study turtles my mother asked him if there was a medicine to give pinellipee but the medicine didn't work when I woke up she had died it was sad me and my mother were crying. But I got over it but sometimes I still have moments when I lay down and cry and let my feelings of hurt come out.

The death of a relative or a pet was one thing. Other writings about death had a more ominous tinge. John is a very bright fourth grader, a box-headed Chinese kid who has thus far tended to clown around during most of my visits to his class. His presence, like the presences of a couple hundred other children, is etched only vaguely in my crowded memory. So far he has written about typically boyish topics—computers, planes, wrestling, guns, baseball—none of which has revealed a great deal about his inner life.

February 14: Valentine's Day. For over a week, in class after class, I have been assaulted by hearts of every shape, size, and texture, in candy, cookies, cupcakes, and sheetcakes. In John's class I am relieved to find not a single heart. I approach his desk. The words are written neatly. He makes no attempt to hide them.

My Life is Mixed-up

I have been alive for 9 yrs, and it has been boring. Nothing happened much to me in these 9 years except getting a few medals and awards (everybody gets them now and then). Nothing really special. I feel so bored with life, that sometimes I want to kill myself but I have this thing about death. But still sometimes I don't want to live.

Sometimes I think of death. I wonder about how it feels to die. I don't want to die. I'm only 9 years old (I have at least a good 25 years to live) and I really don't want to die. I don't want to live, neither. I don't know what I want. My life is mixed-up. 3548 days of life and bore and feelings and stuff and stuff and stuff. [The next sentence is crossed out but I can read it.] Instead of swimming and playing violin I'd rather go to space, break a record, or anything exciting to make my life more colorful, or it's just another 9 years of boring life.

I finish reading this piece. For a moment the three of us—John, his teacher, Ruth, and I—are frozen in silence. Ruth touches the boy's shoulder.

"Is this true?" she asks John. Offhandedly, he nods. We avoid each other's eyes. Ruth looks at John. He looks down at his desk. I study his paper, looking for—what? Ruth pulls me away.

"How the hell do you confer with a piece of writing like that?" she whispers.

When I was brand new to the travel business, a veteran tour guide told me, "There's a fine line between service and servitude. Remember that we work on *this* side of that line." Similarly, I was fast learning that in writing conference a fine line existed between being a teacher and a therapist.

"This is serious stuff," I tell Ruth. "We've got to let someone know about it." Bending down, I ask John, "Mind if I borrow this?"

He shrugs. I take the story down to the Main Office, xerox it, give a copy to the principal. She immediately calls John's parents and makes an appointment for him to meet that afternoon with a school psychologist.

Brian is a lanky third grader, a badly dressed kid with an impassive expression that does a poor job of masking his anger. On February 19 I find Brian working away on a story.

"Surprise, surprise," his teacher whispers. "He hasn't written much all year. I worry about Brian."

Over Brian's shoulder, I read his story.

My Buddy Sammy

Sammy is eighty-eight years old   he lives in the city he takes me places and he buys me things and he loves me. he always take me places and fairs and we have a good time sammy is dead now he died at the age of 90 I miss sammy he was my best buddy sammy got shot in 1985.

The End

Below the story, Brian had drawn two smiling stick figures, one much taller than the other. Above the tall figure he has written "Sammy Smith"; above the short one he had written "Brian Smith."

"This is awfully sad," I say to Brian. He doesn't respond. His anger and grief are his and his alone; he will not grant me even a razor-thin slice. "Was he your grandfather?"

Brian nods. Barely.

"Do you know how it happened?"

Another nod.

"Think it's important to tell how it happened?"

Nothing.

"Look, if you want to—and it's up to you—you might just tape a blank page over on the side, like I did with Melanie, so you have all this extra room to write."

By way of answer he tapes the blank sheet of paper onto the page he has already written on. I know I should move on to confer with another kid, but I cannot. When he finishes taping, he picks up a blunt pencil and begins to write.

Sammy got shot by a white man and all of a sudden the amble came I was running in front of Sammy I saw the man shot Sammy and Sammy Died the man came from behind a big tree Then he pulled out a gun and he shot sammy for no resin Sammy is Dead

Sammy did not have a funeral

Some kids managed to write about death with grim humor, or even cheerfulness. One Thursday Dan Fiegelson, the researcher at the Writing Project, shares with us a story written by Aisha, a precocious third-grade girl in Brooklyn. Aisha, Dan explains, was the first student in Mrs. Long's class to try a poem. She was the first to try a short story. So it shouldn't have been a big surprise when one day Aisha decided to write her final will and testament:

"To Tracey I leive my pretties. I hope you take good care of it and adore it. If some body ask you where you got your pretty face from say Aisha.

"To Billy I leive all my brothers toys. I hope you take good care of them. If somebody say where in the world you get all these nice toys from say Aisha because they might belong to my brother but I gave them to you.

"To Mrs. Long I leive all my dresses even dow they might not fit you hang them up so you would remeber to wear a dress and you would remeber me.

"To Karen I leive my skirts because you look good in skirts and have a pretty face to be wearing skirts and dresses than parnts. I know you told me sevrel times that your ugly buts that's your openyou [opinion] my openyou is your pretty."

Aisha read her will to the class. The kids were mesmerized.

"Why did you write a will?" one girl asked Aisha.

"When my great aunt die she have lots of money, right? She can't take it with her so she have to write a will to tell the police who should get her money when she die. So I made a will, too."

Kathy raised her hand.

"Aisha, I know some people get mad when other people copy their ideas," Kathy said delicately. "But would you mind if I wrote a will, too?"

"Oh, no, that's all right," Aisha replied in dead earnest. "Look, you got to get your good ideas from someplace, right?"

Be Here Now

February 26, 1986. My car heater is on the fritz; I am cold and tired when I arrive at PS 201. Some kid has taken a nasty spill in front of the school; a bunch of kids are gathered together on the sidewalk.

"Look, Mr. Fletcher, blood!" they call, cheerfully pointing out a spot of red-blotched snow.

"That's great," I say. "Wonderful." The kids stare at me, unfamiliar with my sarcasm. I get my schedule in the Main Office. Usually the ash-gray secretaries make a feeble stab at welcome. Today they ignore me, and that suits me fine. Only the office monitor smilingly offers to hang up my coat.

"That's OK, I'll do it," I tell her. In the past I have been charmed by these office monitors. But today there is something about this girl, her privileged position behind the big gray desk, the utter complicity with adult authority, that I find chilling.

I file into the auditorium for Norm Sherman's State-of-the-World address. Norm's voice, a blanket tightly woven with firmness and clarity, has never failed to calm me. I sit with the other kids, waiting for it to work its familiar magic. It is not so much what Norm says as what he does *not* say, the soothing weight of intelligence and insight beneath his words. He is a man of ballast, and ballast is precisely what I crave.

"The big news of the international scene is that there was a bloodless revolution in the Philippines," Norm is saying. "A large number of people were not killed. President Marcos voluntarily resigned and has left the country."

The kids listen—or do they? Maybe they are daydreaming, like me, alive more to the soothing sounds and cadences of Norm's words than to their substance. I try to gather my strength, sipping his voice along with my coffee.

"I want all of you to be looking for signs of spring," Norm tells the kids. "Watch for the days getting longer now. Watch the buds, which have been growing all winter on the trees and are now getting quite fat. Watch for the birds. You'll see more and more birds returning from their winter homes. ...."

Spring. In the past the word unearthed in me thoughts of baseball. Paunchy veterans limbering their hamstrings down in Florida, groaning through calesthenics and wind sprints, oiling up their gloves, roughing up baseballs. But this year the thought only makes me sad.

Batter up. I trudge up to Sylvia Dunsky's second-grade classroom. Sylvia is the union rep and resident musical talent, a strong, frontal-style teacher who has thus far resisted my suggestions that she adopt a workshop format during writing time. Hers is an old-fashioned class-room, all the desks facing forward and carefully spaced apart, so as to avoid any critical mass of students. I have suggested she cluster the kids' desks: she has politely but firmly resisted this idea. A veteran teacher, Sylvia has seen the likes of me come and go many times during her twenty-six years in the system. Still, we get along. I cannot quite resist her high-strung enthusiasm. When I walk into her room, she runs to the piano and bangs out an impromptu melody:

> What're we gonna write
> What're we gonna write
> What're we gonna write to-day to-day?
> What're we gonna write ...

I smile but the muscles in my face feel stiff, cold. The smile actually hurts.

Slowly, we ease into our work, I, coach/trainer, Sylvia, teacher/learner. Writing process draws a great deal from the way writers work. Many writers have found that they separate out into two people when they write: the writer/creator and the critic who stands back to evaluate what has been written. Much has been said about the "creative tension" between these two persona. (Gail Godwin has written a marvelous essay, "The Watcher at the Gate," on this idea.) While working with teachers, I want to encourage something similar: I want them to be able to stand back from their own teaching, to question it, to think and rethink it.

Work of this kind involves a great deal of simultaneity: watching teachers, diagnosing classrooms, appreciating kids, appraising writing conferences, making suggestions. Meanwhile, a part of myself stands next to me while I work: watching, considering, critiquing. This detached "other self" carries on a continual dialogue with my active self.

"C'mon, Fletch, wake up."

"I am awake. Just a little slow this morning."

"If you're awake, then act it. You're sleepwalking."

"I'm going through a hard time."

"You're feeling sorry for yourself. Come on. Get centered. Be here now."

"Thank you, Baba Ram Dass."

"I mean it. Roll up your sleeves. Sylvia's got questions. Respond to her. Respond to these kids."

"I can't. I'm sick of looking at kids' writing. If I see another I-went-to-the-park story, my-head-got-busted, I-went-to-Florida, I'm-having-a-birthday-party, my-mom's-having-a-new-baby story, I'm going to throw up."

"My, haven't we gotten cynical. Maybe you're burning out."

"Maybe I am."

"Look. You're here to do a job. Do it. It's called 'being a professional.'"

"Look at this room, look at the desks. How much of an effect have I really had since I've been working in her class?"

"Poor, poor pitiful me."

"But what's the point? I mean, what am I doing here?"

"Change is slow. Remember what Lucy says."

"*You* remember what Lucy says. Lucy's not hustling from class to class, day after day. I am."

A dialogue like this might go on all morning and become quite acrimonious. Sometimes it gave me a pounding headache; on days like this one it would only deepen my fatigue.

That afternoon I drag myself over to PS 120. Terry deBeavernet has the fourth grade "gifted" class. She is around thirty, athletic and energetic, if unfocused at times.

"Did you want to talk to the kids first?" she asks.

"Well," I counter, "did you have anything planned?"

"I was going to talk to them about how to make the beginnings of their stories better, but if you . . ."

"No, go to it," I tell her. A good sign. At the beginning of the year, teachers like Terry were too frightened to teach under my scrutiny. Today, Terry's willingness to teach suggests that she is beginning to find her "voice" teaching writing. I want to encourage it. Also, truthfully, teaching is the last thing I feel like doing. Terry goes to the blackboard and writes, "The team made a touchdown."

"All right," she says loudly. "Here's the beginning of my story. *The team made a touchdown.* Who can help me make this beginning better?"

A flock of hands shoot up. These IGC kids are confident; they want to show me how smart they are about this writing business.

"The boy zig-zags through the other team and scores a touchdown," says Jessica, a very bright, blond-haired girl with crinkly blue eyes. Jessica has confided to me that she dearly wants to be older, preferably sixteen or seventeen.

"Well, all right, that's using descriptive language. . . ." Terry replies uncertainly. "But that's not exactly what I'm looking for. Anybody else?"

"The man scored a touchdown in the last second of the game," Anthony says.

"Well, OK, you've added time. . . ." Terry says. The glance she throws my way makes me wonder if I shouldn't jump in and save her. But how?

"The magnificent team won the crucial game with a touchdown at the very end," Otari suggests.

Terry looks frustrated.

"I want you to try and work with what I've given you. . . ."

"How about if you *tell* us what you want us to say so we can understand what you mean," Jessica says with exaggerated politesse. The class laughs.

"You've got to admit it, Miss deBeau," Carlos says. "She got you there."

Other kids shout out suggestions. What on earth is she getting at? And while she stands at the front of the room, amidst the confusion, a short Indian boy sitting at his desk in front of me keeps mouthing in a low, foghorn voice: "BOO-RRING . . . BOO-RRING . . . BOO-RRING . . ."

What ailed me? Sure enough, I was depressed, but not all my work went badly. I had plenty of Steve Meyerses, Janice Bentzes, Meryl

Natellis, Deena Golds, and Norm Shermans to cheer me up. I still got my beard trimmed by the ancient Russian Jews at my neighborhood barber shop, letting the sweet mixture of Russian and Yiddish wash over me while one of the old barbers deftly applied a razor to my neck.

I didn't know whether to blame my depression on the short dark February days. Or the friction created from eating/breathing/sleeping writing day after day and yet not writing myself. Or simple marital woes. The good news on the home front was that Marian and I had stopped fighting. The bad news was that we'd largely stopped talking. I would come home from work at 4:00 and start typing up my notes. Marian would arrive an hour and a half later, immediately crawl into bed, and take a two-hour nap. At night, without a trace of irony, we'd watch reruns of The Honeymooners.

I did spend one marvelous day with Ralph Peterson, the whole language specialist from Arizona State University. Looking at Peterson, you understand why they call it a "shock" of white hair. Long, pulled straight back, Peterson's snowy hair made a striking contrast with his tanned face. He darted around the classrooms, delighting in what the kids were writing.

"Look!" he'd exclaim softly to me, pointing to one child's piece of writing. "Read that. That's book-talk! She's got book-talk in her writing!"

Peterson listened hard to the kids he spoke with that day, and did not simplify his language one iota when talking to them, whether explaining how to build suspense in a story or how to find the right ending for a poem. He seemed incapable of talking down to a child. He continually pulled out books and referred to them while talking to kids about their writing.

"I think kids need that reference point," he told me. "I talk to kids about their writing in terms of literature. I talk to kids about literature in terms of composing."

Racing from classroom to classroom with another professional man assuaged my own gender disorientation, if only for a day. The day with Peterson was as exhilarating as it was unsettling. He was old enough to be my father, yet he seemed vastly more energetic than I did. He seemed *fresher.* A quote by Peterson I had heard earlier—"You can't affect someone unless you first let them affect you"—kept ringing in my ears. That sounded great. The problem was I didn't feel like I had any room left inside for anyone to affect me. I felt numb.

On Thursday afternoon a bunch of Project trainers gather at the Amsterdam Café for drinks. Sipping a beer, I notice that my fingers are shaking. I can't decide whether to attribute this to shot nerves, the day's exhausting meeting, or too much caffeine.

These informal Amsterdam Café meetings have become the high-light of my week. Today, per usual, the conversation flows into a catalogue of bizarre moments in the schools. These conversations often verge on the irreverent—I find myself laughing about issues I might not have found funny earlier in the year. But there's a stubborn comfort knowing we're not going through the city school madness alone.

"I have this one teacher, a gifted kindergarten teacher, the nicest lady in the world, and blind as a bat. How she functions in that classroom ... I come into her room and she looks right at me and doesn't see me."

Laughter.

"One day, just for fun, I decided to see how long I could be in her room without her knowing about it. I was there for twenty-five minutes! It was a little secret between the kids and me."

More laughter.

"I have this one teacher, this guy? He's crazy. He really is. One day I came into his room, and he's wearing this space suit with a helmet. There was this clear globe in the middle of the room filled with different colored strands of yarn.

"'What is that for?'" I asked him.

"'To teach kids their colors,' he said. Colors! In third grade!"

We crack up; nobody is laughing harder than me. I'm laughing so hard I can barely stop. Jesus, I'm thinking, I need this.

"I have this one teacher who uses a stoplight—with the three colors—to keep his kids quiet," Jim says. "When it's red, absolutely no talking. Yellow means quiet talking only. Green means the kids can talk freely. One kid told me it hasn't been green all year."

"A traffic light? Does he draw it—"

"No, a real standing stoplight that actually works!"

That afternoon my car moves sluggishly when I ease it out from the curb. I jump out and survey the damage: two slashed rear tires and a smashed back window. The back seat is encrusted with jewels of glass and glass slivers. The two flat tires make my one spare tire worthless, though it looks like there might still be just enough air in the tires for me to make it to the gas station on 96th Street. I decide to chance it, driving dead slow, gritting my teeth the whole way, praying I'll avoid any permanent damage to my tire rims. The incident ends up costing me 378 dollars.

Next day I wake to steady snow, wrench myself out of bed, and turn on the radio. "The New York City schools are all open today with these exceptions. . . ."

With two new rear tires, my Toyota handles admirably on the snowy road. I crawl over the Triboro into Queens. Snow-wrapped and somnabulant, PS 433 looks deserted as a snowed-in airport: nothing in, nothing out. What if school was cancelled after all? Then I spot a cluster of bundled kids running past.

Inside, the school is warm, bright. I revel in the cozy feeling of being inside a school during a snowstorm.

"Coffee?" one of the office monitors asks, pointing a finger gun at me.

"Sure, why not?" The phones ring steadily. A perfect day for calling in sick: a snowstorm, and a Friday, to boot.

"How come we never get snow days anymore?" Lindsey, the secretary, asks.

"It's Quinones," the other secretary mutters back. "He wouldn't close school during a nuclear war."

"That was Fran Thomas," Lindsey says, hanging up. "She's having trouble starting her car. Wants to know what it means when the engine just clicks when she turns the key."

I find the principal in her office on the phone. She covers the receiver and speaks to me.

"Be with you in a sec. It's an emergency. For a change." She smiles and motions to a chair. "Sit."

I sit and sip my cup of coffee. She hangs up the phone.

"Through ice, sleet, and snow, the Writing Project will deliver the process." She stands in front of me. "Do you realize that yesterday I had twelve teachers out sick? That was before the storm. How do you stay so healthy?"

"Beats me." The schools were cauldrons of Flu Stew as of late. With so many teachers out, there were never enough subs to go around, and some classes had to get divided up. Meanwhile, I imagined myself striding through invisible clouds of germs, keeping my record of perfect health miraculously intact. Pete Rose must have felt a little like this when he got a hit in his forty-second or forty-third consecutive game.

"Ralph, today is a day I need teachers," the principal says. "How would you like to take a first-grade class?"

I laugh.

"I'm serious," she says. "Think of the article you could write about it."

"You mean for the whole day?"

"Why not?"

What the hell, I figure, half of the teachers I'm scheduled to work with have already called in sick. As a tour guide I was frequently called on to be babysitter, bartender, blood donor, bouncer, bus driver, luggage schlepper, cook, flight attendant, matchmaker, marriage counselor. So today I'm a first-grade teacher. In room 134, twenty-one kids look me over carefully, I can feel them scrutinizing me: face, beard, gender.

"Have fun," the principal says, smiling.

I gather them in the front of the room to let them begin to get to know me. I start by telling them about the vandalism of my car. I speak softly—my voice has become patchy in places—and the kids listen, eyes growing wider and wider as I speak.

"Don't worry, Mr. Fletcher," one boy tells me, his dark eyes flashing. "My Daddy will get those bad people. He's a policeman!"

"I think God is going to kill those bad people," says Carmen.

Other children start chiming in.

"Please, boys and girls." I try to speak loudly but the words come out as a whisper. "I need your attention."

Now the kids are trying to outdo each other in their proposed punishment of whoever vandalized my car.

"I'm gonna punch them in the belly!"

"I'm gonna screw their heads off!"

"I'm losing my voice," I tell them. "Shhhh."

"Quiet!" one boy shouts. "Can't you hear the man? He's losing his voice!"

The kids quiet and look at me closely. I manage to survive the morning. But by lunch my voice is gone. Useless without it, I head home and spend the rest of the afternoon sipping herbal tea. A strange stillness enters my body.

This is the stuff from which superstitions are stitched: just as I had commenced gloating about my robust health, my immunity among swarms of germ-laden children—wham! Saturday morning I wake up shivering, sheets soaked, with a high fever. I pass the next two days in a haze of delirious dreams and the chicken soup Marian feeds me. On Monday I phone my schools to cancel visits.

"Sounds like a massive case of Teacher Flu," Deena Gold says. "I've got ten teachers out with colds, strep throat, the Russian flu. Stay in bed. Eucalyptus tea."

All that week I huddle in bed, sleeping and sweating. The virus affects my stomach, too; soup and crackers are about all I can hold down. On Tuesday, I feel a little better and consider trying to go to work. But Deena was right about dubbing it "Teacher Flu," for whatever afflicted me seemed particularly suited to the teaching profession: no sore throat or runny nose, just an achy, low-energy feeling, and a ball of phlegm hugging my vocal chords that transformed my voice into something between a falsetto and a whisper. This made it impossible for me to sing in the shower, let alone teach.

So I settle in to ride it out. It's actually cozy lying in bed during the day, dozing and watching the snow gather on my windowsill. I nap a lot—I am not a napper by nature—and these cat naps expose me to an unexpected peril: dreams.

I am in some kind of open-air workshop jammed with writing process people. Trees and bushes. A crowd of people studying several large spiders that are energetically making their webs. The workshop is titled "Natural Writing;" it's about how creatures in other species communicate in their own language.

"The web building you are observing is the perfect articulation of this idea," a lecturer is saying. "The spider's lines and the writer's lines are, for all intents and purposes, the same thing. Through the lines of its web, the spider releases its passion, its creative instinct, its purpose."

People write this down. Everyone is watching, taking notes, trying to stay out of the way of the spiders zooming up and down. Two spiders begin vibrating, moving around their webs in a rapid, circular motion. "Ah!" people murmur, scribbling notes....

I wake up. To forget about writing, I start remembering some of the worst disasters I lived through as a tour guide. A plane filled with food-poisoned tourists, vomiting everywhere. A hotel fire in Rio. A tourist mangled from a boating accident in Acapulco: I rushed him to a hospital where he needed an emergency pint of blood (mine). A man who threatened to "take a contract out" on my life for not giving him preferential seating at a Las Vegas burlesque show. A tourist in a hotel lobby who spat in my face saying, "I am *not* a standard person—I will *not* stay in a standard room!"

I fall asleep and dream about one tour I'd had six years earlier with a group of undertakers. This deluxe trip included four days in Brussels, four days cruising down the Rhine River, and four days in Lucerne, Switzerland. For the most part the tour unfolded without a hitch. There had been only one serious problem: the water level on the Rhine had gone dangerously low. This had brought certain objects near the river's surface, among them several unexploded mines from World War II. After a day's delay, the ship carrying the undertakers and I proceeded, cautiously, downstream without incident.

Tours are surprisingly fragile. Some are jinxed from the beginning and never go smoothly. Others are done in by a series of small snafus. In this case, it wasn't until the final day that the tour fell apart. In Zurich we were informed that our plane had a serious mechanical problem and would be delayed at least seven hours. Spare parts were being flown in from Frankfort; the delay would ultimately last twenty-eight hours.

Until that moment the undertakers had been cooperative, even friendly. Now they went berserk, pressing forward, belching out curses and shouted cries. Take my word for it: having two hundred undertakers turn in unison against you is a frightening experience. I felt a tinge of the Death Chill.

"Get us another plane, goddammit. We want to go home!"

"I am exploring every possible option—" I began.

"You're not doing a damn thing!"

"I've got a lot of business at home, and I'm going to lose that business if you don't get me home on time!"

I tried not to think too hard about what he meant by "business."

"Look, there's a plane right there on the runway. A goddamn jumbo jet. Why don't we sublease that jet right now? Huh?"

"It's not that easy—"

"Lemme tell you something that *is* easy, son, and I mean this from the bottom of my heart. If we don't get home soon I'm going to sue your company, and I'm going to sue you, personally, for incompetence."

"You've got that right," I told him. "But there's not too much I can do about an engine that needs repairing. It's an 'Act of God' and—"

"Don't you give me that 'Act of God' bullshit, you son of a bitch!" The man screamed at me, his face bright red. "There's a wild animal out there that needs killing, and I'm not the least bit convinced that a big enough gun has been brought in to kill it with. I want you to lean all over this goddamn airlines so they *do* sublease us a plane. Show them some muscle! Do it now!"

I awake, sweating hard, with a fierce thirst for some cold club soda. I search the cabinets: nothing. Recklessly, I bundle up and head outside to the supermarket. The sidewalks along Lydig Avenue are narrow rinks of ice ventilated by air so cold it burns my lungs. Ominous changes in this neighborhood of the elderly. Two new doctor's offices have opened (MEDICARE WELCOMED), along with a store selling gravestones. At a discount. I stand in the supermarket checkout line, breathing slowly, fighting off waves of exhaustion.

Two lines over, a chubby, freckled girl waves at me. Catching my eye, she flashes a gap-toothed, irrepressible grin. It is Erica, from PS 105, a second grader with lovely pale blue eyes who once bragged that she had so many ideas to write about she "worked magic" by helping her classmates come up with ideas for their own writing. When she starts to approach me, her mother holds her back.

"Where do you think you're going?"

"I'm going to talk to Ralph."

"Who's Ralph?"

"Over there. He works at our school."

The mother glances over at me. Pale, bleary-eyed, with uncombed hair, I try to look harmless. She looks singularly unconvinced.

"You stay right here. I don't want you talking to any strangers."

"He's not a stranger, Mom, he's—"

"Stay here."

Erica rolls her eyes and grins at me. Then her grin softens. She slowly mouths, Where *were* you today? Weren't you supposed to come to our class?

I'm sick, I mouth back. I've got the flu.

Oh, she mouths sympathetically. Too bad.

Erica's mother turns to me with a glare that says, keep your eyes off my daughter, creep.

I pay and trudge home. The experience has been exhausting; I barely have the energy to open the club soda before I fall back into bed.

Returning to work, I find the schools exactly as I have left them. But something has changed: maybe it's me. The flu has left me leaner, weaker, wobblier. There is a funny taste in my mouth. I hear a disembodied, high-pitched tone in the schools; it seems to float above the chattering of kids and the bleating of their teachers. Or maybe it's in my head.

On March 17, my first day back, Meryl Natelli greets me at PS 121 sporting a neon green ribbon in her hair and a monstrous birthday card that has been signed not only by the six teachers I am working with but the 150 kids in their classes as well.

"You look like a ghost!" she says. "Happy birthday!"

"Thanks," I stammer. How had they known it was my birthday? I am surprised by the gesture, and even more surprised by how much it touches me.

Time to make my rounds. My appearance is a signal for the kids to break into a raucous chorus of "Happy Birthday." During my visit, kids keep sneaking up to hand me green homemade birthday cards, green jelly beans, green cupcakes.

One second-grade boy named Kami hands me a present with a card. When I open the present, I find one of those religious plaques. It reads:

> I asked Jesus,
> "How much do you love me?"
> "This much," he answered.
> Then he stretched out his arm
> and died.

"Thanks," I tell him, not quite knowing what to say.

"You're welcome," he says seriously.

In Cera Northern's class, the first graders burst into applause when I show up. The combination of that sound and the kids' faces warms me like a fire. Some kids have written letters to me along with birthday cards. Eric has written:

Dear Ralph,
I'm glad you are coming agen.
I'll be glad to see you.
I'll bet the Hole class will be glad to see you.

Tomor be prepard for a story.
I'll write a good story. And I mean good.
Beter than eny story youv herd. Better even than
Goldy loks.
Like I sed see you tomoro Ralp.

From,
Eric

Parrish, a "low-functioning" child, has written:

Dear Ralph,
You are the Bas Sore   You are the best story
teler I eforsors.   teller I ever saw.
Ralph, er the Bast   Ralph, you're the best
fand I wae er find.   friend I will ever find.
And I we ol was be   And I will always be
ther wan you ned me   there when you need me.

"Hey, I love that," I tell Parrish. He flashes an immense grin up to me. Many of Cera's children have recently lost one or two of their front teeth. In my notes I scribble, "Explore the possible relationship between writing development and dental development."

I am very tired.

Something is happening, not only that day but during the weeks that follow. In the schools I find myself dwelling on small, dark things. A kid wearing dirty pants. A girl with a bruise like a storm cloud on her neck. A teacher who hasn't done writing with her kids because she's run out of paper. A broken window on a classroom door that lets in a stream of corridor noise and remains unfixed, inexplicably, for several weeks. Six teachers waiting silently in the Main Office because they cannot punch out a moment before 3:00 P.M. Newly fed children being reprocessed to dump off their trays. Bullhorns. Stay in line. Don't let me hear a word out of you.

And scattered better moments. A boy giving me a baseball card for a present. A girl giving me a dried piece of her Christmas tree. Three kids who write a song about me ("He writes on the land, and he writes on the shore . . . He writes and he writes till he can't write no more . . .").

Michael Cuiselli is a kindergarten child. He has a pale, perfectly round and angelic face, pug-nosed, with wispy eyebrows that won't stay down but insist on hoisting themselves up in perpetual delight at the world. Enormous glasses, just bordering on the ridiculous. A tiny, soft voice. And the kind of gentle, miniature, other-worldly gestures that draw us to koala bears and baby chimpanzees. "We call him our Cabbage Patch kid," Pat, his teacher, told me earlier in the year. You want to take this little one home, just for one evening, to see if your crustiest, most cynical friend could resist. Incredible: that a man must start so small, so tender, raising his trusting, lens-covered eyes and voice to the hubbub of the class: "Mrs. Cosgrove, Mrs. Cosgrove. . . ."

Today Michael runs up to me, brandishing a piece of paper nearly as big as himself.

"Ralph, c'mere. I gotta show you my shark story. . . ."

He is wearing a button-down white shirt with a bright green tie. His story is vibrant with color and complexity.

"Where on earth did you get the idea for this?" I ask.

He points to his head.

"In here," he says, giving me a sudden fervent hug. He whispers, "I wish you were my father."

Moments like this had been easy to brush off earlier in the year. Today such sincerity seems almost dangerous. Very seriously I thank Michael, disentangle myself from him, and turn away, hoping he does not notice the tremor in my voice.

Footprints in the Sand

On Easter Sunday Marian and I finally decide to separate. The fact that it happens at the beginning of Easter vacation buys me time to find a new place to live. I move some of my stuff out to my parents' house on Long Island. A few days later, Hindy List calls to tell me that her Manhattan apartment will be vacant for a month or two and asks if I want to sublet. I spend the next two days moving in. The place is tiny, mauve-colored, and as intricately furnished as a kindergarten classroom. The studio looks out on Grammercy Park, a lovely and private square with an imposing black gate, peopled with aristocratic tulips, reeking of privilege. Under the circumstances, I am not unhappy to be there.

I move my computer in last. Driving, with the monitor snugly seatbelted beside me in the passenger seat, I feel giddily futuristic, just another fellow taking his computer out for a ride. This whimsy lasts about as long as it takes me to plug the thing in. I wake each morning with a nauseous stomach and a distinctly metallic taste in my mouth. Unadorned lethargy invades my limbs. With all my books, records, clothes gathered around me, my life feels like a hodgepodge of reassembled parts. Relieved when vacation ends, I force myself to get up, go to work, go to therapy, get on with the business of putting my life together again.

Have you ever seen a dead fly resurrect itself? Imagine: you have just dealt a common housefly a tremendous wallop with your hand or rolled newspaper and, to all appearances, killed the pest. Watch. If you have not totally flattened the thing, if the fly has not leaked too much bodily fluid, the following events will take place. One leg twitches. Another leg. Keep watching. Did you just see that wing jerk, stop, jerk again? Sure enough, the fly moved. And the twitch of life spreads. Bit by bit the fly comes back to life. In five or ten minutes, the fly you just killed is standing on its two feet, limping around. If you watch a few minutes more, you'll see it impudently grooming its wings, washing its face. In a matter of minutes, all bodily parts appear to be in reasonably good working order. Reborn, it flies away.

On April 15, tax deadline day, I drive to PS 402, my car radio aflame with reports of the U. S. attack on Libya, rumors of a coup in Tripoli, even the death of Quadaffi himself. Inside the school, Brenda Scott, one of my writing process teachers, is watching a group of her second-grade kids walk down the hallway and into their classroom. Though she sees me, she does not acknowledge my presence; she is too intent on making certain her students walk in a straight line. I stand there watching while my eyes readjust to the dim interior light.

Suddenly, as if by prearranged signal, two little figures, one boy and one girl, stop, turn, throw their arms tightly around each other, and glom their mouths together in a hot, sticky kiss. The kiss is awkward—for a moment they have trouble circumventing the bulky winter coats. For one shocked instant Brenda Scott seems nailed to the corridor. Then she rushes forward, wildly pulls the offenders apart, and drags them both into the classroom. Even from the hallway her voice is piercing.

"WHAT DO YOU THINK YOU ARE DOING? WHAT? WHAT? WHAT? ARE YOU SOME KIND OF ANIMALS? HUH? HOW DARE YOU ACT LIKE THAT IN THIS SCHOOL? LOOK AT ME! LOOK AT ME! I'M TALKING TO YOU, MISTER! WHAT DO YOU THINK YOU'RE DOING? WHERE DID YOU LEARN TO ACT LIKE THAT? HUH? WHERE? WHERE? WHERE? DO YOU THINK I'M GOING TO STAND FOR THAT? DO YOU THINK MRS. GOBSTEIN WILL? SHE IS OUT THIS MORNING BUT I'LL TELL YOU ONE THING—AFTER LUNCH I AM MARCHING YOU BOTH DOWN TO HER OFFICE. THEN WE'LL CALL YOUR PARENTS AND SEE WHAT THEY HAVE TO SAY ABOUT IT. IN TWENTY-ONE YEARS OF TEACHING I HAVE NEVER SEEN SUCH DISGUSTING BEHAVIOR IN MY ENTIRE LIFE!"

Moving closer, I can see that she is directing most of her tirade toward the boy, her face so close to his that tiny specks of spittle are spraying his cheeks. She finishes by dragging him by the ear back to his desk.

"SIT THERE! AND DON'T LET ME SEE YOU OPEN YOUR MOUTH!"

My first class of the day. I enter. Brenda Scott avoids me, her face still beet red. I wait. She cools down by taking attendance. Moments like this one cut gaping holes in whatever energy reserves I have in me—it is everything I can do not to turn and bolt from the room.

In the silence that follows, I watch the boy. For a long moment he remains motionless, his face perfectly still, his hands flattened on the desk. Two whole minutes pass. I watch for any twitch, any spasm of emotion. Nothing. Then, very quietly, he reaches into his desk, pulls out his writing folder (marked "Unfinished"), and opens it up.

Painful times. Moments of deep learning, Piaget has said, involve a great deal of confusion on the part of the learner. A great deal of *disequilibrium*. If so, I must have been learning a bundle. Mostly, I tried to survive.

Adrift, I set my bearings by the steadiest thing in my life: my job, the daily rhythms of city schools, my principals and my teachers. Particularly my contact with kids. For months I'd noticed how needy city kids were; now it is clear that I need them at least as much as they need me. Like some weary, oversized bumblebee, I move from child to child, drinking up their affection and humor, their courage and honesty, on some days surviving on that nectar alone.

Witness: In one second-grade class, Rita approaches me. She is a chubby girl, a halo of tight golden curls, a face given to sudden bursts of secret mirth. She has had a bad year. Both her parents are alcoholics. Early in the year, Rita often came to school unclean and poorly dressed. She would fall asleep in the middle of the day—her parents often kept her up until well after midnight. The school psychologist classified her as a child "at risk" and, in this case, the classification helped. Rita, her father, her mother, went through family counseling together. During the last two months, she has been far more alert in class.

Now Rita gives me a story she has just written. She waits while I read it.

"I was in a wedding. It was not fun. I was a flower girl. The nice thing was that I got to be with my sister. The not-fun thing was that I had to dance with a boy. That was not fun. When I came out of the church they threw rice on my dress."

Ha! I laugh out loud and squeeze the girl's shoulder; the other kids wheel around to see what the commotion is about. If you want to affect someone, you have to allow yourself to be affected first.

Witness: I am spending the day with Jim Sullivan, watching him read Nancy Williard's *Nightgown of the Sullen Moon* to a rapt group of kindergarten children. He is a big warm man; by the end of the book he has worked up a passionate sweat on his forehead. The kids burst into applause.

"How many of you think the moon really might have to go shopping for a nightgown in a store?" Jim asks the kids.

Every single child solemnly raises a hand. Jim glances at me, his eyes ablaze with restrained delight. By some Herculean effort, I do not burst into amazed laughter at the kids' boundless sense of magic. Innocence. After my separation I need to start replenishing that in myself.

Not that kids are all magic and innocence. The darker sides of children recur frequently enough to keep me from romanticizing them.

April 20, I leave PS 105 and head to my car. I walk along Lydig Avenue, past the Jewish bakeries and fruit stands of my ex-neighborhood. Ten days earlier I would have been walking home; now it feels strange to have to drive all the way into downtown Manhattan to go "home." I walk gingerly, praying I won't run into Marian. There are a dozen or so fifth or sixth graders bunched together on the far side of narrow Pelham Park. Though they are far away, I can clearly hear the ferocious menace in one boy's voice.

"You better watch your fucking face or I'll break your fucking jaw just like I did with Tony Scardelli," the boy yells, taking a step forward and jabbing a finger at the other boy's face. His face is swollen with a hatred that seems monstrous in proportion to his size. He draws back to throw a mock punch; the other boy flinches and backs off a step, stirring up laughter in the other kids. I watch, my own jaw frozen into silence, a sick feeling in my stomach.

A few days later, outside PS 402, I spot a big boy chasing a smaller boy. The victim-to-be throws a few hapless fakes while the older boy closes in. He grabs the other boy on the sidewalk and puts his prey into a ferocious headlock. Working quickly, he twists his opponent's head around so that the younger boy is facing skyward. Through my windshield I can see his face getting red as he struggles for breath. Then the bigger boy hoists up his prey and proceeds to deliver a violent "back-breaker": pulling the other boy down hard onto his own back. From a distance, I can feel the tremendous force of the blow; the younger boy's eyes roll up into his head. He crumples onto the sidewalk. I stop to see if he is all right. After a moment, he stands unsteadily and begins walking. The older boy has already walked away.

"Machine Gun" Mosely and Bill O'Reilly, my old tour guide buddies, come into town, fresh off a cruise on the *QE2*. At a restaurant in Little India, on East 6th Street, Mosely and O'Reilly share their latest tour adventures. Machine Gun claims to have just become a card-carrying member of the Mile High Club, thanks to the cooperation of a willing Singapore Airlines flight attendant. Though I only half-believe him, the story makes fine entertainment. And in the aftertaste of a very spicy fish head curry, the lexicon these tour guides use to pepper their dialogue suddenly sounds very foreign: group manifests, no-shows, grats (gratuities) and pax (passengers), "fam" (familiarization) trips, ground handlers, charters, and sched air. . . . I've come a long way from the world of tours and detours. Our talk is lopsided. Mosely and O'Reilly talk Paris, Kaui, Singapore. I talk Bronx, Brooklyn, Queens.

"Let me tell you what happened today," I tell them. "I'm in the Bronx, and this kid finds a razor blade in the playground—"

"Wait a sec," O'Reilly interrupts. He glances over at Mosely, pauses, then looks back at me. "Question: how serious are you about this business of teaching teachers?"

"Real serious," I say. "I've never been more serious about anything in my life."

They look at each other, surprised by my remark, but no one is any more surprised than me.

But just when my work matters most, I begin to sense something wrong in the classrooms I visit. My students (say it ain't so!) seem sick of writing.

One afternoon I sit before Laura Poulos's third graders at PS 154. Great kids. I have repeatedly let their applause and enthusiasm lift my spirits like a hot cup of espresso. But not today. They look washed out. Mentally, I fish for the problem. Citywide tests? Spring fever? The end of the school day?

"Writers write about the worlds they know about," I begin, "and that's why you've been working mostly on personal narratives this year, writing the stories of your lives."

The phrase *personal narratives* provokes a kind of subtle shudder, an almost imperceptible collapsing of shoulders, among the children. A shade less polite, they would have groaned. In fact, for grueling months they have mined the stuff of their lives, sifted for gems among the debris, cut and reworked and polished their narratives until they shone, more or less. Now the kids look written out. I imagine each kid as a rickety mine shaft, all the precious ore taken out, in danger of collapsing from within. On an impulse I write the words *personal narrative* on the blackboard.

"That's one kind of writing," I tell them. "What other kinds of writing are there?"

The kids look at each other, surprised. Other kinds of writing? Carlos raises his hand.

"Mysteries?"

I write that down.

"Plays?" Amanda asks.

I put that down, too. Encouraged, other kids speak up; I have to write quickly to keep up with them.

"Poems."

"Romances."

"Science fiction."

"Folk tales."

"Nature writing."

"How-to books."

"Horror."

"Real fiction."

"Biography."

"Letters."

"Sports."

Soon there are so many writing genres on the blackboard that the words *personal narrative* are mercifully obscured.

"Go to it," I tell the kids.

The kids just stare at me.

"You mean we don't *have* to write true stories?" Socrates asks softly.

"Right. Try something new, if you feel like it."

The kids race back to their seats. Four girls start working on a play. Konstantin and Socrates begin a teaching book about dinosaurs. Robert, Cindy, and Shayma begin poems. Two boys want to collaborate on writing a picture book. Another pack of boys works on a sci-fi story. The kids are wired, and their energy infuses Laura Poulos and me. We race around the classroom trying to answer kids' questions. Do poems have to rhyme? How many scenes are in a play? Where can we learn more about dinosaurs? In a picture book, do the words and the pictures always have to go together?

After my last class I gather my things and go to my car. Ten minutes pass before I realize I am driving nearly seventy. Slow down, Fletch. The passenger seat is piled with a stack of poetry books I've been reading for my own healing purposes: Rilke, Dickey, Kinnell, T. S. Eliot. All year during Thursdays, Georgia Heard has been discussing her work teaching poetry in the city schools. She has repeatedly encouraged me to try getting some poetry going in the classrooms I've been working in. I swing from the Triboro Bridge onto the FDR south. Maybe it's time for something new.

The next day, as it happens, I begin a two-day consulting job in Mamaroneck, an affluent village in Westchester, New York. Carpeted teachers' room with free coffee, decent-looking prints, even a meeting room with a large, solid oak table. The teachers like my suggestion that we work with kids on writing poetry. I tell them I'll start by reading a variety of poems to the kids: serious and light, rhymed and unrhymed.

"You have to marinate the kids in lots of great poems before they start to write," I tell them. The teachers nod. They seem to like that word—*marinate*—with its juicy connotations of barbeques, suntan lotion, steamy bestsellers devoured on the beach. Maybe summer isn't so far off after all.

In the first class I visit, I begin by reading poems by my favorite authors of poetry for kids: Myra Cohn Livingston, Lee Bennett Hopkins, Lillian Moore, Richard Margolis, Eloise Greenfield. Next, carefully selected poems by the likes of Sandburg, Frost, William Carlos Williams. The kids listen. I read the poems twice and ask the kids two questions.

What feeling did this poem give you? What picture did you get in your mind?

Some responses are surprising. In a third-grade class, I read "Nantucket" by William Carlos Williams:

> Flowers through the window
> lavender and yellow
>
> changed by white curtains—
> Smell of cleanliness—
>
> Sunshine of late afternoon—
> On the glass tray
>
> a glass pitcher, the tumbler
> turned down, by which
>
> a key is lying—And the
> immaculate white bed

"What feeling did you get from that poem?" I ask the kids.

"Nice," one girl says.

"Happy," says another.

"Peaceful."

"Clean."

"Boring," a boy in the back says. The kids giggle and turn around to look at him. I study him closely, trying to gauge how much trouble he'll be.

"What do you mean by boring?" I ask.

"Well, see, I like to play my radio real loud, and, you know, ride around on my bike and laugh loud and have fun. That place Nantucket sounds like you always have to be quiet and can't make any noise. I don't think it would be that fun being there."

The observing teachers, the other students, even a part of myself all wait to see my reaction to this challenge. I am, I realize, being tested. Not for the first time, either.

"The poem made him feel bored—it made you feel clean," I tell the kids. "That's all right, there's no right answer. That's his reaction to the poem. Poems give different people different feelings."

The classroom ambience darkens while I read "His Dog" from Richard Margolis's *Secrets of a Small Brother*:

My brother shuffles through the door
carrying little Sandy in his arms.
His tears make Sandy's fur wet.
When I try to pet her head,
he pulls away. "Don't," he says.
"She's dead."
Then I pet my brother's head.
She was his dog.

Stunned silence.

"How many of you have had some kind of pet die?" I ask the kids. Every hand goes up. Instantly, the kids are talking dead dogs, flattened turtles, kidnapped cats, stolen snakes, a rabbit who died of a heart attack, a parakeet who expired from a broken heart, goldfish who died from overeating. With great effort I quiet the class.

"How did that poem make you feel?"

"Like I wanted to cry for a thousand years."

"My favorite part of that poem was the last line," one girl says. "'She was his dog.' He had a *right* to hold her, even though she was dead, because he loved her so much."

But in the second class I visit, a bevy of well-groomed second graders, the marinating process goes less smoothly. One blond boy, Sean Reynolds, contorts his face while I read the poems. I read "His Dog" and ask the kids what feeling the poem gave them.

"Happy," Sean replies with a sinister grin.

Giggles. At the back of the room, Sean's teacher loudly rolls her eyes.

"What do you mean by happy?" I ask him.

"Dead things make me happy." More giggles.

"What picture did you get?" I ask, getting angry.

"I saw this boy carrying a dead dog," Sean says, "and holding it so long that after a while all he was carrying was a bunch of bones." Loud laughter. This, I realize, is my second test. I have never encountered such cynicism in such a young child; I don't quite know what to do with it.

"You can go back to your seat," I tell him.

"Why?" he asks, suddenly contrite.

"Go ahead," I tell him. "I don't have time for your kind of fooling around." In utter silence, he stands and goes back to his desk.

After that, the kids settle down. The second graders seem eager to start writing poems, so I let them write. I ask the kids to close their eyes and think of a time when they had a strong feeling. Scrunching up their eyes, they enter worlds of memory and imagination. Georgia Heard calls this "writing from darkness."

"Try to get that feeling in your whole body," I tell them. "Can you do that? Now, try to get a picture in your mind that's connected to that feeling." I pause. "When you've got something, whisper it to the person beside you."

A few minutes later, all the kids are whispering the seed ideas for the first original poems they will ever write. This excites me. I send them back to their desks to start.

Jasmine's first poem will be about Valentine's Day. The poem begins:

> "On Valentine's Day you get presents,
> And sometimes you get nesents"

"What's a 'nesent'?" I ask her. She smiles and gives me a nervous shrug.

"It's just a silly word I made up to rhyme with present," Jasmine says. Time out. I stand and ask for the children's attention.

"Remember: not all poems have to rhyme," I tell them. "Rhyme is great—the problem is that sometimes it makes you pick a word you don't really want."

To the teachers I say, "It's the Shel Silverstein Syndrome. Kids have trouble breaking out of the sing-song rhymes because they have a narrow idea of what poetry is. They need new models of what a poem might look and sound like."

Next, we move to Andrew, a very serious and thin boy who looks like a miniature version of David Stockman. Slowly, in a voice just above a whisper, he reads his poem:

> Wan i run in a
> field in the samar
> i fil like i am
> runing on aer
> tan i siy a playgon
> i fil my salf
> bak hom in my
> bed and my
> mom is koling
> miy for
> brafex.

"'Running on air,'" one teacher says excitedly. "That's terrific. Just look at how he plays with perspective. And time!"

On a roll now, I move next to Rhashida Yizar, a black girl in a lovely red dress with white lace at the sleeves and neck. Her teacher whispers to me, "Let me forewarn you: this kid is as bright and as stubborn as they come."

Wordlessly, the girl slides her poem in front of me.

"Would you read it to me?" I ask.

"You can't read it yourself?" she asks. So I read it out loud:

A nice, cute, safe, second-grade poem. Rhashida looks at me warily.

"I can see you love bread and jam," I tell her, stalling until I can think of something more profound to say.

"Yeah," she says, smiling to herself. "And you know what? This morning I put so much jam on my toast that when I took a bite I had a jam mustache!"

"That's wonderful! What a great image: a jam mustache!" I laugh. "Maybe you'd like to add that to your poem. I could help you—"

"Nope," she says. "I'm finished, It's done."

"But—"

She looks at me, shaking her head. No.

"Now I'm writing a poem about my dog Cleo. That's short for Cleopatra." She looks deep into my eyes. "Cleo died over the weekend. Got hit by a car."

"Boy. That's terrible. I'm so sorry."

"And guess what." A dreamy stillness comes over her face. "I have this sandbox in my backyard? And even though Cleo is dead, her footprints are still in the sand. You can still see them."

This shuts me up. For a moment the other teachers and I stare at each other.

"That's ... so ... powerful," I tell Rhashida. "Are you going to put that into your poem?"

"Nope," Rhashida says. She shakes her head, no, no, no, and by the way she shakes her head you know she is not kidding: she will not add this image, or any image, to her poem. The teachers and I look at one another, our eyes filled with despair.

"She comes up with these gems all the time," the teacher tells me. "But she practically never writes them down."

That night, on the phone, Georgia listens to the story of my day and my woes about Rhashida.

"Maybe you were a little too laid back," Georgia says. "You could have said, 'Rhashida, that's so beautiful, so sad; poets work hard for an image like that.' Let her know that she has just said something important."

Emboldened by my success at Mamaroneck, I start launching poetry workshops in city classrooms. What with the wounded condition of my own life, there is something comforting about talking to children about the emotions that lie at the heart of poetry. Spring is about beginnings, after all, and I'm grateful for this fresh new focus to my staff development. I'm hoping that the kids (and teachers) who sleepwalked through the writing of tedious personal narratives will perk up when we work on poetry. The earliest returns are promising. In Helen Winstral's second-grade class at PS 105, Becky writes:

The Dark

Tears in your ears
Are fears.

"D'ya like it?" Becky asks me.

"I love it," I reply, "even though I'm not sure I understand it."

"Well, see, sometimes when I go to sleep I get a bad nightmare," Becky says. "And when I wake up I'm crying and there are tears in my ears. So that's what gave me the idea."

For Charles Emanuele, a precocious and outspoken first grader in Barbara Finkel's first-grade class, poetry seems to provide an organizing form for his ideas. His first poem is about the rain:

O To The Rain

ho rain you pateter on my window like a summer day
derop derop derop
your rain makes me LAFE.

An ode? I have no idea where Charles got exposed to this form. But next day he is back at it again:

O To The Sun

o sun I edor you
we hant met rel clos.
you redle cep
me wom. zoowes you BENN BAD.
I LOVE YOU.

Ode to the Sun

o sun I adore you
we haven't met real close.
you really kept
me warm. Zowie you BURN BAD.
I LOVE YOU.

After finishing a poem Charles waits at his desk, sucking his thumb, staring straight ahead.

At Meryl Natelli's school, I'm surprised when even the first-grade teachers want to try poetry with their children. When I show up in Llewellyn Berk's class, she is reading to her kids "Ode To Spring":

O Spring O Spring
you wonderful thing
O Spring O Spring O Spring
O Spring O Spring
When the birdies sing
I feel like a king

Llewellyn's voice is harsh and passionate. No need for a voice transplant here. Her kids, mostly black and Hispanic, go wild while she reads: laughing, standing, slapping their thighs, wiggling their hips in response to the rhyme and driving energy in Llewellyn's voice.

"Why did you laugh?" she asks the kids.

"Cause you read the words funny."

"How?"

"Cause you loved it," Willie says.

"Right," Llewellyn says. "I do love these words. And that's what happens. Sometimes it makes you feel a little funny when you open your heart to something."

"Yeah," Unique says. "It's like when you go to a party and you hear some fresh music but you're afraid to get up and dance."

Writing poetry presents older kids with a dilemma: to reveal themselves or to hide. In a sixth-grade class at PS 105, Melissa Gonsalez writes:

Stuck

Stuck to the door
let it go
Stuck to happiness
let it show
But stuck to someone's heart
just can't let go

Poems like this one had a personal impact on me. I was trying hard to be honest with myself: about my marriage, my guilt, my suffering, even about the relief I felt being out of the marriage. Poems like Melissa's gave me courage to persevere.

I find myself expecting the most tender poems to be written by girls. Fortunately, I'm often proven wrong. Matthew Oh, a fourth grader at PS 154, writes:

My Mom

My mom takes good care of me.
She's the gardener,
I'm the rose,
She waters me every day.
When it gets cold

> She puts me in a pot
> And brings me inside.
> I love her
> As much as she loves me.

This simple poem fills me with equal amounts of wonder and envy. Wouldn't I love to have written those lines! During the marble craze of my youth, I would return from school on certain days with a few unusual specimens, orbs aglow with fragile, other-worldly light. I'd bring the marbles up to my room, shut the door, and spend hours studying them, the smooth surface tension, their somber weight, the exotic language of clicks they made bumping into each other. Now, as a man, I find myself leaving the city schools on particular days with a stash of poems by children, filled with the boy's thrill of hiding them away until I can get home to study them at my leisure.

Poetry conquers class after class; for the next few weeks I throw myself into it. It's not perfect. Kids fall into all the predictable traps: silly rhymes, strained snytax, poems that become stories, banality. Still there is a new energy, a new rigor, to my work, and my teachers pick up on it. Now my talks with teachers are flavored with words like metaphor and simile, rhyme schemes, white spaces, compression, image, and meter.

For some kids, poetry comes hard. Darel is a sinewy nine-year-old wearing a blue and white Mets shirt with the faded letters, STRAW-BERRY, stenciled on the back. When I come to his class the other kids are all writing, but Darel's paper is blank. He favors me with a sleepy smile. Slides down on his seat.

"I dunno what to write about," he says.

"Why don't you make a list of four or five things that you care a lot about, that you might write about. Then, put a star next to the most important one."

His nose wrinkles at the word *care*, and I wonder if I have lost him. But after a few moments he does start a list:

1. When I went down south I saw a lot of my cousins.
2. When I went to the beach my sister all most drowend.
3. When I went to my aunt's house she had a cat.

4.   I went to my friend house and he had three cats.
5.   When I had a rabbit my cousin through the rabbit.

"Great, now which one is the most important?" I ask Darel. I'm sure he will star the second topic. Without looking at me, he puts a large star next to number three.

"Go to it," I tell him, trying not to sound too surprised. Darel begins writing his poem. In a few minutes he is finished.

The End
When the dog was chasing the cat
the cat turned around and the
dog bit the cat. and the cat died.
and my rabbit had lived.

and my father had died.

Every day I read kids silly poems, funny poems, lovely poems, angry poems, clever poems, tender poems. Still, it is remarkable how many kids rise to the darkest bait: the grief of death. Within a short time I collect a stack of death poems. I discuss this one night on the phone with Georgia Heard.

"What about you?" she asks. "Have you shared any of your sad poems with the kids?"

"No," I tell her. "I haven't read them any of my poems."

"Why not? Kids need to know that adults write poems, too. Why don't you bring in your book?"

Good advice. I hang up. Marian calls. We argue. I hang up. She calls backs. More arguing, worse this time. She hangs up. Finally, on the fourth try, we hang up on a civil note. But now I'm wide awake. My Grammercy Park neighborhood is noisy tonight, and there is a menagerie of old anxieties and new ones gnawing on my heart. I cannot sleep.

The next morning, on less than three hours' sleep, I head off for work with my stomach full of bile. Only my destination, the calm ship of PS 79 captained by Deena Gold, prevents me from calling in sick.

The kids in Janice Bentz's third-grade class gather around where I sit in the big stuffed armchair. I know these children and they know me; I was earlier witness to the remarkable scenes that took place when Carmelina read her book to the class. Now there are oohs and ahhs when I pull out my book of poems, *The Magic Nest*. The kids pepper me with questions.

"When did you write it?"

"Did you paint the cover yourself?"

"How much money did you make?"

"Was it a bestseller?"

I raise my hand: the kids respond with instantaneous silence.

"Driving here I was trying to decide which poem to share with you and it was hard," I tell them. "I think I'm going to read you one about my brother Bobby, who got killed in a car accident when he was just seventeen. I wrote this poem—and a lot of other poems—to try and make some sense out of that tragedy. A funny thing. On the day he died something really wonderful happened. These friends of my family, Barbara and John Leckie, had a baby boy born into their family. They decided to name the new baby Bobby, after my brother. And even though we were awful sad, it made my family feel a tiny bit better—I mean, my parents don't believe in reincarnation or anything—but just knowing that there was a new life, a new baby boy, named . . ."

The kids' faces swim: my eyes crowd up with tears. Damn! What do I do now, Lucy? Nothing in my training had prepared me for a moment like this. This is either my high point on the job or my low point, one or the other, I can't say for sure. Maybe it doesn't matter. Later, rethinking this moment, I will understand for the first time why other kids started crying in similar situations while reading their work out loud; not, as I had suspected, because some innate human need to speak, to state the truth, to bear witness, to open one's heart, had been satisfied at last. No. It had far more to do with the audience provided by all these children, the compassion in their narrowed eyes, the extraordinary quality of the silence as they listened, that finally broke through whatever membrane remained between my emotions and the outside world. But that insight would come later. Now I am choking back sobs, fussing and swabbing and blowing my nose with the tissues Carmelina has handed me.

"It's all right," Mrs. Bentz is saying. "It's all right."

And she is right: it is all right. In a few minutes we are all exchanging smiles and deep breaths and I am calm enough to read my poem about Bobby out loud:

That Keeps Us Warm

My brother Bob died
while golden corn stalks
were plowed under
to make fertile soil
for next year's crop.
Blond strong Bobby Leckie
born the day my brother died.

One cool night two years later
I carried him on my shoulders
through dark-dewed grass
to a small wood campfire.
His face fat flushed cheeks,
purple-streaked by the grapes
we'd been picking and eating,
and wide flaming eyes
mutely gazing at the source.
Bob
through the heat of this fire
the light in this child's eyes
you come back to us

from *The Magic Nest*
Northwoods Press, 1980

A Teacher Kind of Person

April 30, 1986, is a gorgeous day. Sweet spring air, greening meadows, bulbs stirring beneath the moist earth. The pea-green hue of new leaves on the trees. Sixty-nine degrees. A Ford truck cruises by, somebody's bare foot sticking out of the open window, Springsteen blaring: "The screen door slams ... Mary's dress waves ... like a vision she dances across the floor while the radio plays ..."

In the auditorium, Norm Sherman addresses his sleepy charges.

"Good morning, boys and girls. Teachers. The weather today will be warm. We will have outdoor recess. The major event in the news is the accident at the nuclear power plant near the city of Kiev in the Soviet Union. Information on this event is still scarce. As some of you know, the Soviet Union is not a free country like the United States. There is no such thing as a free press in that country, and the rest of the world is having trouble finding out exactly what happened. What seems clear so far is that there has been some kind of fire in the nuclear reactor and the Russians are having trouble putting it out. This is a dangerous fire best put out by robots, and the Russians may not have the kind of advanced robots that we have. ..."

Norm continues, explaining to the kids how Soviet helicopters have been dropping bags of sand on the damaged reactor. Reports so far about Chernobyl have been alarming—explosions, radiation, severe contamination—and wildly contradictory. The *New York Post* (bold red headline: NUKE CLOUD SPREADING) quoted an unidentified source saying that two thousand Russians had been killed in the disaster, while Tass claimed only a few people had died.

I listen, preoccupied with my own problem: Eleanor Bosch, my original nemesis at PS 414. Against the backdrop of Chernobyl, the Eleanor Bosch problem should seem trivial. But it doesn't feel trivial. This afternoon I must return to her class for the first time since the Easter vacation. I dread this visit. As much as possible, I have tried to avoid thinking about Eleanor Bosch. It now occurs to me that not thinking about her has been nothing less than a Trojan horse for allowing her to feature prominently in my most nightmarish thoughts.

There is no other way to put it: my work with Eleanor Bosch has gone badly. I think back to January when I walked into her classroom and found her sitting at her desk. Wall-to-wall kids, the desks in five long rows. The fifth graders burst into half-hearted applause at my arrival. Out of sheer relief, no doubt, at seeing another face in front of the class. Eleanor sat at her desk, magic-markering words (FREEZE, QUIET, VACANCY) onto large cards.

She barely looked at me when I walked in. Working with New York City teachers, I had become fluent in the body language of resistance and hostility to my ideas. I thought of their gestures as the grammar to this language, a grammar I had come to know only too well: the glazed eyes, crossed arms, chewed lips, frozen jaw, mischievous wisecracks during workshops out of the corners of their mouths. Some gestures were subtle (the muted sighs, the discreet glance at the wall clock) while others less so (the teacher who noisily corrected a stack of homework papers while I talked to teachers about editing student work). Such gestures weighed heavily on me, far more so than any spoken utterance.

The students were working on one of Eleanor's dittoes when I entered the room. Marlon Hauser was right. Before the first day of school, Eleanor had prepared a long, time-intensive worksheet for every school day of the year. These dittoes were numbered in decreasing sequence so that ditto #179 got handed out on the first day of school; ditto #1 was given out on the last. On any particular day, a glimpse of those worksheets would tell me exactly how many days were left in the year. Today the kids were plowing through ditto #102.

"All right!" Eleanor yelled upon seeing me. "Put away the ditto! Carlos, Rhonda, pass out the writing folders."

Soon the kids had writing folders in front of them. Some started writing, but most began chattering. Eleanor remained at the front of the room. It was apparent that Eleanor would permit the kids to talk so long as the noise did not get too loud.

The scene depressed me. I had my good days and bad days as a teacher trainer, and these fluctuations had a direct impact on how effective I was with teachers. But with Eleanor Bosch it didn't seem to matter. Good days, bad days, my work with Eleanor always went poorly. How had I ever allowed things to deteriorate to such a level? Earlier in the year Eleanor agreed to give writing process a fair shot in her class, to let kids choose their own topics, to confer with them while they were writing, to have them write three times a week. Now she sat without embarrassment at the front of the class, magic-markering words onto large pieces of cardboard.

"How is it going?" I asked.

"So, so," she replied. Even when at ease, her knotted brows and grim mouth suggested extraordinarily well-developed facial muscles, features held tight together by tremendous internal pressure. The sound of her voice made me clench my teeth. Prime candidate for a voice transplant. Or, if that was impracticable, why couldn't I buy a couple of earplugs to at least deaden the sound? I made a mental note to bring up this idea at our next Thursday.

"I'm not getting much writing out of them. And the kids refuse to share. Watch." To the kids: "Who wants to read to the class something they've written recently?"

A single boy, Carlos, raised his hand.

"See what I mean? They don't want to share, they can't come up with topics to write about, and they don't revise. Editing? Forget about it. Writing time is social time."

"Why do you think that is?" I asked, stalling.

"Writing's just not their thing. Frank wrote a composition, said he didn't want to be a writer when he grows up. And he's bright. I tell him he'll need writing for junior high. He says he'll worry about it then."

Eleanor and I stared at each other.

"Part of it is the number of bodies we have in here," she said. "Thirty-eight. Putting thirty-eight kids in a class—what kind of sense does that make? You can't teach thirty-eight kids at one time. You can't keep thirty-eight kids quiet unless they're shoving pizza into their faces."

"You're right, it's a ridiculous number," I told her. "I don't know how I'd do it. But come on. Let's see what we can do. Let's try conferring with a couple kids. I'd like to see what they're writing about."

Sighing, she got up to follow. As soon as we went, Frank, a handsome black-haired kid, quickly moved to the large pieces of cardboard on Eleanor's vacant desk and started flashing cards at his classmates. FREEZE. They froze. Only when Frank put down the card did the kids start moving again. QUIET. Utter silence. Distracted by the sudden decibel drop, Eleanor looked up.

"EXCUSE ME!" she yelled at Frank, planting the seed of a migraine in my medulla. Classroom schizophrenia: the striking dichotomy between this polite phrase and the strident voice. Smirking, Frank returns to his seat.

"Did you see that?" Eleanor stage-whispered, pointing at Anitra, a very pretty Indian girl who was writing a story about a girl's first date with a 'real make-out artist.' "Last week by accident I read her journal. The journal was bad enough: 'John can't have me because he had me last month.' What the hell does that mean? Then I intercepted a note from her to Danielle. It was disgusting. No wonder these girls are so popular with the boys."

This particular visit to Eleanor's class quickly beat me into speechlessness. Why *was* I working with this woman? Marlon had encouraged me to continue working with her: she was a key person in the building, the UFT representative, etc. But that didn't justify it. I can't explain, even to myself. At moments like this I had an uncontrollable hunger for Andrew O'Reilly's luxurious bathroom: that poetry and classical music, that wood-grained toilet seat, the resounding *thwump* of its heavy door.

A man I know, the father of a close friend, has this philosophy about life: "When you take away all the worthless jobs and errands and chores we do during the day, there's probably only about one minute each day when we do something even remotely important. Think of it: one minute. In fact, if you get right down to it, there's maybe only one minute in your *whole life* when you ever do something really important, something that really matters. The trick is to be ready for that minute when it comes."

These sobering words came back to me often as I made the rounds through the city schools. I figured that during any given forty minutes I spent with a particular teacher, only about one minute of that time would make even a little difference in his or her teaching.

What would they remember from any one of my visits? A word of encouragement and reassurance, maybe, a new way of looking at a particular child's writing. Not much more.

I liked this idea: it kept me in touch with the long-term perspective in staff development. But the usefulness of such a thought ended with a teacher like Eleanor Bosch. The minutes ticked by while I worked in her room, the number of my visits decreased with the numbers on the dittoes Eleanor handed out. But in the dynamics of the classroom itself, nothing changed.

One day I suggested that Eleanor celebrate kids' writing by putting their stories up on a bulletin board. She listened for a moment before blurting out, "I don't like to have a lot of junk on the walls."

Junk! The word struck at me, deeply. I glanced around the classroom and noticed for the first time that the richly detailed bulletin boards and solar systems and job lists and colored charts and posters and attendance sheets all were *her* creations. There was no evidence of her students' work anywhere.

Once, in the teacher's room, I heard Eleanor complaining to another teacher about her students.

"Following directions? Forget about it. If you want to get anywhere with these kids you've got to hit them with it three times. You tell them what you're going to tell them, then you tell them, then you tell them what you've just told them."

"And they still don't get it," the other teacher put in.

"These kids are surface thinkers all the way," Eleanor said. "You wind them up and they clutter ahead. Ask them to really think and solve a problem? Give me a break. Sometimes I feel like holding a mirror under their mouths to see if I get any fog."

"Tell me about it," the other teacher said. "Anything you teach has to be real specific, real concrete."

"Yeah," Eleanor said, pointing at her head. "Concrete. I've got a pair of first cousins. Brian and Jonathan. Boy are they some piece of work."

"Slow?"

"Slow?" Eleanor snorted. "They share a brain. Ask Mr. Fletcher over there. Eleven years old and they couldn't write their way out of second grade."

I had had enough.

"I don't think *I* could write in your class either," I told Eleanor. Startled, the two teachers looked up.

"I mean it."

Why not?"

"Because you're always telling me what your kids *can't* do. What the hell ever happened to believing in kids?"

"You're a fine one to give advice," Eleanor said, standing. "You come to my class for less than one hour, once a week, and the kids give you a big welcome. And you know why? Because you're new. That's why. You try standing in front of them hour after hour, day after day. Try it. Tell me then if they clap when you come into class. See how far you get. Try working with these kids month after month. See how friendly you feel towards them."

With that she left. Slammed the door behind her.

On my next visit to PS 414, I wondered if Eleanor was angry enough to take her name off my scheduled visits. No such luck. I walked into her classroom. She didn't mention the incident. Instead, she started complaining that her kids weren't revising. Fine, I told her, let's see if we can encourage more radical revisions in their stories. We conferred with Bavesh, a portly and bespectacled Pakistani boy who was writing about the sun. His piece contained some promising sparks ("The sun never goes on vacation,") but was badly disjointed, and Bavesh knew it. I showed him how to cut up his story and use Scotch tape to put it back together in the right order. Eleanor exploded into sarcastic laughter.

"Ha! You must be joking! Are you? Just give these kids carte blanche to use my tape whenever they choose to! Are you kidding? You must be."

"I'm not kidding," I said. "Are you trying to tell me Marlon wouldn't—"

"Ha!" She laughed again. "I can tell that you don't know anything about the New York City schools. Let me explain something to you: I get two rolls of Scotch tape and they have to last me all year long. Two! If I let them use it up it'll be gone in two days!"

Subterranean teaching again. We weren't arguing about a fifty-nine cent roll of tape. We weren't arguing about writing process. I wasn't even sure we were arguing about teaching. We were arguing about something else, something deeper than any of that. But what was it? Until I could get down to whatever that was, I knew I would never make any headway with Eleanor Bosch. And the truth was that I didn't want to go any deeper inside this woman's psyche. As far as I was concerned, I had gone plenty deep enough.

In my early flush of enthusiasm for the writing process, I had this hypothesis: if kids latch onto writing process, maybe it can succeed despite a bad teacher. Maybe writing process was as "teacher-proof" as the IBM "Write To Read" writing program purported to be. Eleanor Bosch put this theory out of its misery.

One Thursday I had lunch with Lucy Calkins and spelled out my job woes. I told her all about John Federico, the third-grade teacher whose classroom was dominated by the continuous stream of healthy snacks he fed his kids, his bad jokes, his stupendous passivity. I also told Lucy about Eleanor Bosch, her toxic dose of negativity, the bizarre roll-of-tape episode.

"Why don't you drop them?" Lucy asked, surprised.

"What do you mean?"

"What on earth are you doing in there? It doesn't make sense for you to be working with teachers who are that resistant. You're wasting your time. I mean it. You can tell them if they want you to, and if your schedule permits, you can work with them next year. But you shouldn't be working with them. Your time is too valuable. There are too many other teachers you could be working with instead."

Drop them. I loved the clean guillotine sound of those two words. And I resolved to do it. Immediately. The next time I entered John Federico's classroom, his eyes lit up.

"John, I want to talk to you for a moment."

"Mr. Fletcher, glad to see you. We've been participating in a stop-smoking campaign, and I've come up with some animal sayings I'd like to share with you."

"John, I—"

"Wait a sec, now. Listen. How do you like this one: 'Hippos say stop smoking: it makes you hippoactive.'" He looked at me hopefully.

"John. We need to talk."

"Or this one: 'Ducks say smoking makes you quackers.'"

The kids groaned. John turned his back on them. When he looked at me, I saw something in his face I had never seen before.

"I'm having a hard time right now," John said softly. "Maybe this isn't a great time for me to be working with you."

"You know, I was thinking the same thing," I told him. I took a deep breath. "Maybe, if things are going better, we can work together next year. I'll be in this school a long time."

We were both relieved. Genuine smiles. Bracing handshake. On the way out, I allowed John to press into my hand two little packets of macadamian nuts. Leaving this room, I felt light, free, and enormously grateful to Lucy Calkins.

I decided to give Eleanor the ax. I put a bright red circle around March 28, Drop Eleanor Day, bought a bottle of good dry champagne, and looked forward to the occasion with dark anticipation. The day approached. I honed my resolution to a razor's edge.

March 28 dawned clear and cold. Unusually light traffic en route to PS 414. I parked my car, got out, and strode into Marlon Hauser's office. The moist air, the profusion of greenery, confused me, and I stood for a moment getting my bearings.

"Marlon? You in here?"

"Over hear," came the muffled reply.

I found him in one corner of the room, tending a big cactus-like plant that had long, sharp green leaves.

"Feel that," Marlon said without looking up. I touched one of the plant's sharp points. "Bet you could think of a few teachers you'd like to introduce this to."

"As a matter of fact that's what I want to talk to you about," I began, clearing my voice. "I want to drop Eleanor from my training. It's just not working, Marlon. It's going nowhere. It's a waste of time."

Marlon looked up at me, then down at the plant.

"Lucy suggested I drop her, and I realized she's right."

"You know anything about these plants?" Marlon asked me.

I did not.

"A century plant," he said. "*Agave americana.* Grows in the desert. Would like it a lot drier than it is in here, ideally. These babies get big, leaves as big as a man, with a big yellow flower spike. Know how often these plants flower?"

I shook my head.

"Once every ten to fifteen years. Then it dies. I hope to be out of here before this one blossoms, but you never know." He stood up and looked at me meaningfully. "Once every ten to fifteen years."

"Aw, come on Marlon, you're not—"

"I *am*. A teacher like Eleanor Bosch just isn't going to blossom in a month or two. No way. For some teachers, it's going to take longer. It may take years."

"Marlon," I stammered. "Let's talk reality. The training didn't take root. The seeds fell on barren soil. However you want to put it. I am wasting my time with this woman."

"Eleanor's got a husband, kids, a couple cats. Try not to forget that she's a person, too. You're seeing her in the worst possible setting. She's had a bad year. Varicose veins, some bad investments, union tensions, God knows what else."

"I know she's a person, Marlon." I spoke testily. "I really do."

Marlon approached, eyeing me with measured sympathy. Then he made an expansive gesture to the room around us.

"Lemme tell you something, Ralph. I find myself spending lots of time in here, more time than you would imagine. Sometimes I wonder if I'm not hiding, you know? People around here know if they can't find me where I'm supposed to be, they can find me in here. The plants, the muggy air, kept lots of people out at first. They didn't know what to make of all this. But now most of them barge right in here, bringing all their bad air with them. I just hope the plants don't suffer. Did you see my Venus flytraps? C'mere. They're growing like crazy. I just bought a bunch of flies. Live. That's the thing, they've got to be live. Every time I solve a major problem, one of my Venus flytraps gets to eat a fly. Soothes my nerves."

We stared at each other.

"Do what you've got to do, Ralph," he said softly. "You've got a hard job. I trust your decision. But think about it. I've given Eleanor every chance to bow out of the training, and she's refused. I think in a crazy way she likes you. Promise me one thing: think about it before you pull the plug on her."

"I *have* thought about it."

"Then let me know when you do it," he said, shrugging. "Afterwards, if you want, you can feed one of my Venus flytraps. You'll be amazed how good you'll feel.

I went upstairs and quietly reviewed my conversation with Marlon. Was I doing the right thing? You bet I was. I reminded myself of Eleanor Bosch's wheedling, complaining, foot-dragging. Her nasty tone with children. I did not like this woman; I got headaches from her Black 'n Decker drill of a voice. Today was Drop Eleanor Day. The lady had to go.

I was scheduled to go to another teacher's room first, and had to pass Eleanor's room to do so. I made a habit of moving quickly past the doors of teachers like Eleanor; sometimes, however, a kind of morbid fascination compelled me to look inside, and I did so now. I peeked in just as Eleanor looked up from behind her desk. Our glances met, and I saw in her eyes a look of such wounding sadness and defeat that I could do nothing but hurry past. Five steps later, I froze. I took a deep breath. I turned around and went back. Eleanor looked up when I walked into the room.

"Will I see you at 1:30?" she asked, lowering her bifocals.

1:30," I told her. And when I returned to her classroom at 1:30, I couldn't do it. I couldn't drop her.

The next time I returned to Eleanor's classroom, I saw that she had written on the blackboard an assignment for her kids to write a thank-you letter to the PTA for some playground equipment. There was also a list of words for the kids to plug into their letters: basketballs, swings, ropes, softballs. Kids were writing listlessly. When I glanced at the stories, I saw that most of them began, "I like the swings" and "I like the softball equipment." Paint-by-numbers writing.

"Why did you do that?" I asked. "I thought we agreed to let the kids pick their own topics."

"I figured they probably forgot how after the long vacation."

"Forgot?"

"Mr. Fletcher's time is valuable so let's not waste it!" Eleanor yelled at her kids. "Carlos, do you hear what I'm saying?"

"I'm not at all sure that giving them a topic is the right way to go," I told her, motioning toward the kids. "They're not doing much writing."

"No, you're wrong," she said. "This is more than I've got from these kids all year. I'm happy with the results."

But she didn't sound happy. The unhappiness in her voice was the most genuine thing in that classroom. Such moments filled me with the rinsing sadness of public schools, a sensation palpable and indelible as the floor-wax scent in the hallways. The bleak light streaming in through the old, tall, unwashed windows.

April 30. I drive from the relative sanity of Norm Sherman's school to PS 414. At the corner of Kissena and the Long Island Expressway service road a man is hawking an extra edition of the *New York Post*.

"Extra! Extra! Reds battle nuclear fire! Radiation spreading to Sweden and Norway! Get your paper right here!"

Driving, I try to prepare myself for Eleanor. Having lost my one chance to drop her from my training—the end of the year was all but upon us—I no longer allowed myself to feel the slightest bit sorry for myself. Instead, whenever I got depressed, I used her persona to punish myself for my own shortcomings. Eleanor Bosch epitomized my own colossal inability to deal decisively in the world. I worked in her classroom without hope, without any prospect of change. I deserved Eleanor Bosch.

I had launched Eleanor's kids in poetry writing. As expected, she has not waxed enthusiastic about the quality of their poetry, or about anything they have written all year, for that matter. When I arrive at her class, precisely at 1:30 P.M., Eleanor is fuming.

"C'mere," she tells me. "I just want you to see something."

She brings me over to a table where two girls are sitting, decorating poems they have written. With most of my disagreeable teachers, I survived in their classrooms by enjoying their students and "bonding" with them. But Eleanor even managed to spoil her kids for me; she somehow made it impossible for me to enjoy them. Eleanor stands between us like an unbreachable barrior. Her smile barely conceals her rage.

"Diane, maybe you'd like to share your poem with Mr. Fletcher," she says with a flourish, like a matador, stepping aside so I can see the poem.

Fish?

The little fish eats the tiny fish,
The big fish eats the little fish—
So only the biggest fish get fat.
Do you know any folks like that?

by Diane Gereck

"Ask her who wrote it," Eleanor hisses in my ear, loud enough for the girl to hear. "Ever hear of Shel Silverstein? Ever hear of a book called *Where The Sidewalk Ends*? It's right in our classroom library. She didn't even go to the trouble of changing the title."

This reminds me of a discussion about plagiarism we recently had at one of our Thursday meetings.

"Kids will lift a poem," Georgia Heard had said. "It's not such a horrible thing. It depends on how you handle it."

"Kids will lift a poem," I tell Eleanor Bosch now, shrugging. "Sometimes they don't even know they're doing it. It's not such a horrible thing. It depends on how you handle it."

"How would *you* handle it?"

"Would you like to see one way of handling it?"

"Can't wait," she replies.

I return to Diane. The girl watches me carefully.

"I wanted to talk to you about this poem." I smile at her. "It's a great poem, and a great illustration, too. You know, I used to do the same thing, copy down my favorite poems and stories. So I'd always have them."

The girl watches me, blinking, wondering if she is in trouble or not. I try to ignore the sight of Eleanor Bosch behind her, snorting and furiously rolling her eyes.

"You might even start a folder where you can collect all your favorite poems," I suggest. "Maybe even make an anthology. Think you might like to do that?"

Diane nods and offers the tiniest of smiles.

"Have you written any of your own poems in here?"

The girl looks down, compressing her lips.

"Not yet," she says softly.

"Why not?"

"I can't think of any ideas."

"Maybe while you're reading through poetry books and copying out your favorite poems, you can be thinking of a poem you could write. What do you think?"

The girl smiles. Not a bad conference, I'm thinking, standing up.

"Oh give me a break," Eleanor says, walking away.

May 1 is a superb specimen of a day: neighborhoods ablaze with tulips, lilies, forsythia. This day contains a test of character for me—yet one more encounter with Eleanor Bosch. Marlon Hauser has set up a lunch meeting in his office greenhouse to plan for next year. Next year!

I park my car and walk into the school. Inside, while my eyes adjust to the dimness, I can hear a teacher berating her children in a large, shrill voice, "Stay in line, hup, two, three. You know how the Marines are looking for a few good men? Well I'm looking for a few good students. . . ."

As I stand there, something surfaces in my memory, some advice my Uncle Ed Collins once gave me when I was a boy: "Take great risks to do what you love."

I listen to that teacher's voice.

Is this what I love?

I spot Eleanor in the Main Office. Too late to duck.

"Are you meeting with us for lunch?" I ask her.

"Sorry, I never stay in school for lunch," she says with a funny smile. "I make a point of going out."

She glares, daring me to disagree. I try to mask my pleasure at her impending absence.

"I can understand that."

"Can you? I've been teaching for thirty years. I'm a damn good teacher, but it's pretty clear that I made a big mistake when I went into teaching. My husband and I have been married for twenty-one years. He's an executive vice president with a big insurance company. I've grown, too, in lots of ways, but I'm still teaching fifth grade in this school. He's a vice president and I'm still mucking around here."

I nod. I'm listening to her. She looks at me suspiciously, but continues.

"When my husband does a good job he gets rewarded with a raise, a bonus, a promotion, a nicer office, tickets to see the Knicks or a Broadway play. I do a good job and they reward me with the kid nobody else can handle. Rewards like that I need?

"No, sir, I don't stay in for lunch anymore. I go out—to the nicest restaurant I can find. It started about three years ago when I had this impossible kid, this punk who drove me to the brink. By lunch I figured if I didn't go out I'd snap. So I went out. Felt so good I started making a habit of it. It's funny, but I don't feel like a teacher kind of person anymore. I've grown. My friends are professional people. When I leave here I put on my fur coat and become a person again. My husband and I go to the museum, to the ballet, to the opera. We collect antiques. We entertain a lot. Does any of this make sense to you? There's a lot more to me than you can see here."

She turns around and walks away.

Walking Trees

The morning kicks off with a Shelter Drill precisely at 9:00. Children answer the rhythmic alarms by filing out of their classrooms and huddling in the hallways. Welcome to the Nuclear Age, kids. Then a chubby boy gets his knee stuck between two bars of a hallway radiator; four teachers and I struggle for fifteen minutes trying to extricate him. A sixth-grade class gets infiltrated by a yellow jacket; a half-dozen kids chase the bee with small cans of hairspray until one boy shoots it down.

At 9:30 I work in a second-grade class with an unusual breed of disturbance: Natasha, an oversized girl with ravishing good looks, wearing a battery-powered computer shirt. It features colored lights that flash across her chest. There is even a small keyboard beneath the computer. While I try to keep the class focused on writing, kids keep running up to Natasha, giggling, pretending to type on her shirt.

10:15. A third-grade class is putting on a play. Tonight. The kids are sky high. When I gather them in a corner of the room—next to a cardboard box containing two small chickens—the kids wiggle, fidget, drum the floor. Just as I begin to talk, one of the chickens flies up to rest on the top of the box. The bird flaps its wings, lifts off, and lands directly on my right shoulder. Everyone roars.

In another class, a boy vomits. The teacher shakes her head, apologizes to me, calls for the janitor. He arrives promptly: a long-boned young man with bad skin and a silver loop earring. I try talking writing to the kids but they cannot keep their eyes off this man. His earring, the allure of physical work, the exotic aroma of the disinfectant, all are pungent reminders of the real world beyond the school building.

One more class until lunch. My head swims with images of a good local diner: great cheeseburgers, a leisurely perusal of the *New York Times*, unlimited coffee refills and, just maybe, a piece of rhubarb pie. Now I am conferring with Heather, a shy first grader with a sleepy smile. An ordinary child except for one thing: Heather does not have a last name. Knowing this, I would award her the same celebrity status as other one-name wonders like Cher, Madonna, Marisol, and Aliki, except that it turns out that the girl's truncated name has far more sinister origins.

"Her parents are divorced—a terrible custody battle there," Heather's teacher explains. "Her mother was afraid the father would try to steal the girl away. So she had Heather's last name removed. Legally. Just took it off. That way, she figured, the father couldn't check through any student lists and find the girl. She drops the girl off at school herself every morning, and picks her up at the end of the day."

Heather is working on a large piece of beige construction paper, on which she has drawn several trees, widely spaced with great twisting Van Gogh roots, with her name in the upper righthand corner of the page. All her lines are infected with the same wobbly tremor. I try not to read too much into it.

"What are you writing about?"

She smiles without looking at me, bearing down with a brown crayon on the tree she is coloring in. Her teacher crouches down beside me.

"Can you tell me about your story?" I ask, gently taking the crayon out of Heather's hand. She looks at me.

"It's about the walking trees," she says in a near-whisper.

"Walking trees?"

"Yes." When she looks at me, her eyes are illuminated; I can see that the idea has captured her imagination. "See, me and my mommy and daddy went to Florida, and we saw the walking trees down there. They walk with their roots. They take one step in a hundred years." Significant pause. "We didn't see them walk while we were there."

Walking trees! Earlier in the year I would have feverishly scribbled down this phrase and the accompanying anecdote as a perfect illustration of a child's magical literalness, her transformational wonder at the physical world. Now, after John Federico, after Eleanor Bosch, after Fern Resager and Florence Smith, after my own separation, the words have a newer, darker ring, a precise evocation of the tremendous effort implicit in even the smallest amount of growth in the teachers I worked with. And in myself.

Walking trees. The phrase articulates an idea I have so far been unable to articulate to myself. It occurs to me that this is precisely what I have been trying to do all year long: to encourage big and ponderous trees to lift up their roots and take a step, even a small step, even if it would be the only step they would take the entire year. This was my job: to take those rough old trunks by the hand, to coax them to uproot themselves from that tired dirt they'd been stuck in, to leave their familiar terrain, to take a chance, to go someplace new.

I thank Heather profusely. She gives me an askance look and continues working. But I am grateful to her. Her words have given me a new metaphor for the issue I have been grappling with all year: how difficult it is to make real educational change in the face of the economic disparity between schools, teachers with low morale, political polarization, monumental inertia, the scarcity of high quality personnel, inefficiency, knee-jerk testing, daily interruptions ... Walking trees. Walking trees. Walking trees. I repeat the words over and over to myself, like a mantra.

Heather's phrase gets me thinking about my work in this year: how much real growth has there been?

"We're a slow-growth project," Lucy said again and again at Thursday meetings. "Deep change takes time. Some teachers won't start changing their teaching until next year, or the year after."

Fine. Those words had given me the patience to persist in my work throughout the long year. But now it is May. The school buildings, the classrooms, even the kids are beginning to blur, dangerously. I suddenly find myself needing something concrete to show for my year of slogging through city school buildings.

I have been working in one school where the secretaries invariably answered the telephone, "Hello, PS 422, Partners For Excellence." There were Partners For Excellence posters in each classroom, a Partners For Excellence Bake Sale on the last Friday of every month, even a gigantic Partners For Excellence mural in the main hallway as you entered. During my visits the principal always showed up in at least one of the classrooms where I was working. She was a petite woman with heavy makeup and ramrod posture. Seeing her enter, the children would rise, no matter what else happened to be taking place in class, and respond en masse.

"Good morning, boys and girls."

"Good mor-ning, Mrs. Brad-ley."

"What are we, boys and girls?"

"Part-ners For Ex-cel-lence."

"Very good. And who can tell me what a partner is . . . Tim?"

"A partner is someone who works with someone else."

"Very good . . ."

Partners For Excellence. Who could be against that? Me, that's who. Such ritualized scenes (for whose benefit? mine?) pushed me to the very brink. Slow-growth model or not, it had become clear that certain teachers like Eleanor Bosch, principals like Ellen Bradley or Andrew Reilly, would not change. Ever. Having grappled with some of the massive forces involved, I knew that there was nothing accidental about the attitudes most adults carried into schools. They were the product of their own personal demons coupled with too many years spent breathing the city school air. I understood that so clearly that professional growth of any kind seemed almost miraculous. Maybe that was it. Maybe I was looking for miracles.

I stop in to talk with Miranda Sklar. My selective mute had grown taller since the fall, and had written some gorgeous picture books during the year. She looked right into my eyes when I spoke. She heard every word I said. But she still withheld the miracle of a single spoken word.

My favorite baseball team, the Boston Red Sox, opened their season on April 9 by drubbing the Yankees at Fenway Park. Homers by Armas, Boggs, Evans. On April 11, they crushed the Yanks again, 14–5. Next day they completed the sweep, 6–4. Great start: I succumbed to an early dose of pennant fever. But by April 18, their record had slipped to four wins, four losses. Same old story: the Sox archetypal pitching weakness would prevent any miracles at Fenway this year.

On May 8 I am sitting in the Main Office of PS 121 having just completed a workshop (Weaving Literature Into The Writing Workshop) for teachers at noon. The workshop is tortuous. Starving, I drool while I talk and watch the eight teachers munch from containers of cold pasta, curried chicken salad, tuna salad, ratatouille. When the workshop ends the teachers thank me, pack up what remains of their food, and return to their classrooms. One teacher lingers to ask me about mini-lessons. I don't care a hoot about mini-lessons; I want to eat. Now, I've got thirty minutes until I visit my next class. There is a decent diner a few blocks away, but my wallet is empty. No CitiBank cash machine nearby, either.

A teacher and two boys rush into the office wielding large, foil-covered trays. Groaning, they set them down on the counter.

"You're not by any chance hungry, are you?" the teacher asks me. "International Food Day. My kids brought in foods from around the world and we've got tons left over. What are we going to do with all this stuff?"

"Well, I suppose I could eat a little. ..."

"Great! Wonderful! It'd be a shame to let this go to waste. Here. I've got some paper plates."

Miraculous: to be ravenous one moment, listening to my stomach growl, and the next moment wielding a huge plate of spicy paella, spanikopita, moussaka, Italian sausage and peppers, stuffed chicken wings ...

Fine and well. But had my teachers grown during the year? You never step in the same river twice, Hippocletes once said. During my follow-up visits with teachers, I wanted to believe that. I wanted to believe that during the course of the year the rivers of the classrooms I worked in had grown deeper, clearer, swifter, maybe even a bit more dangerous.

Teaching writing, Donald Murray has said, involves teaching reading; that is, teaching children how to skillfully read their emerging drafts. Being a staff developer, I now realized, also involved "reading" teachers' classrooms as they emerged. And, eventually, teaching teachers how to read their emerging classrooms. I read carefully, looking for clues.

Teachers like Cheryl Steinberg and Steve Meyers had made dramatic breakthroughs with me. At the other end of the spectrum were the teachers who had not budged. My other teachers fell somewhere in between, having made fitful progress in ceding bits of classroom power to their kids, learning not to write all over their students' papers, trusting that kids could take more responsibility for their writing. The ambiguous growth of these teachers was harder to decipher.

I enter a dirty first-grade classroom. Bits of paper and a green sweatshirt on the floor. Chairs of absent children are upended on their desks, giving the room a particularly ugly look.

"Rhoda, I've got a great list of books for you," I tell the teacher when I walk in. She holds up her hand and stops me dead.

"I don't need it," she says emphatically. "I've become emancipated. Look." She points at a box of picture books. "Classics, all of them. I bring them in from my library in Westchester. That solves the first problem of getting classroom literature for my kids. Second emancipation: the stapler. From now on we use these brass fasteners. See? No more of the kids putting a million staples in their booklets so they can't even open them. Plus, I give out the writing folders at the beginning of the day. No more of this craziness at the beginning of the writing workshop. And you know what? It's working like a charm. I'm totally emancipated. . . ."

"Great," I murmur, looking around the ugly classroom. A breakthrough doesn't always look like a breakthrough.

Veray Darby is a first-grade teacher at PS 121, Meryl Natelli's school. She is a handsome black woman with smoldering black eyes. Something angry and uncompromising in her demeanor, but a great deal of kindness as well. Earlier in the year, Veray sat stone-faced through a demonstration I ran in her classroom. When I asked for her reaction, Veray shook her head.

"I run a very quiet, very structured classroom," she told me. "And my kids learn. I can't imagine doing this writing process thing with my kids."

At Meryl's suggestion, I visited Veray's class several times during writing time. On nearly every important issue—topic choice, inventive spelling, decentralized classroom management—Veray and I vehemently disagreed. I gave her articles to read, I loaned her a copy of Calkins's *The Art Of Teaching Writing*, all to no avail.

"This inventive spelling makes me crazy," Veray said. "I can't have these kids going into second grade spelling 'went' 'yt.' It's like sending a daughter out into the world knowing her slip is showing. It doesn't make sense."

"It's based on the way kids learn to speak at home—"

"But this isn't home," she countered. "This is school. It's a big difference. In here I want my kids to know how to spell words right."

This angered me. When I replied I spoke slowly and with more force than I had intended.

"Veray, if teachers like you expected the same amount of perfection in kids' early *talk* as you do in kids' early *writing* there would be a lot of people walking around who don't even talk at all."

This happened in early February. After this, Veray asked Meryl Natelli to remove her name from my schedule of classroom visits. Now Veray made a point of avoiding me and didn't speak to me when we passed in the halls. In early April, Meryl called me in to talk with her.

"We've had a tragedy in Veray's class," she said with a faint smile. "She's been studying tadpoles with her kids. Over the long weekend, the tank somehow got placed in direct sunlight, the water heated up, and all the tadpoles died. The kids took it pretty hard. Go take a look at the wall outside her class."

Outside her classroom, Veray had taped up a printed sign: WE ARE SAD. This sign was surrounded by a profusion of stories, poems, and letters kids had written in reaction to this incident. I was surprised and pleased to see that Veray had taped them up in their original uncorrected versions. Raymond had written:

> Dear Mrs. Darby,   the frogs may had died but at lese the butterflys made it.
>
> I am sorry that the frogs died but there are owes new things that are in life to opserv.
>
> I lked the tadpoles verey mach. Everything has to diey some times.
>
> And I am going to pray for the tadpoles. Evey day in my life in tell I gowe up.

I read all the writing. Then, feeling very much like an intruder, I walk into the classroom.

"Mr. Fletcher," Verary smiles with a genuine grin. "Welcome, welcome, welcome. Are we glad to see you! This writing process of yours has really taken off with these kids. I've set up a writing workshop, and they write every morning, and I'm telling you it is amazing!"

"It's not really my idea—"

"Some of the kids have even written letters to Mrs. Natelli to tell her that they want the right to wear shorts on hot days," she says, shaking her head in mock dread. "I hope this writing thing doesn't get us all into big trouble!"

"What happened?"

"Well, I thought about what you said last time you were here. About how we've got to support kids' beginning writing just like we do when they start talking. I didn't agree with it—I guess you noticed I'm pretty stubborn—but it stuck with me. I kept thinking about it. So about a month ago I started trying it. Secret, you know; I didn't tell anyone about it. Then the tadpoles died and the kids just needed to write about it. I had nothing to do with it. They just poured their hearts out on paper." She shrugs. "When they'd finished writing it seemed like the thing to do was just put the writing up so everyone could see it, spelling mistakes and all."

"Did any of the other teachers say anything?"

"No!" Veray laughs. "I guess that was my hang-up. And it's just gone on from there. The kids are pulling me along—I'm just trying to keep up with them! Last week, for one hour every day, I took the whole class outside to write. You should've seen them. They spread out on the ground with pens, paper, crayons, and clipboards. It was a beautiful day. And did they write! One boy saw an ambulance rush by and made up his own story about an ambulance. Eric heard the subway and wrote a story about a runaway train: 'The Ghost Train.' Here. Let me show you this."

Veray gives me a long piece of writing, apparently a poem, written by Toshana. She calls the girl over.

"C'mon, Toshana, read your poem to Mr. Fletcher."

Toshana reads shyly, with a trace of a Caribbean accent. While she reads I try to imagine her, sitting on the grass on that perfect morning, opening herself to the world of sounds around her.

The Ceps

The sun is shine.
Cars are passeing.
And vans too.
Peple walking by.
And there sabow.
trees too.
also nocks on boor.
Tunr passeing.
every thing shadow shien.
Trees saking all of them.

The Creeps

The sun is shining.
Cars are passing.
And vans too.
People walking by.
And their shadows.
Trees, too.
Also knocks on doors.
Trains passing.
Everything shadow shine.
Trees shaking all of them.

Maynes thing jup.	Many things jumping.
Peopel trnuing and walking.	People turning and walking.
Peope working hard.	People working hard.
Bers bowing.	Breezes blowing.
every thing cold.	Everything cold.
I am in the school yard.	I am in the schoolyard.
Cepe house.	Creepy house.
Jeps going dy too.	Jeeps going by, too.
Plan nosis.	Plane noises.
Two mans walking by.	Two men walking by.

It has been said that there is something strange at the heart of all great art. I detect this strangeness in Toshana's poem: the closely observed details, the hint of something sinister.

"Marvelous!" is all I can say. Veray hugs the girl against her.

"Isn't that something? Listen, I'm sorry I gave you such a hard time earlier on." She lowers her voice. "And it's too bad that now, just when I'm getting comfortable with first grade, Mrs. Natelli is planning to move me to second grade next year."

"Why?"

She motions me outside. When she speaks, Veray has a wide grin and sparkling eyes.

"The parents in this class petitioned the superintendent to keep me as their teacher in second grade. It happened just last week. I'm taking the whole class next year!"

I show up in Eleanor Bosch's classroom for my second-to-last visit. There is a silver-haired woman standing in front of the class. She has the rosy cheeks of an English nanny.

"Is Mrs. Bosch absent today?"

"No, Mrs. Bosch has left the school for good," the woman tells me. "I'm Mrs. Smith, and I'll be taking over this class for the rest of the year."

I stare at the children. They look up at me—Frank, Carlos, Anitra, all the others. Studying my expression.

"The way I understand it, on May the second Mrs. Bosch became fully vested for her pension," Mrs. Smith explains. "So she left. That's the way it is in the city system."

The children look back at me gravely. The entire class is deadpan. No one cracks even the hint of a smile.

"I've heard all about you, Mr. Fletcher. Mr. Hauser says you do some wonderful things with writing. If your schedule's not too full, I'd love to work with you. Just to get my feet wet, you know. I know it's late in the year. Next year I'll be ready to really get started."

"Well, sure, that might be okay," I say, still trying to get it through my head. Eleanor is gone. Gone. She dropped me. Dropped the whole system. "Have you taught before?"

Mrs. Smith laughs, a musical, silvery note. I start. Until then I had never heard real laughter in that classroom.

"Oh, my, yes, I started teaching back in 1959," she says. "Twenty-seven years ago. I had one little girl two years ago who came into my class and said, 'My Daddy said he had you as a teacher!' On Open School Night he came in, sure enough, all grown into a man. I gave him a big hug. Isn't that something? But I don't like to think of it as twenty-seven years. I'm always trying to learn something new. When Mr. Hauser hired me to teach here and told me about all the new ideas he's bringing into the school, well, I just said to myself, 'Dorothy, you're a new teacher, just getting hired. It's time for a new start.'"

Carlos raises his hand.

"Yes, dear?"

"Can I go to the bathroom?"

"Yes, but hurry back. We've got a lot to do today."

Dazed, I leave the classroom and head straight for Marlon Hauser's office. Seeing me, he bursts into laughter and runs to hide behind a stand of ferns.

"Merry Christmas, Ralph, and don't be too mad at me for not mentioning this earlier. I couldn't be positive she would actually leave until she did. Will you forgive me?"

In one poem, A. A. Ammons writes, "New leaves to old give the releasing push . . ." Ammons is invoking a scientific fact: autumn leaves do not fall off the trees merely because they turn brown and brittle, but rather because the new buds appear on the branches and literally push the old leaves off.

Moving from class to class, I thought of this line often in terms of children, their relentless growth. Even in my worst schools I could feel the minds of children pushing at my own mind, swelling, crowding me out. It was there in their writing, a burgeoning intelligence of the future generation, an evolving conscience making sense of a new world. Whenever I got frustrated by the teacher's slow rate of growth—or by my own—I took refuge in this fact.

I return in Fran Rogers's first-grade class and ask about the progress of Denise, the loose-jointed girl who had lagged so far behind her classmates earlier in the year.

"Take a look at that," Fran says, pointing to Denise's story hung up on the bulletin board. "I can still hardly believe it."

Next to a huge red house, subdivided into six rooms, Denise has written, "My fatr jigld me awak. He nibld on my sholdr."

"'My father jiggled me awake'" Fran reads. "'He nibbled on my shoulder!' Can you believe that?"

I read the words over and over again. Nibbled. Jiggled.

"Terrific. She did it!"

Fran and I look at each other. When we look over at Denise, she looks quickly away, but I can see the pride on her face.

"Does this mean she won't have to repeat first grade?"

"No," Fran says, smiling sadly. "She still needs another year of first grade under her belt. But it's a tremendous accomplishment for her. I had her run down to show the principal." She pauses and laughs. "Plus, you just know that it's true. Her father *would* nibble on her shoulder. Anyone's shoulder."

All year long I reexperienced that tangible tug I had known as a boy that pulled me through neighborhoods along with children and teachers, past the driveways and little houses, and irresistibly into the schools. Now, as June approached, I felt this force counterbalanced by another, more insistent pull: summer. The classrooms where I worked were invaded by the exotic smells of flowers and moist, freshly-cut grass. Kids' eyes grew dreamy while I talked, and wandered off to the windows and the explosion of greenery beyond.

PS 105, my ex-neighborhood. While I am working in Helen Winstral's second-grade class, the voice of Dr. Gold, the principal, comes over the loudspeaker.

"This will be Mr. Fletcher's last visit to our school this year," she intones. "We want to thank Mr. Fletcher for his work, and also all the teachers and boys and girls who worked with him. We look forward to working with him next year."

A minute later, while Helen and I are conferring with Murtzar, Jennifer Cillafarno approaches and tells us: "Ralph, Selena and Erica are both crying. They don't want you stop coming to our class."

The sobbing girls are sitting one behind the other. I approach them just as a school photographer enters the room, saying, "Oh, you're Ralph Fletcher! I must get a picture of you with the children for our PTA newspaper. My last chance!"

Cherie takes my hand and won't let go. I half-walk, half-drag her with me over to Selena and Erica; when we get there Cherie bursts into tears. Wordlessly, the other kids gather around the three sobbing children. With one arm around Cherie, I flash Helen a what-do-I-do-now? look. The photographer snaps away.

"Boys and girls," Helen says, "you'll still see Ralph. He's going to be working at PS 105 next year. He says he's going to stop in and see us from time to time. Maybe Ralph would be willing to put his address on the blackboard so you could keep in touch with him. Would you do that, Ralph?"

I would. Sniffling, the kids race back to their desks to begin copying down my address.

"Wait, you forgot to put your phone number up there, Ralph," Murtzar says.

"Well, I'm just getting a new phone," I lie vaguely. For the remainder of the class, kids keep sneaking up to me with scraps of paper on which they've written their own addresses.

I am quite touched by all of this.

Some teachers ask their students to write evaluations of the writing process. The first graders have uniformly positive things to say; among other things, they express relief at not having their writing corrected all the time.

Jynell (first grade): "I like to write Beecors it is ezeey if you make a mustak you don't haft to Be sad and I don't like when pepol tees me when I make a mustake Becors I am lorning and one day I made a mustake and a boy thot I cuddn't read and He made two mustaks and He was sad like I was so I tod Him you sudn't tees nobode no more o.k.? Becos you can make mustaks."

Demitris (first grade): "I like to write because it is fun. And everyone can read my booklets. And I like it because when ever I make a mistake whith spelling nobody can tell me to do it over. I like writing!! I like what I write in my booklets. And sometimes my stories go on the buleting board. And when I forget a word I can put a currat. It is fun to write. And I like to read my classes booklets. Everyone can be an author even little children they just have to put their ideas on the paper they don't need to spell the words right."

Marianna Kalinic (second grade): "Ralph is a good writer he makes nice books he helps people alot I like storys what he reads I am glad that he is coming to PS 79. You larn alot of things from writing proses and when you grow up you could be a good writer and be fames ralph is a fames man becouse he writs storys."

Bhavesh (fourth grade): "I think writing lab is a good session in class, and at the end of the year we should have a writing contest—the best story should win."

Carmelina DePietrantonia (third grade): "Writing process has been the most important part of my day. It will be very interesting to see how I write when I am 20 to 40 years old. I hope Writing Process will be around for a long, long time."

Some of the most remarkable evaluations came from Bill Gregory's third-grade class.

Janson: "I like it because my mind is like a floppy disk. I store in my head what happens over the weekend. Then I can call it back up and write about it on Monday or Tuesday."

Rhonda: "I like writing process because it's like I can have the excitement of what happened all over again when I write about it."

Jennifer: "Writing process taught me that I could go deep inside myself and come back with something important to write about."

Christian P. (fourth grade): "I didn't like that much of the program because we could not write whatever we wanted to write. It always had to be real—boring! When I write about real stuff I either get Writers Block or Writers Cramp. Mr. Fletcher seemed like a nice guy but he was always a thousand miles away from me."

Jessica (fourth grade): "To me writing process means I'm going to grow up to be the best that is (me and my very best friend Andy) because we know we can conquer the world of authorization. I don't want me and Andy to sound conceited but we think we have the skills and the luck it takes to be the best writers of all."

I say goodbye to all my teachers. I say goodbye to Derek, Felicia, Carmelina, Miranda, Bhavesh, Lauren, Konstantin, and about a thousand other kids. I do not get a chance to say goodbye to Gabrielle, the chubby girl in Robin Cohen's kindergarten class. She has been moved out of the class; I have lost track of her whereabouts.

On June 6, Jenifer Hall, Shelley Harwayne, and I go to PS 230 for one last day of training, a kind of debriefing for the year. Jenifer, who used to teach at PS 230, greets old friends all over the school. We spend a great deal of time in one second-grade class that is a laboratory of scientific projects: models of various spider webs, germinating seeds, animal homes. There is a classroom terrarium with a dozen butterflies just about to emerge from their silken purses. The kids are writing furiously about fossils, crystals, leaves, spiders, fish, turtles, butterflies . . .

2:45 P.M. Shelley and I are standing outside, in direct summer light, waiting for Jenifer. The door opens, loosing a flood of kids: the second-grade class that has been doing all that nature writing. The children jostle for the privilege of holding the door for their teacher, who is carrying the terrarium with the hatching butterflies. Excited, the children follow her down the cement stairs and into the grassy area behind a black wrought iron fence.

"Stand back!" she tells the kids, and gingerly lifts off the tops of the terrarium. The kids hold a collective breath. But the butterflies don't leave.

"Go ahead!" one boy urges. "Fly away!"

"Go! Scat!"

"How come they're not going?"

"Maybe they don't know how to fly yet."

"Give them a few minutes," the teacher says.

Shelley and I watch, our heads pushed against the fence. The children start a sponteneous countdown.

"Ten! Nine! Eight! Seven! Six! Five! Four! Three! Two! One! Zero! Blastoff!"

The butterflies do not blast off, preferring to stay at the bottom of the terrarium, stretching, drying out their new wings. A little eddy of disappointment ripples through the children. Then one butterfly timidly flutters its way up the side of the glass and stops, perched on top.

"Go ahead!" one girl says. "Fly!"

The butterfly lifts, starting a jagged flight path over the iron fence, over my head, maybe even over the school. The kids burst into cheers.

Heads tilt back trying to follow the disappearing monarch through the sky. A minute later, to more applause, another butterfly flutters out of the terrarium.

I watch the kids' faces, utterly absorbed, radiant with energy and excitement. Asians, blacks, Hispanics, Orientals, whites, and who knows what else. Americans, every one.

"These kids will never forget this," Shelley murmurs.

A rare moment: I actually envy this teacher her job.

Epilogue

September 28, 1986. A new year. The best part about being back in school is reconnecting with the Deena Golds and Norm Shermans, the Veray Darbys and Gail Falcoffs, not to mention the kids like Derek, Carmelina, Felicia, Lauren, and dozens of others.

I am looking forward to working with Steve Meyers, the flamboyant lawyer/teacher I enjoyed so much last year. But Bill Scott, the principal, has decided to pull out of the writing process training.

"My teachers have got it," he tells me over the phone. "It was great. Now it's time for something else."

Working in many new buildings, I encounter a batch of new kids, many with exotic names like Pacifico, LaStarr, Chastity, Windur. After a few visits, they burst into applause, on cue, whenever I show up. More than me, I realize, they are applauding the presence of something new in their classrooms: their own decisions, their own words and stories, their own voices. They are applauding themselves.

One morning I leave two crisp Macintosh apples on the front seat of my car. When I return, at 3:30 P.M., the car is an oven; the apples on the front seat are hot, literally baked, from sitting for hours on the broiling black vinyl. I pick one up and take an apprehensive bite. Underneath the skin, the apple flesh is almost unbelievably sweet, even better than the baked apples I used to make as a Boy Scout. A fine omen for the year.

I am working in Mamaroneck, New York, with Gwen Mahoney and her first-grade class. Gwen's most fascinating student is a boy named Christopher, a child who is as unusually bright as he is small. His parents have hired a physical therapist to help him with his motor coordination. At the end of the writing workshop, during share time, Christopher shrewdly and persistently questions the child sitting in the Author's Chair.

"Why were you sad then you left your Grandma's house?" he asks, narrowing his tiny eyes to slits.

"Because I had fun there."

"But *why* did you have fun? What did you do?"

One day Christopher approaches me the moment I step into the classroom.

"Would you like to buy one of my stories?" Christopher asks. He speaks in a low, disembodied voice, the voice of an elf.

"How much?"

"Fifteen dollars."

"Wow, that's a lot. How about one penny?"

He considers this for several seconds.

"All right," he says. "But it has to be a *real* penny."

"You've got a deal," I say. When I give him the penny, he hands me three pages of large, wobbly writing.

"Christopher wrote that piece after the art teachers Mrs. Pappalardo, came and did an activity with the class," Gwen explains. "You know, she took colorful leaves and ironed them between sheets of wax paper. It's the oldest thing in the world—my teacher did that when *I* was in school. But I guess it captured Christopher's imagination."

> "It is october.
> The leafs are changing colors now.
> And soon they will fall off the
> trees and die. But the most
> buwtyful leafs will stay alive
> longer. So let us all giv thanks
> to the person who had this great
> idea. Her name is Mrs. Pappalardoo.
> Yes the plan is in action. They
> will not live forever even with the
> plan. But they will last longer

thanks to Mrs. Pappalardoo, leaf
specialist. For it is all because
of her great idea—wich is the iron.
Now give thanks to the best we can do
and give thanks to leaf specialist,
Mrs. Pappalardoo."

This piece of writing has a strange melody—somewhere between
a tribute and a prayer—that delights me. Another good omen for
the new year.

In PS 26, Queens, I visit Carol Cossins's first-grade class and encounter Juliet, a dark-haired girl who decides to write a book about
rainbows. She writes with astonishing speed and confidence. By the
third day of my demonstration teaching, the book is finished. Though
this text cannot convey the same cumulative, page-turning effect of
Juliet's book (which includes rainbow stories, rainbow poems, rainbow
dreams, even a section titled "Find The Hidden Rainbows"), I have
included my two favorite pages:

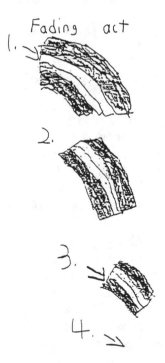

Fading act
1.
2.
3.
4.

A THREE ACT PLAY.
Act 1, Rain
Act 2. Sun.
Act 3. Rainbow.

I fall in love with this book and carry it everywhere, pulling it out and passing it around like a proud father with photos of a new baby to show teachers, principals, colleagues, friends, parents, anyone willing to take a look.

"The definitive book on rainbows," I brag to one group of teachers. I stand aside, basking, as they ooh and ahhh at the humor and inventiveness of Juliet's book.

"This kid's a real writer," one teacher says.

"Don't worry," a male teacher nearby mutters. "They'll find a way to beat it out of her."

He looks straight at me. Something inside me stirs and rises toward the dark truth of his words.

In Ruth Zander's third-grade class, in Norm Sherman's school, there is an elderly woman, perhaps seventy years old, in the back of the room.

"Hello," she says to me, grinning.

I shake her hand, wondering who she is: volunteer, paraprofessional, PTA representative, Board of Ed?

"Nice to meet you."

"I'm Mrs. Webster," she says. "Mrs. Zander's student teacher."

"Really!"

"I know what you're thinking." She looks at me closely. "That I'm pretty old to be starting a career as a teacher. I was a school secretary for thirty years. I retired two years ago. And you know what? I missed the job. I missed working. I kept asking myself, what was it about the job that I missed? And I realized it was just being around kids. I always envied the teachers their close relationship with kids. So, I decided to go back and retool myself. Become a teacher."

I was wrong, after all, about the Red Sox. They would beat the Angels in the American League playoffs, stumble into the October Classic, the World Series, and come one pitch away from victory over the New York Mets before they would finally break my heart.

I am sitting outside the principal's office. A black boy, maybe eleven, takes a seat on the bench beside me. After a moment I can feel his gaze upon me.

"Do you mind if I ask who you are?" he asks.

"Ralph Fletcher. How about you?"

"Michael. Michael Vallo." Pause. "Do you mind if I ask what you do at this school?"

"I teach writing. I teach teachers how to teach writing. Do you like to write?"

He considers this, and lowers his eyes.

"Yeah. 'Cept when we have to write for punishment."

"Does that happen often?"

"All the time."

"Well, in the classes where I work, we try to get kids to write about what they know, what's important to them, what they care about."

"That's our best subject," he replies, nodding.

New year, new place to live (Manhattan's Upper West Side), and new challenges at work. In addition to my regular work in various city schools, I start working as an independent consultant at the Yeshiva of North Jersey, in Teaneck. I'm initially apprehensive about how the Jewish kids and teachers will relate to a goyim like myself. Not to worry: Rabbi Goldstein has deemed writing to be of major importance in the yeshiva. Thus am I endowed with celebrity status.

The classes at the yeshiva separate boys from girls. I begin by talking to the kids about becoming an author: making decisions, writing about important topics, writing for real purposes. The rooms are small and noisy; the kids are better dressed if not discernibly better behaved than the kids in New York City schools. Several second-grade boys write stories about being in the Israeli army and shooting at Arabs out of tanks.

One day I have an afternoon meeting with two third-grade teachers at a building next to the yeshiva. Leaving the building, I spot a man approaching the door, carrying a large heavy box. When I open the door for him, I can see that he is none other than Jim Bouton, ex-big league pitcher/author/sportscaster and New York Yankee persona non grata.

"Jim Bouton!"

"That's me," he admits.

"Wow," I'm saying. "I mean I loved *Ball Four*. It reads like a novel. I love the beginning: 'I'm thirty years old and I have these dreams . . .'"

"Thanks," he says, grinning with those boyish good looks of his. On the way toward his car, we chat. Ecstasy: to be talking baseball with a flesh-and-blood Jim Bouton on a radiant fall day. I tell him how unfair it is he's been banned from playing in the Yankee Old-Timers Games. He has just started a company, he says, that makes business cards in the style of baseball cards. He hands me a brochure.

While we talk, the doors to the yeshiva open and kids start spilling out. Some of them spot me and come racing over.

"Mr. Fletcher! Mr. Fletcher's here!" Eight, maybe ten kids flock around me. Having seen my poetry book and magazine articles, these children know me as a writer, a real author. Now they whip out pieces of paper and crowd around, begging for my autograph. I'm eager to continue my talk with Bouton and try to shoo the kids away, but this only makes them plead more loudly. Bouton watches all of this in perlexed silence. Finally, he clears his throat and takes a careful look at me.

"Who are you, anyway?" he asks.

October 15, PS 154, Queens. As I'm leaving the school at the end of the day, a boy hails me from the end of the corridor.

"Mr. Fletcher! Mr. Fletcher!"

I stop and peer at him. His figure makes a silhouette against the far window, and it takes a few moments for me to clearly see him. Smoke-skinned, chubby, otherwise nondescript. I cannot quite place him.

"Carlos, from last year," he says. Pause. "Don't you remember? I was an author last year."